Rose Kennedy and Her Family

Rose Kennedy
and Her Family

The Best and Worst
of Their Lives and Times

Barbara Gibson and Ted Schwarz

A BIRCH LANE PRESS BOOK
Published by Carol Publishing Group

When Mrs. Kennedy suggested to me that I keep a diary of my days working for her, she said, "It will be nice for your children to have, to look back on." And so, as Mrs. Kennedy suggested, I would like to dedicate this book to my children, Kathleen and Kevin, and to their children, and to posterity—B.G.

To Leslie, Raheem, and Clifford. See, I really was working when I buried myself in the office all day.—T.S.

Copyright © 1995 by Barbara Gibson and Ted Schwarz
All rights reserved. No part of this book may be reproduced in any form, except by a newspaper or magazine reviewer who wishes to quote brief passages in connection with a review.

A Birch Lane Press Book
Published by Carol Publishing Group
Birch Lane Press is a registered trademark of Carol Communications, Inc.
Editorial Offices: 600 Madison Avenue, New York, N.Y. 10022
Sales and Distribution Offices: 120 Enterprise Avenue, Secaucus, N.J. 07094
In Canada: Canadian Manda Group, One Atlantic Avenue, Suite 105, Toronto, Ontario M6K 3E7
Queries regarding rights and permissions should be addressed to Carol Publishing Group, 600 Madison Avenue, New York, N.Y. 10022

Carol Publishing Group books are available at special discounts for bulk purchases, sales promotion, fund-raising, or educational purposes. Special editions can be created to specifications. For details, contact: Special Sales Department, Carol Publishing Group, 120 Enterprise Avenue, Secaucus, N.J. 07094

MANUFACTURED IN THE UNITED STATES OF AMERICA

10 9 8 7 6 5 4 3 2 1

Book design by Robert Freese

LIBRARY OF CONGRESS CATALOGING-IN-PUBLICATION DATA

Gibson, Barbara.
    Rose Kennedy and her family : the best and worst of their lives and times / Barbara Gibson and Ted Schwarz.
        p. cm.
    Includes index.
    ISBN 1-55972-299-1 (hc)
    1. Kennedy, Rose Fitzgerald, 1890– . 2. Kennedy family. 3. Presidents—United States—Mothers—Biography. I. Schwarz, Ted, 1945– . II. Title.
E748.K378G52 1995
973.922′092—dc20
[B]
                                                                    95—19926
                                                                        CIP

Contents

Preface

I never expected to write a book about Rose Kennedy when I began working for the family in 1968, first as a secretary and later as Rose Kennedy's personal assistant. I was always too busy with Mrs. Kennedy. Already an old woman, she was set in her ways, concerned with her family's image and their maintenance of power. Her days were filled with the religious rituals that had been the focus of her life since she graduated from the Sacred Heart schools as a Child of Mary. Part of her time she spent continuing her correspondence with the world's rich and famous, from members of the British royal families to Nelson Rockefeller. Part of her time she spent with political campaigns. And part of her time she spent shaping the family image by hiding its history, such as putting her daughter Rosemary's diaries in the trash, from which I rescued them, discovering in them perhaps the darkest of the Kennedy family secrets.

Although raised in a small Ohio town, before entering the odd mix of isolation and sophistication that comprised the Kennedy family, I thought I had experienced the world. My husband and I had lived in cities ranging from Manhattan to Cleveland to Tokyo, Japan. My first job had been with the FBI during the height of J. Edgar Hoover's power. Headquarters was filled with secret files, though the ones that related most intimately to the Kennedys I would not know or read about until many years after the director's death. Even then I only discovered the material when working with my co-author, Ted Schwarz, whose research uncovered transcripts, letters, and other documents Hoover had once retained for blackmail. These included details of Jack's love affair with the alleged Nazi spy Inga Arvad, a Nordic beauty whose apartment Hoover had wired for sound. Everything from the couple's passionate coupling to their pillow talk about their postwar plans was recorded and transcribed.

Preface

I lived and worked in Washington when Jack Kennedy was in Congress. I moved from the FBI to Capitol Hill, and Jack moved from the House to become the junior senator from Massachusetts. In those days, congressional representatives, senators, and their staff members used to frequent certain popular "watering holes" after work. The most popular was Mike Palms, located just east of Capitol Hill. There were also hotel cocktail lounges, and almost always a weekly party in the House Caucus Room. Everyone had a favorite spot, and in one of these I first watched the junior senator from Massachusetts make a fool of himself in his quest for a date.

Years later I learned from Jack's cousin Joe Gargan, Mrs. Kennedy's nephew, that Jack was extremely shy. He never had the nerve to approach any of us young women, though we were all quite available. But you had to make the effort to try, something Jack Kennedy could not bring himself to do. Instead he would send one of his aides to approach the woman he desired, letting the middleman try to arrange a date. Although he occasionally got lucky, we used to gripe because he couldn't approach us himself. However, rather than recognizing his shyness, we thought he was an arrogant, spoiled rich kid who was used to someone else handling every phase of his life, including picking up women.

Later I learned that it was typical of the Kennedy men to use others to do their bidding. However, in those days it seemed that Jack was also afraid of rejection.

We laughed at Jack in those days, for we felt that anyone that timid was not going to be very successful. What I did not expect was to one day work for the matriarch of a family that, by then, had become one of the most respected in America.

Mrs. Kennedy's attitude toward both the help and the family amused me. She had spent so many years striving for respect that everyone who regularly was in the family home had a title. I was The Secretary to distinguish me from The Cook, The Chauffeur, and even The Ambassador and The Senator.

Being the secretary should have left me at the low end of the pecking order, but Mrs. Kennedy was an intensely lonely woman by 1968. Four of her children were dead—one in war, one by accident, and two by assassination, most recently Bobby. Her husband was dying from the effects of a stroke. And Teddy, her sole surviving son, the last Kennedy hope for the presidency, had a sham of a marriage and a penchant for blondes, alcohol, and, it was rumored, occasional recreational drugs that constantly endangered his political aspirations. She needed someone in whom to confide, with whom to talk about times past. I was never a total family intimate, of course, but we would go swimming together, talk together, and over a decade our relationship made me privy to Kennedy triumphs and scandals as seen through her eyes.

Not that Mrs. Kennedy and I were close at first. I had too much turmoil in my own life to be concerned with much more than rearing my two children. My marriage had come to an end the previous year, and I had moved to Cape Cod for a more pleasant environment in which Kevin and Kathleen could grow up with a single parent.

Mrs. Kennedy had her own problems during those early days, since Joe was dying from the effects of his stroke. As a result, the house was filled with visiting Kennedy children and a staff that consisted primarily of a cook; a downstairs maid; an upstairs maid; a chauffeur; a secretary; John Ryan, who provided the muscle to move Mr. Kennedy; Rita Dallas, RN, the private-duty nurse; and Ann Gargan, Rose's niece.

Immediately following Joe's death, everything changed. Mrs. Kennedy fired the entire staff except for a combination cook/maid and a gardener, who was also expected to act as chauffeur. The children and the grandchildren had their own lives. As a result, Mrs. Kennedy, one of the most admired women in the world, had little social interaction. I was The Secretary, but that position required more education than the only other two positions that continued in those post-Joe years.

Gradually my life became filled with Kennedy facts and trivia. I filled notebook after notebook with correspondence and other information Mrs. Kennedy had me record for her. I learned about the lives and loves of the children and the grandchildren. Mrs. Kennedy coped by talking, and I learned to listen and remember.

In 1985 I first agreed to write a brief memoir about my time with Mrs. Kennedy. Yet that book, *Life With Rose Kennedy*, was grossly incomplete. Not only was much personal history not yet known, the publisher edited out all but nice comments so as not to upset the still-powerful family.

And there was much that *was* nice about Mrs. Kennedy. She could be warm and caring, which enabled me to survive ten years in the midst of what I eventually felt was America's most prominent dysfunctional family. I would have stayed at least a decade more had a series of what were called pencil strokes not left her as if she were senile. She had come to need a full-time nurse, not a secretary or personal assistant. I left when only the shell remained of the woman I had grown to love/hate as did all truly intimate staff members. I left when she had days when she was not lucid and days when she would talk for hours, the stories no longer accurate, her awareness of her surroundings so limited that she sometimes did not know whether she was living in Hyannis Port or Palm Beach.

As Mrs. Kennedy entered the last months of her life, I realized it was time to tell the full story of her 104 years. Hers was a deeper story, richer, more colorful, awe inspiring, scandalous, and tragic than had ever been discussed by me or her other biographers. And when I decided to tell it, I turned to author Ted Schwarz, whose work has ranged from true crime to history to biography, including members of the Kennedy family.

Ted had begun his in-depth research into the history of the Kennedy family when he wrote the biography of the "first brother-in-law," the actor Peter Lawford. Peter had married Pat Kennedy, and though their marriage ended in early estrangement and eventual divorce, he was the delight of the rowdy Kennedy brothers. He introduced the men to Hollywood in a way Joe Kennedy had known but never discussed with his sons. Peter brought them starlets delighted to have sex with one or another of the famous brothers. And he introduced Marilyn Monroe to Jack and Bob, leaving them with the greatest lingering scandal before Teddy's erratic driving sent a woman to her watery grave.

Peter also acted as unofficial family historian, documenting facts the family was so anxious to hide that the Peter Lawford files became part of the archives of Arizona State University rather than the Kennedy Library. Peter's widow, Patricia S. Lawford, helped Ted Schwarz gain access to hundreds of family friends and acquaintances, most of whom he was able to interview. And later, when he and I wrote a book about the Kennedy family's third generation, we were able to interview even more.

By the time we decided to tell the full story of Rose Kennedy, tape recordings, file cabinets filled with notes, seemingly countless books, and other resources had been acquired. I was able to supply personal anecdotes and my own files. Ted focused on the history that predated my involvement and the awareness of us both.

What you are about to read is a carefully researched biography combining a historical narrative with my notes and comments. Other Kennedy biographers arrived too late to interview a lucid, fully rational Rose Kennedy. Most seem to have gone back to earlier interviews, pulling together snippets of previous work and writing as though all of it were learned in one sitting. At the time when one of the more famous biographers claimed to have conducted many of his interviews, strokes had left Mrs. Kennedy confused at best, showing the inaccuracies of the senile at worst.

Although we have read all these works when pursuing our research, we have eliminated that which we know is false. There was no need for sensationalism or pretense. Mrs. Kennedy lived in a fascinating world of love and hate, desperately grabbing for power and respect, while in a lifelong pursuit of proper humility before God.

As you read this book, I will share throughout the intimate secrets known only to those of us who were there to ask questions, listen to answers, and to always be a sounding board to a powerful, lonely woman trying to come to grips with her past.

Rose Kennedy is dead. I hope through the reading of this book she will again come alive, neither saint nor devil, but a fascinating woman in America's recent history.

Barbara Gibson

To give you the most effective possible understanding of Rose Kennedy's remarkable life, the historical narrative of this book will periodically be interrupted by Barbara Gibson's comments about the lives and times being discussed. She will add information obtained during her ten years with the Kennedy family, during which she saw the triumphs, the tragedies, the scandals, the pettiness, and the adoration that makes them so unique in American history.

Ted Schwarz

Acknowledgments

Thanks to the staff of the John F. Kennedy Library for helping us find the often overlooked critical documents that helped add flesh to the skeletal information available concerning the often hidden aspects of both the political skills and the personal life of Rose Kennedy; the staff of the Boston Public Library; the staff of the Special Collections Division of the Hayden Library of Arizona State University, Tempe, Arizona; and the staff members and friends of Rose Kennedy and the Kennedy family.

Rose Kennedy
and Her Family

1

The Death and Life

Another Kennedy funeral. Another crowd. Strangely silent this time, they pressed against the Boston police line that ringed Old St. Stephen's Church on Tuesday, January 24, 1995. Many were quietly weeping, an elderly woman dabbing at her eyes, a teenaged girl with a tear-streaked face staring straight ahead at the closed doors of the Catholic church, a man in his forties, wearing a leather jacket and baseball cap, blowing his nose in an oversize bandanna. Others stood respectfully, oblivious to the still and motion-picture cameras bearing the logos of CBS, NBC, ABC, CNN, CBC, BBC—television broadcasters from throughout the world.

Many of the people present were uncertain why they had come. Rose Kennedy had been alive in name only for the last ten years. A stroke had left her mind in whatever nightmare of limbo exists for those who lose all ability to communicate. For the previous two years she had been comatose; the pneumonia that ultimately ended her days on earth could only be considered a blessing to those who loved her.

Yet somehow she was important to the crowd that stood in silence. She had given birth to what once seemed a dynasty—rich, powerful, handsome children whose desires took them to the peak of power. Ultimately Rose Kennedy's legacy could be seen in the White House, the Senate, the House of Representatives, in educational institutions, on television news shows, television soap operas, and in motion pictures. Some of her children and grandchildren had died in wartime, through assassination, and some from drug overdose. Others had become the darlings of tabloid television shows, the A-list party guests for Washington power brokers and New York socialites.

But the gathered crowd was not there to remember the tragedies of the past or the glamorous images of the new generation. They were there to pay homage to a remarkable woman, the matriarch of an American family that once came as close to being royalty as has ever happened in a democratic society.

Finally the eulogies and the mass were over, the doors to the church where Rose Kennedy had been baptized opened to let out her casket, her pallbearers, and the mourning survivors among her children, grandchildren, and great-grandchildren.

That was when you saw the men, Kennedy men. Some were there by blood. Others by marriage. Yet their contrasts, their successes, and their excesses made them familiar faces to all those present.

Somehow the sudden shift of focus was appropriate. Rose Kennedy had always been known by the men in her life. She was the daughter of John "Honey Fitz" Fitzgerald, Boston's first and perhaps most powerful Irish Catholic mayor. She was the wife of Joe Kennedy, an intensely driven man who had amassed great wealth and great power in pursuit of the presidency he wanted first for himself, then for his sons. And she was the mother of John Fitzgerald Kennedy, a man who, despite his weakness for women, had had a presidency so popular that the press and public dubbed it Camelot.

But those men were gone. The men who stood before the crowd seemed suddenly to overshadow her for different reasons.

There was Ted Kennedy, her only surviving son, the youngest of her nine children. She always called him "The Senator," a title spoken as though he were unique in the halls of Congress. In his prime, Ted Kennedy had been the heir apparent to the image of Camelot, the tragically brief White House years of older brother Jack, as well as of his murdered brother Bob.

Nobody thought of Ted as a statesman. Even his most ardent supporters would later say that the only reason they wanted him in the White House was to keep the memory of his more respected brothers alive. Yet at one point that might have been enough to take him all the way to the Oval Office.

In stark physical contrast, there was John F. Kennedy Jr., the grandson so handsome that *People* magazine named him "The Sexiest Man Alive." One generation of Americans would remember him as a little boy saluting the passing caisson pulled by a riderless horse and bearing his father's coffin. A younger generation, many of whom were born too late to experience his father's presidency other than through history books, knew the tabloid darling from his exploits with movie star Daryl Hannah, singer/actress/sex-symbol Madonna, and other glamorous women.

Arnold Schwarzenegger was there, a mountain of a man who had parlayed his Hollywood success to move from title roles in the likes of *Conan the Barbarian* to marry Maria Owings Shriver, Rose's granddaughter and goddaughter.

Near the rock-solid Arnold was William Kennedy Smith, now a doctor of medicine, who had brought the last of many scandals into his grandmother's life when he was charged with rape in Palm Beach during Easter weekend, 1991.

And there was Christopher Lawford, whose dashing, handsome father, Peter, had made millions in the movies, then squandered it on drugs and alcohol. Christopher had also been an addict, though unlike his father he had managed to become straight and sober before finding steady work as an actor in the soap opera *All My Children*.

There were more, of course. There were Joseph Kennedy II and Patrick Kennedy, congressional representatives from Massachusetts and Rhode Island respectively. There was Ted junior, who had triumphed over the cancer that took one of his legs and the alcohol abuse that almost took his life.

Rose's men. So many men. And as had always been the case, they were gathered together because of the matriarch.

It would be the last time, of course. Her strengths would no longer sustain them. Her weaknesses no longer mattered. She had experienced the best and worst that life could offer. One hundred and four years of faith, family, and tragedy.

———————

BG: I DIDN'T ATTEND the funeral. Had I done so, Mrs. Kennedy would have wanted me to sit in the back. She didn't want to be seen with the hired help, and I was just The Secretary. The few times she asked me to come to church with her, I was expected to remain several pews behind her. Even in death I was certain I would hear her disapproving voice admonishing me for my actions.

Instead, a week later I attended her memorial service in Palm Beach, an area that was more her home than Hyannis Port. She enjoyed more acceptance there, even though she was too uncomfortable with others to take advantage of the seemingly endless invitations to parties. When Joe was still alive, she used the disability of his stroke and his need for assistance as her excuse to avoid going out for more than her often solitary game of golf. When he died, she used the shabbiness of the Palm Beach mansion to justify her reclusiveness. But in death there was a gathering she could not put off, a gathering of family and friends, of her former chauffeur, of merchants, businesspeople, and others who could squeeze into the gathering. Although solemn and sad, it was one gathering Mrs. Kennedy had ultimately not been able to avoid.

Afterward, as I stood in front of Green's Pharmacy, facing the church across the street, I watched some of the congregation lingering to talk with the priest, with Ethel, her daughter Courtney, and her son-in-law, known to the press as "Black Jack" Hill, a member of the Irish Republican Army who once served prison time for a murder conviction.

I did not want to be noticed. I just wanted to watch the people as they drifted from the church. But as I did, some regular customers left Green's Pharmacy, passing me in their tennis clothes, running clothes, and other Palm Beach "uniforms."

"What's going on?" one woman was heard to say.

Another woman said, "Oh, it's for Rose Kennedy."

A couple passed behind me. The woman paused, looked, and said, "The end of an era." Then they walked on.

Perhaps life would have been different for Rose Kennedy had she been born a few years later. A girl born in Boston in 1890 faced a world filled with social conflicts. The Protestants held the Catholics in disdain, and Irish Catholics were hated most of all. Historian Francis Parkman wrote *Our Common Schools* that year, stating: "New England Protestants will do well to remember that the Catholic population gains on them every year, as well by natural increase as by emigration. New England families have dwindled in numbers generation after generation through all this century, and it will be folly to provoke collision till the race returns to its pristine vigor, and promises a good supply of recruits for the war."

The Protestants were socially divided as well, but the poorest of laboring Protestants often felt themselves better than the most successful of the Irish Catholics. Among the Irish Catholics, the social hierarchy was based on education, financial success, and political influence.

Attitudes toward women were also changing, and a growing number of them would soon be entering skilled professions. When Rose was born, women worked almost exclusively as domestics, factory workers, or store clerks. By the time Rose was a teenager, daughters of the domestics commonly sought higher education. Many had become teachers, nurses, and small-business owners, the latter often funded by the savings of their frugal, self-sacrificing mothers.

The opportunity to obtain an education was a radical change from life in Ireland, where the Catholics had been denied by law the right to go to school.

Rose herself not only graduated from high school at the age of fifteen, having been encouraged by her father, John Fitzgerald, to apply herself, she expected to go on to study at Wellesley College. Wellesley was proof of how much women had achieved in New England. The faculty included such notables as Emily Green Balch, who would win the Nobel Peace Prize for her work in abolishing sweatshops and improving the lives of laboring women. Throughout the faculty were internationally respected scholars, and political economics, psychology, mathematics, and the arts were among the many subjects offered. By contrast, most other women's schools focused on domestic skills, such as "physics for homemakers."

BG: MRS. KENNEDY'S SUCCESS in school was always a subject of amusement for the children. She was far more intelligent than her husband, Joe Kennedy, and had times been different, the family fortunes might have been greater than he ever imagined possible. She also used to both fascinate and horrify the friends of the children because mealtimes and long drives in the car were considered perfect occasions for learning. She would drill them on everything from the catechism of the Catholic Church to American history. She would clip and post articles for them to read, then discuss them to prove that they had learned from them.

"What is a sheikh?" "Why does Lent last forty days?" "What does Passover mean?" "Where is the Middle East?" "Why is the

Middle East different from the Far East?" I was not present when the children were growing up, of course, but I was present when she carried on this tradition with her grandchildren. I once heard her ask Bobby Shriver, Eunice's son, why he did not speak proper English such as "If I were he" instead of "If I were him." Bobby complained that it sounded too affected.

It was Sen. Ted Kennedy who had a laugh at his mother's expense about the lessons. The first time I visited his office in the Capitol Building, his administrative assistant escorted me to the private office where the wall had several framed letters from his mother. Some offered personal advice. Some were reproofs for one misstep or another. A few, written about incidents where she feared she either might be mistaken or where her children might be angry with her for sending them, were typed. At the bottom, where her signature should have been, she had all her secretaries type, "Dictated, not read." And in the midst of all this was a report card Ted had found somewhere. It was from Mrs. Kennedy's tenth grade, and though most all the grades were high, algebra was marked C-.

Prior to framing the report card, the senator had circled the grade in red, then written in the margin, "What happened, Mother?"

Only later would I learn how daring the stealing of the report card had been. Mrs. Kennedy had the strength of her immigrant ancestors, and if her son ever thought she would discover his humor, he would have hidden the card until after her death. For her entire life, she was a woman not to be challenged.

But the pull of the progressive era for New England women was countered by bigotry and the growing conservatism of the Catholic Church in Boston. The best, the brightest, and the wealthiest Catholic schoolgirls were being encouraged by the bishop to seek a convent education to train them to be proper wives and mothers. Ironically, the nuns running the convent schools were often more intellectually liberated than their students. Yet no matter what an Irish Catholic girl of Rose's generation might achieve, Boston society refused to accept her as worthy by their standards.

In many parts of the country, the hostility to the Irish Catholics could be directly related to the vast influx of immigrants following the potato famine of the 1840s. But in Massachusetts, the hatred manifested itself as early as 1688. That was when an Irish servant girl, Mary Glover, was accused of being a witch by local Puritans, who considered her Gaelic utterances to be the devil's language, and her habit of crossing herself to be the work of Satan. She was convicted, then put to death on the Boston Common by hanging, the standard punishment for witches.

The hatred directed toward Mary Glover in 1688 lingered in the community. The Irish who were descended from those earliest of settlers learned to keep a low profile. However, the later immigrants, the ones who arrived as a result of the potato famine of the 1840s, would dramatically challenge the old order, wresting power from the entrenched Protestant Brahmins.

Fifty thousand Irish immigrants arrived in the United States in the decade between 1820 and 1830, two hundred thousand following over the next ten years, and almost as many again by 1844. From the end of the War of 1812 until just before the potato famine struck, approximately a million Irish arrived, most of whom sought jobs in Boston and New York.

As early as October 21, 1837, the *Boston American* editorialized concerning the growing number of Irish immigrants: "Instead of assimilating at once with the customs of the country of their adoption, our foreign population are too much in the habit of retaining their own national usages, of *associating too exclusively with each other*, and living in groups together. These practices serve no good purpose, and tend merely to alienate those among whom they have chosen to reside. *It would be the part of wisdom, to* ABANDON AT ONCE ALL USAGES AND ASSOCIATIONS WHICH MARK THEM AS FOREIGNERS, *and to become in feeling and custom, as well as in privileges and rights, citizens of the United States.*"

To the Brahmins, the Irish seemed boisterous and noisy. The Irish men worked hard and afterward liked to spend time in bars, drinking, arguing, and sometimes brawling.

BG: THERE WAS AN IRONY to the lives of the Kennedys I would learn as I worked with Mrs. Kennedy for more than a decade. From the time Rose Fitzgerald married Joseph Kennedy, one of the driving forces behind their life together was the seemingly desperate desire to become accepted by the Protestant elite. Despite this, they were rearing sons whose antics were often similar to those of early immigrants. The police regularly chased the unruly Kennedy kids around Cape Cod, and few of their neighbors liked the boys. A state highway patrol officer, Jack Dempsey, was regularly called by Joe Kennedy senior to cover for the children. Years later, in retirement, he would talk about the way he made certain the Kennedy sons never had to pay for actions that would have landed less well connected young men in jail for at least a few days.

Joe Gargan, Rose Kennedy's nephew, has related how young Jack frequently stripped to his underwear, got on the prow of his motorboat, and rode around the harbor in Cape Cod while drinking beer and shouting obscenities.

Not that Jack was a saint when younger. In Mrs. Kennedy's diary, an entry for Tuesday, September 11, 1923, reads: "Boys went to school. Staying with Moores. Jack said that night, 'Well, here I have been home only a few hours and the cops are chasing me already.' He later explained he was teasing a little girl who told policeman and he hid in a cellar."

On October 28, 1923, Mrs. Kennedy wrote: "Boys stole false mustaches for Halloween from shop—Anna Shop."

Rose's youngest son, Ted, managed to stay in political office long enough to become one of the nation's most powerful senators, all while being known for heavy drinking and extensive womanizing, both during and after his first marriage, as late as 1991. Even Rose's grandson Dr. William Kennedy Smith years later admitted to drinking in a raucous bar, picking up a girl, then engaging in "rough sex" with her. (She charged him with rape, though a jury found inadequate evidence to convict. The Kennedy habit of having friendly law enforcement officers protect them from their own actions wherever they were living paid off in the Smith case. As much as the family would have liked to have distanced themselves from the unruly, hard-drinking, hard-fighting Irish Catholics of early Boston, their family behavior would not have been unfamiliar to the immigrants of the 1830s.

Mary Josephine "Josie" Hannon, Rose's mother, came from a family who did not patronize the Boston pubs. Unlike so many of the Irish Catholics who came to America, she was raised on a farm after immigrating. Her family, including her cousin Thomas Fitzgerald, had moved from Ireland to South Acton, a tiny agricultural community near Boston where many people were quite poor. Mary Ann and Michael Hannon were among the least successful farmers in the region, and though they were in better financial shape than the Irish peasants fighting the potato famine, they barely survived. Only three or four other families in the area were Irish Catholic. They lacked the numbers, the social organization, and the religious support others had found in the cities.

The Hannons stayed in the farming community, but Tom Fitzgerald, who had been working as a hired laborer on various farms, abandoned the rural life for the North End of Boston. He became a street peddler of fish, so poor that he could only afford handbaskets for his wares and not even a cart. The peddler's life was hard, profits limited, and survival always in question. Many of the pushcart operators worked such long hours for so little return that they could barely feed their families. This was certainly true for Thomas Fitzgerald.

Tom Fitzgerald's dreams never matched his reality. He claimed to be a lover of the rural life and would frequently talk of saving the money to buy his own farm. First he was going to buy in South Acton. Then, after moving to Boston and marrying Rose Cox in 1857, he planned to move to the Midwest, where many immigrant farmers were migrating. However, following his marriage, he had the first three of his children and the offer of a business venture with his brother James. Together they would sell groceries and bottle goods (liquor) at 310 North Street.

James Fitzgerald, the younger of the two brothers, was also the more knowledgeable businessman. Tom was little more than a clerk and an investor in the business. James's desire for success and understanding of the business world as practiced in Boston's North End where the brothers had their store led to great wealth.

Rose's father, John Fitzgerald, was born before his father Tom's success. It was February 11, 1863, and his earliest years would be spent in a Hanover Street tenement building in Boston's North End. This historic area, the location of Paul Revere's home from 1770 through 1800 and of many other historic buildings, had once attracted the wealthy and socially powerful. The nearby Burying Ground on Copp's Hill held such famous bodies as those of Edmund Hartt, who built the USS *Constitu-*

tion, as well as Cotton, Increase, and Samuel Mather. However, by the time John Fitzgerald was born, the Irish poor dominated the area. They had migrated following the Famine of 1847, and tenement houses, bars, and similar evidence of a laboring class were everywhere.

Even among the poorest and most oppressed there was discrimination. The Irish Catholics of Boston differentiated among themselves based on their county of origin. Men in supervisory capacities, such as construction-crew foremen, would only give jobs to men whose ancestors were from their same section of Ireland.

Thomas and Rosanna Cox Fitzgerald had been born in County Wexford, Ireland, although they didn't meet until they were both in Boston. John, their fourth of ten sons, knew well his parents' origin, but once he entered politics, whenever he spoke before a group, he would adapt his family history to suit the background of his audience. He traced his roots from County Wexford for one audience, Cork for another, Sligo or Mayo or Galway for a third. During the rare occasion when the audience was mixed, he might claim that his mother was from County Kerry, his father from County Mayo. No one compared what he was saying, and the newspaper reporters never mentioned it.

John Fitzgerald was a bright youth who excelled in various athletics. A short-distance runner, he was strongest in quarter-mile races, though he competed in distances up to a half mile. A fierce competitor who pushed himself to his limits, after beating those racing against him he would collapse from exhaustion. Later he would use this intense energy to enter politics. He was popular, being nicknamed both Fitzie and Johnny Fitz. Later he would also be called Honey Fitz.

John Fitzgerald and his siblings were reared in the back of his father and uncle's store. In the evening the men of the area would drop by to drink and talk, and John would listen to the stories of personal problems and politics.

The Irish poor had no one to look after them in a crisis. A widow with no resources could starve.

John learned about all this from the men and women who came to buy food or to drink. He also learned about the ward heeler, the local politician whose success came from helping those in need in exchange for their votes (sometimes several votes in the same election by the same voter) for whichever candidate he supported. The system was corrupt, but it so benefited the struggling immigrant community that not even the Church dared to challenge what was taking place.

Thomas Fitzgerald was so successful that he moved his family out of the tenement when John was only three and a half years old. The family's new quarters had separate bedrooms for parents and children, a clean toilet, good lighting, and other amenities. The family had none of the stress of the past, none of the stress of the childhoods of many who voted for John. However, he was a master at making voters feel that he was a kindred spirit. Thus he regularly referred to the tenement life he had long forgotten, not the childhood of great comfort he knew well.

While John thrived in the saloon environment, his mother worried constantly about both the children and her husband's owning such a place. She knew that alcoholism was rampant among the working-poor Irish Catholics. And she felt that those who supported the liquor business, including her husband and brother-in-law, would ultimately pay a price. Had she lived long enough to see three of her ten sons die premature deaths from alcoholism, she would not have been surprised. When she died in 1879, John, her fourth son, was just sixteen and not yet out of Boston Latin high school. She was forty-five years old, had given birth to twelve children, the most recent a girl named Mary, who died that winter. Two months later she was pregnant again, extremely weak, and in poor health. One of the several stories about the cause of her death is that she was terrified by a false report that some of her family were killed in an accident. She died on March 10, 1879, from, according to her death certificate, "cerebral apoplexy."

Only one important change occurred in John's life after he lost his mother. Now his father took him regularly to the country to see his relatives, the Hannons, with whom he had previously had only a brief acquaintance.

John had met Josie Hannon for the first time when she was thirteen and he was two years older. He later claimed to have experienced love at first sight, but as with everything John Fitzgerald talked about once he entered politics, this was probably a fabrication. What was certain was that Josie was uncomfortable with the city youth and fled to her room within moments of spotting him on that first visit.

Josie Hannon was a bright, quiet, rather withdrawn child who was a radical contrast to the gregarious Fitzgerald, her second cousin.

Josie may have been uncomfortable with the Fitzgerald boy, but she could empathize with some of his experiences. Of the nine children in the Hannon family, Josie was the sixth, born on October 31, 1865. The physical demands on parents trying to feed and rear their young were intense, and it was not unusual for farm women to age prematurely, as apparently was the case with Josie's mother.

When Josie was just eight years old, she was present when her sister Elizabeth and a neighbor girl accidentally drowned in a frozen pond.

There is no record that Josie was blamed for the deaths, but it would be impossible for a child that age not to feel responsible. Her father, distraught with grief, arrived at the water within moments of the drowning.

In horror, he pulled the corpses from the water and carried them to the house.

Josie saw her father's shock and grief, and the corpses in the parlor where he left them until others arrived to help. She was overwhelmed with remorse.

It is impossible to know the emotions that stayed with Josie Hannon the rest of her life. But from what we know today about children experiencing such trauma, without someone reaching out to Josie, letting her talk through what happened, helping her put the incident in perspective so she could heal, Josie would lead a troubled life, filled with self-hate. This was apparently what occurred.

All the surviving Hannon children endured their pain silently so far as we know. Certainly the times were such that people thought that was the role of a woman. Thus, when Josie dedicated her adult life to her husband and children, to making her home a fortress against the harsh realities of the outside world, it was fully within character. When she eventually married John Fitzgerald, she attended as few social occasions as possible, including after he became the mayor of Boston. When she went away with her husband on vacations at spas, where they were just another couple relaxing, her focus was on him, not others.

Her only regular local outing was going to church. Catholicism and its rituals became the focus of her life. After her marriage, she built a shrine to the Blessed Virgin in her home. Though it was decorated with fresh flowers and used for nightly prayers each May, the month of the Blessed Virgin, it was maintained year-round. She also gave her children regular lessons on Catholicism, in contrast to her husband. John saw in the Church more its social and political opportunities rather than a spiritual temple.

Public awareness of young Fitzgerald's political and business success first came when he was publicized for founding the Neptune Associates boat club when he was twenty-one. Always creative, he rented the Boston Music Hall, then sold tickets and advertising in the program for the club's dance there.

The night of the dance, Fitzgerald went early to the Music Hall and shut off all the water, having previously stocked the Hall with tonics. With no free alternative, the thirsty dancers paid and paid and paid for tonics. At the end of the evening, the club had made a substantial profit and Fitzgerald was gaining a reputation as someone who could accomplish things, even if he had to be devious.

Fitzgerald soon became well-known in social circles, being mentioned periodically in the newspapers. He increasingly realized that his chosen field of science was wrong for him, however, and his father's death gave him the opportunity he needed to change careers. He had only been in Harvard for nine months and could easily have continued. A local merchant offered to pay for the rest of his education, and there was a few thousand dollars in the estate to help educate his younger siblings.

John put his own twist on the story. In theory nine children were orphaned by their father's death, though John conveniently ignored their ages at the time. Instead, he became known for the emotionally moving quote: "For some reason or other, it used to be my trust to boss the family. I even washed the faces of the other boys every day and oftentimes dressed them, even the babies."

The statement brought a tear to the eye of many a voter, and Fitzgerald himself may eventually have come to believe it. Still, he was already an adult and was the fourth-oldest son. His mother had died when several of his brothers were grown, and his father died when they were in their mid to late twenties. Certainly he was not washing their faces or dressing them. And it is also logical to think that the brothers could easily have worked together. As it was, the older children hired a housekeeper to care for the younger ones, and all of them were working as soon as they could.

* * *

Editorial in the *Boston Evening Transcript*, March 5, 1880: "Let them come, then, as the waves come, and cause the absentee English landlords to mourn over their deserted glebes. It is very easy for every man of them to have a farm which they can soon call their own. . . . If politics are necessary to the existence of Irishmen, they can get plenty of the needful in this country, in some parts of which they vote so soon as they touch the soil. Our Celtic friends are good at voting, they vote early and sometimes often, and as a general thing can be relied upon for the whole Democratic ticket. With all that drawback, we say the cry in Ireland should be, Young men, leave Erin for the American shore."

* * *

When Fitzgerald first entered the world of city politics, he took for a teacher Matthew Keaney, the local North End ward boss. It is likely that John had been watched by the power brokers, who knew him first from his father's store and saloon. But he had proven himself capable in the rough-and-tumble world of corrupt Boston on his first job, that of a newsboy.

In John Fitzgerald's day, newsboys in Boston, New York, Cleveland, and elsewhere were subject to extortion and violence at best, corrupted by the whorehouses and gambling joints at worst, as they attempted to earn a living on the streets.

A paper route paid more than many better-educated adults could earn, especially in the Irish Catholic, Italian, and Jewish ghettos of Eastern cities. In September 1877, when fourteen-year-old John Fitzgerald was licensed to sell newspapers in the city of Boston, a high school graduate working as a clerk earned less than fifty cents a day. Newsboys usually averaged more than the $2.50-a-week salary on which that clerk often supported a wife. Selling papers at the end of the nineteenth century had the same appeal for low-income street kids seeking a fast dollar as drug dealing would have for boys from similar backgrounds a century later.

Newsboys began their day at three o'clock in the morning, making the rounds of the various newspapers to buy copies of the first edition. The Boston papers were numerous—the *Globe*, the *Traveler*, the *Transcript*, the *Herald*, the *Journal*, and others. Every reader had their favorites, each paper aimed toward a different type of person. The publications championed different political parties and ethnic and income groups. They featured radically different styles and focus. Every newsboy had to purchase several copies of each of the most popular papers for the people who passed the street corners where they worked.

Fitzgerald was a natural salesman. He scanned all the papers he carried, seeking the featured stories that would most interest the readers of each type of paper. He learned to spot which papers would appeal to his potential customers based on the way they dressed and carried themselves. Then he would shout the headlines that would get that buyer's attention. Because dress and demeanor were so rigidly adhered to in the

city, and because the ethnic groups were so diverse, this was less difficult than it seemed. However, many of the boys lacked Fitzgerald's
business sense, taking far longer to sell their papers.

Fitzgerald analyzed city traffic during his wanderings, ultimately lo-
cating the best locations for selling papers. However, he found that
older boys, known as hawks, had long ago conducted their own analyses
and arrived near the best locations about the time the newsboys had
sold their papers and had pockets filled with coins. The hawks would
mug the carriers, beating them and taking the day's receipts. Since the
money earned by the newsboys both paid for the next day's papers and,
in many instances, determined whether a family would have food on the
table, such muggings were a serious concern. The hawks knew just how
often to steal, eventually giving the carriers the chance to pay only a
percentage of their day's profits, the amount calculated so as to allow
the carriers to pay for their papers and have some of their profits left for
their families. The carriers, usually younger and weaker than the hawks,
generally concluded that the extortion charge was tolerable.

In 1878, when Fitzgerald had advanced to better sales areas and had
learned his way around the community, he began organizing the
younger and smaller newsboys into groups of six or more. They would
meet after selling their papers, before the hawks could stage their attacks. Then they would walk home together, outnumbering and defying
the extortionists. This ingenious solution earned Fitzgerald the respect
of the other boys.

As a newspaper boy, Fitzgerald observed all aspects of Boston, not just
the Irish Catholic ghetto. He was fascinated by the fine clothes, the
elegant homes, and the expensive possessions of the Boston Brahmins.
He wanted power, respect, to be able to live in the grand style of the
Protestant elite. Willing to work for it, to study hard, he combined the
long hours and difficult life of the newsboy with the diligence needed
for success in school. This drive attracted the ward boss.

Keaney showed Fitzgerald how to make every waking moment a potential political triumph. He learned to attend every wake in the North
End, using the occasion to talk politics. He learned to be certain that he
or others representing Keaney were kept aware of every potential crisis in
the ward. Was someone going to court? Keaney or one of his men would
be there to stand by him, to put in a good word, or to provide a bribe if
necessary. Did someone need rent money? Food? Clothing? A job? All
would be provided at a price—political support in the form of one or

more votes for the ward boss's candidate. And usually the key was to have a man vote several times.

Boston elections were always corrupt. Sometimes the ballot boxes were stuffed. At other times the loyal supporters would rush from polling place to polling place, voting repeatedly throughout the day. A man working to win the favor of the ward boss would rarely vote fewer than a hundred times, and that was when the race was *not* close.

Fitzgerald's political idol and primary mentor was Martin Lomasney, Keaney's boss, a man called the Mahatma. Lomasney was an anomaly among the sons of Irish immigrants. His father had been a tailor in Ireland, not a potato farmer, yet he was not interested in traditional business of any sort. He wanted power and practiced what would eventually be called machine politics.

The Mahatma developed simple, highly effective methods for maintaining power. He maintained a headquarters at the West End Henricks Club located near the wharves where immigrants were arriving in Boston. Greeting people as they landed, he would take them to his office and help them with everything they needed. He explained required paperwork. He assisted with housing and jobs, with medical care and all other concerns. Then, he registered them as Democrats and told them to vote for his candidates.

People were so grateful that they were happy to do what Lomasney desired. They had no political or personal allegiances when they arrived, so if Lomasney wanted them to vote for a particular candidate, they had no qualms about doing so.

John Fitzgerald's dark side first became evident while he was working for Keaney and Lomasney. The ballot was not secret in Boston. In Fitzgerald's day, only the casting of the ballot was a private matter. Once you marked your X, election workers had a variety of ways to learn what you had done before the paper was placed in the ballot box.

Many men had jobs that were secure only so long as they supported the party bosses' candidates. There were also those men who were unemployed and receiving help with food and shelter. The party in power controlled fourteen thousand patronage jobs in turn-of-the-century Boston, and these jobs were often supervisory positions where the underlings knew that their jobs were only as secure as those of their immediate supervisors. A worker quickly learned to vote for any man his boss voted for, and checkers made certain no one acted independently.

Ward heelers were present at polling places, men like John Fitzgerald, who handled anything the ward boss desired. Frequently, the ward heeler was a strong-arm bully who watched the checker to see which men voted wrong. If the candidate was the party choice but not critical to the boss, then the miscreant voter would be beaten as a warning to others. If the candidate was important to the boss's future, and if the errant voter held a patronage job, the heelers would fire him instantly. Those who did not hold patronage jobs would walk away, seemingly unscathed, while the heelers learned where they worked. Then whatever pressure was needed was applied to the employer to assure the voter was fired. No one escaped punishment, which meant that few voters ever went against the system.

In 1888, having proven himself as a heeler, Fitzgerald was promoted to checker by ward boss Matthew Keaney. Not only willing to fire or hurt anyone who had voted wrong, Fitzgerald had gained a reputation for greater vote fraud than any other young heeler in the North End. This meant that he had arranged for men to vote not only under their own names but also under the names of individuals long dead who were "registered" in the cemetery.

This particular election was important because Keaney's candidate for Common Council was not popular among the workers, who found him arrogant and abusive. There was rumor of a mutiny, and Fitzgerald's job was to be certain that each rebel voter was fired—including the uncle of a youth who had once been John's best friend. The youth had died and the uncle was known to be the sole support of a needy family. The uncle's situation was the same as that Fitzgerald claimed to have experienced when his father died. Yet he also understood that the system rewarded loyalists and destroyed rebels. Assuring his own political future, he had the uncle fired, knowing that it might mean homelessness and starvation for the family. And seventeen years later, when he was mayor of Boston, he confirmed his belief at the time of the firing that the end justified the means.

On October 1, 1889, John Fitzgerald married his second cousin Josie Hannon, having checked with church leaders to make certain the relationship was not improper. The marriage was legitimate in the eyes of the Catholic hierarchy, but it would be emotionally troubled.

Because he was away from home most of each day, Fitzgerald decided to continue living in his family's home at 465 Hanover Street. Six of his brothers were already living there, so he assumed that Josie would have plenty of company to keep her happy. He did not understand that she would have preferred a country place and solitude. She wanted a life with John as the center, not a life where she was inserted into the tail end of an extended family. She was shocked to discover that he wanted an active life in the midst of the Irish Catholics of Boston.

At first, there was no convincing John to move. However, when Josie became pregnant, her husband agreed that rearing a family was different from two adults living with other adult family members. The couple moved to their own house, though in typical Fitzgerald fashion, his family owned it. It seemed, at first, that Josie was to have nothing uniquely for herself.

On July 21, 1890, their first child, Rose Elizabeth Fitzgerald was born. Agnes Fitzgerald was born two years after Rose, the same year John entered the insurance business. And then came Thomas Fitzgerald, with three children following in the years to come.

The family could have afforded additional help, but John was not home enough to understand the need. The only compromise he made was a generous one in his mind, though a necessary one in the mind of his wife. In 1897 the couple moved to the country home she had always desired, even though the decision was politically risky because it gave him a primary residence outside his ward.

The house in West Concord included a barn, henhouse, and fairly extensive land just two blocks from Josie's brother's home. Here, Rose thrived between the ages of seven and thirteen, passing from girl to tomboy to budding woman. And since John Francis Fitzgerald and Eunice Fitzgerald, who died in early childhood, were also born there, her mother left her alone much of the time, concentrating on the needs of the less independent younger children, another fact that delighted Rose. She grew to be athletic, outgoing, self-reliant, and independent, traits that were in no way squelched when the family ultimately moved back to Boston.

During these six years, there would also be a conflict between John Fitzgerald and the orders of the Catholic Church. The Boston archdiocese had built its own school system, and all Catholic schoolchildren were to be sent to Catholic, not public, schools.

John Fitzgerald thought that this directive was nonsense. His children had to live in this world, not the next. Josie was deeply religious, leading the children in prayer, drilling them in the catechism. They regularly attended mass. Thus he insisted that they attend public school, learning the ways of the streets, not just the ways of the Church.

BG: DESPITE JOHN FITZGERALD's mixed feelings toward the Catholic Church, he was instrumental in the building of St. Edward's Catholic Church in Palm Beach. He was a regular visitor to what was then a young resort town and joined with other wealthy Catholics to finance the construction of a place for worship.

More than a century later, I attended the memorial service for my former employer held in that church. Old habits die hard. I could easily have sat near the front, a position Mrs. Kennedy always favored. I like pews that are close in, but on those few times Mrs. Kennedy had me accompany her to mass, she insisted I sit near the back. She liked to be seen, and that meant that she wanted to be alone. When she could not be alone, she certainly did not want a younger woman sitting near her. She felt that people might notice how she had aged. As a result, at the memorial I still sat toward the rear, glancing at the stained-glass window just above me. It was then I noticed a small plaque dedicated to John Fitzgerald. How ironic, I thought. When trying to honor Mrs. Kennedy's feelings about not sitting too close to where she would have sat, I inadvertently chose a pew in an area honoring her father.

The same year that Agnes was born, when John was twenty-eight, he decided to seek a seat on Boston's Common Council. This was only a $300-a-year job, but it served notice to the politicians and the voters that he was a man on the move.

In February of 1892, Matthew Keaney died and Fitzgerald became the North End boss. He also decided to run for state senator. Due to a fight between two other ward bosses (Fitzgerald represented Ward 6, with Wards 7 and 8 at odds with each other), Fitzgerald received the nomination. Since the entire area was Irish and Democratic, the victory was assured. On November 8, 1892, John Fitzgerald went from the Common Council to being a Massachusetts state senator.

The change from rural to city life, from relative isolation to being a politician, was not easy for Josie. John Francis Fitzgerald saw the city of Boston as one giant theater, and the rites of passage for its people formed the stages on which he performed. Baptisms, weddings, wakes, and funerals all experienced his presence. He went to picnics, church celebrations, and holiday festivities. He was the first to dance, the first to kiss, the first to sing, and the last to shut up when speeches were called for. His years in Massachusetts politics would be filled with the cultivation of strangers, adultery, and a style of political oratory that both friends and enemies alike dubbed "Fitzblarney." And when he realized he would never convince Josie to campaign with him, he would groom his firstborn child, Rose, to become the most prominent young Irish Catholic woman in Boston.

Rose Fitzgerald's family had long known the family of her future husband. P. J. Kennedy, Joe Kennedy's father, was also a politician. But where John Fitzgerald liked the attention of the public, P. J. preferred the back room. Although he held public office over the years, his power came from controlling how wards voted, who ran for office, and as much patronage as possible. And his money came primarily from running a saloon, a location where men went to both drink and discuss their problems, an invaluable source of information for a politician. His style was radically different from that of John Fitzgerald, and the two men were often bitter rivals.

BG: YEARS LATER I WOULD look at what happened to the Fitzgeralds, and they all seemed so common to me. Mrs. Kennedy thought of them as the Irish Catholic elite, but other than for her father, I had to question her thinking. One of Mrs. Kennedy's brothers became a ticket taker at the Mystic River Bridge in Boston. Jack Kennedy was invariably embarrassed when he had to pass his uncle's post. Dave Powers, Jack's former aide, used to laugh at the way he would slouch down in the backseat of whatever car he was riding in so that his uncle would not see him.

Mrs. Kennedy would help many of the Fitzgeralds with money in later years. She enabled them to travel, to put their children into private schools, and to have luxuries they would never have afforded. However, her seeming generosity had a price. She and her children developed a caste system, and the poor relatives were not respected. The Kennedy children never mixed with the poor Fitzgeralds, their visits as adults carefully timed so a proper Kennedy son or daughter would not have to mingle with a lowly Fitzgerald. Those rare occasions where all the cousins happened to be together at the same time resulted in Pat, Eunice, Jean, and the others barely acknowledging the visiting Fitzgeralds.

I was always amused to see the car of a relative drive onto the circular drive in Hyannis Port. The relative would spot the car of another relative, pick up speed, and continue around the circle, returning to the road in front.

It was 1887. P. J. married Mary Augusta Hickey, whose background gave her full understanding of her husband's careers. Her father also was a saloon owner and businessman prosperous enough to have sponsored an Irish girl who came to America to work as housekeeper for the family. Mary's brothers had chosen careers in medicine, police work, and the funeral business, and one of them was also active in politics in Brockton, Massachusetts. At least as intelligent as P. J., she was outgoing where he was withdrawn. She would delight everyone she met with her wit and friendliness, while he would tend to be off in a corner, enjoying what was taking place, yet too shy to participate to the degree that Mary did. From this marriage, Joseph Patrick Kennedy was born in 1888. And from this child—who inherited his father's business acumen and political savvy but not his compassion, his father's striving for success without the older man's tempering morality—a family of mythic importance would rise like Icarus to reach the sun before crashing in the harsh light of reality.

P. J. Kennedy officially retired from public life in 1893, though his "retirement" made him more powerful than ever. He had served one term as a state senator, attending the sessions with John Fitzgerald. But while Honey Fitz planned to continue in public politics, P. J. moved behind the scenes. He had his liquor businesses to sustain him financially, and he was a member of the Strategy Board, which met weekly in the Quincy Hotel in South Boston.

The Strategy Board sounded innocuous, a group of men who planned the Democratic Party's activities. In truth, they determined who would run for office and controlled money, votes, and muscle. They also controlled incumbent congressman Joseph O'Neil, whom John Fitzgerald decided to challenge for office in 1894.

South Boston meant Ward 7, and Fitzgerald was informed that if he made his move, he would receive no votes whatever in that ward. Any that were cast would either be destroyed or not counted. He might be able to sway the public, but the public experienced only the illusion of a free election. Votes went to the Strategy Board candidate, not the popular favorite.

Rose's father did not waste time fighting in Ward 7. Instead, he looked at the congressional district to see if he could win despite the Strategy Board opposition. If he could take the Charlestown and East Boston regions, areas of the district the Strategy Board could neither influence nor steal, he thought he could win. Using volunteers, many of them friends he had made while running various social clubs, he blanketed the areas where he could make a difference. He ran a strong campaign, taking advantage of the fact that Congressman O'Neil had to remain in Washington during the early days of the campaign.

Finally Fitzgerald made a move that would later be imitated by his grandson and namesake, John Fitzgerald Kennedy. He challenged O'Neil to a debate. O'Neil, confident with his past success and the support of the Strategy Board, declined. Instead he focused on his record, read messages from other congressmen praising his work, and appeared before crowds of loyalists. However, as Fitzgerald had hoped, by demanding debates at every turn and even advertising his challenge in the Boston papers, he created the image that O'Neil was afraid of him. Even the newspaper editors who should have known better began to think that O'Neil was resting on his laurels instead of finding new ways to help the community he was serving. The fear was that O'Neil would practically sleep through the next session, a belief that worked in Fitzgerald's behalf.

Fitzgerald also campaigned on the idea of his youth. He stressed that the people should support a man who represented the new. His grandson would appropriate this theme, too, John Kennedy stressing that he represented the first presidential candidate born in the twentieth century and tempered by World War II. The fact that his opponent, Vice President Richard Nixon, shared the background was irrelevant. Jack said it first, imitating his maternal grandfather's strategy.

Fitzgerald also used another tactic that he would continue in office. He relied upon women, seeing them as so important that when he became mayor, he hired as many as possible to work for him. Again this defied conventional machine policy wisdom.

Traditionally the ward bosses and other politicians ignored women because they could not vote. Why give a woman a job when a man would trade his vote (or several votes in the same election) for a chance to work? But Honey Fitz had a slightly different attitude. He took advantage of political patronage and would one day run a thoroughly corrupt city hall that created unneeded jobs for male supporters. But he made certain he had a strong force of working women behind him.

The reasoning was simple. The Irish Catholic women of Boston dominated their men. They had so much influence that an aggressive daughter could convince a father or brother to vote for the man she favored. She could also counter negative talk that had moved a man to the brink of supporting a different candidate from whom he had backed in the past.

The idea was brilliant. Despite women's not having the vote, Fitzgerald's support of women assured him stronger male support than his opponents. It also brought him close to his growing daughter Rose, who was raised as a liberated young woman ahead of her time.

P. J. Kennedy more than met his match in the congressional Democratic caucus to determine the outcome of the primary election. Every polling place controlled by P. J. would have a Fitzgerald man dispatched by hansom cab to make certain any cheating was fair to both sides. With 163 delegates attending the Democratic congressional convention, an outright win required obtaining 82 of them. In each ward, candidates were pledged either to O'Neil and Kennedy or to Fitzgerald. And in each ward, the turnout was a record for what normally was an election of little interest to anyone.

It was six o'clock in the morning before all the votes were tallied and posted in the offices of the *Boston Globe*. Fitzgerald had taken all of the inner-city wards and had won by five delegates—eighty-seven pledged to him and seventy-six to his opponent.

Two shocks followed the election: first, that the Strategy Board could be defeated, and second, that someone so new to politics could triumph so decisively. Then Fitzgerald added to the surprise by winning a seat in the House of Representatives on November 6, 1894. He would stay for three consecutive terms before P. J. Kennedy regained enough force to block his renomination in October 1900.

BG: Mrs. Kennedy told me of her father coming home on weekends. They would hear the train whistle and take the horse and buggy to meet him. On Sunday he would stay until they heard the train whistle, then race to catch the train.

In 1903, after Fitzgerald's three terms in Congress, the family returned to Boston so he could make a run for mayor. He had kept his voting registration in the North End, but that he lived outside Boston could become a campaign issue, and as a result, the family moved back into the city. They bought a mansion high atop a hill, a property so large as to isolate them from the masses in the rest of Boston. Josie was at last able to experience happiness in the city. John would have the people. She would have the house. And the public man would never let the community intrude on her private world. Or so she naively imagined.

It was 1905, the year that Rose Fitzgerald turned fifteen, that her father fought in the primary for the Democratic nomination for mayor. Again the battle was against the behind-the-scenes maneuvering of P. J. Kennedy, who again underestimated Fitzgerald's political sense.

The Strategy Board chose Edward "Ned" Donovan as their candidate because the man already worked for the government and would go along with the political machine. But Donovan was a sick man and his government experience was as street commissioner. He did not want to stand for election, but he needed a job. He was earning $7,500 a year, an extremely large sum for those days, and he could not afford to be fired. Thus he let himself be promoted, a foolish decision on Kennedy's part. Fitzgerald may not have been the best Democrat for the job, but with his experience at both the state and national level, his robust health, and his "Fitzblarney," he made Donovan look like what he was —a tool.

The final fight was intense. Although Fitzgerald had long been as corrupt as Kennedy, he had been out of politics for the previous five years, and most of the voters either forgot his past, didn't know it, or didn't care. They looked at him as a fresh candidate and he took advantage of that image. For example, on November 8, 1905, the *Boston Globe* quoted him as saying that the election would determine whether the ward bosses or the people determined their candidates. He kept attacking the fact that individual voters had lost their power. They needed to vote for him to prove to men like Kennedy that Boston was still a democracy: "And I now appeal to the people of Boston over the heads of the bosses, and I know that you will not prove faithless."

In the end, Fitzgerald won by almost four thousand votes, taking twenty-one of the city's twenty-five wards. He soundly beat the Kennedy-dominated machine, though he was smart enough that when he took control of city hall, he reappointed P. J. Kennedy as commissioner of wires. What he did not expect was that he would soon have to accept Kennedy's son as his son-in-law.

2

The Beloved Joe

John Fitzgerald was never known for his integrity. But he played by the rules of his times, and he had seen changes in his lifetime, including the fact that an Irish Catholic could become mayor of Boston. And now he wanted a better life for his oldest daughter.

Rose was smart, at least as smart as her father. She was also the mayor's daughter, and as such, she was the social leader of Boston's Irish Catholic community. But she had the outgoing personality of her father with a sincerity that he lacked. He wanted her to marry a man of integrity, of education, and of culture.

Rose had a mind of her own, a situation that was occurring with a growing number of daughters of the rich and powerful.

Rose was likewise a rebel. She fell in love during a Democratic Party outing in Old Orchard, Maine, in 1906. And to her father's horror, the boy was Joe Kennedy.

BG: MRS. KENNEDY SAID to me, "I fell in love when I was seventeen and I never fell out."

John Fitzgerald had taken the measure of Joe Kennedy and had found him wanting. He disliked the youth's father, of course, but he was willing to overlook the parents. Joe was simply lacking in everything Fitzgerald valued. Joe was a step down for his daughter, and when Joe was

28

smitten with Rose, asking her to the first dance of the year at Boston Latin that summer they first met, John refused to let her go.

There have always been two sides to the romance of the teenaged Joe Kennedy and Rose Fitzgerald. For Rose, having Joe wanting to date her, yet being denied the opportunity, was exciting and romantic.

Joe fueled the fantasy by aggressively pursuing Rose, scheming to be together. Rose saw his actions as "true love" and would not willingly date any other boy. She did not deny herself social opportunities, but all who knew her clearly saw that she would never settle for anyone other than Joe.

Joe wanted the mayor's daughter. He wanted her social position. He wanted access to her power.

But Joe was never faithful to Rose. While he had no reason not to date other young women prior to their engagement, he knew Rose was committed to him. By his making certain that, when they were together, she danced with no one else and spent time only with him, he realized she considered him exclusively hers.

Joe let Rose enjoy her fantasies, but when they were not together, he liked chorus girls. He was a "stage-door johnny," one of the wealthy young men who would wait by the back door of theaters and offer an evening on the town to showgirls. He would continue the practice for years.

Did Joe ever love Rose Fitzgerald? It is impossible to know.

In those early days, most likely the self-centered Joe delighted in having the mayor's attractive daughter hopelessly infatuated with him. Had he been more willing to include her in his life, they might have found great happiness with each other. As it was, Joe was a womanizer who had been raised with little physical contact with his parents. He had difficulty showing affection, as would his sons afterward. His lovers found him eager, but of the "wham, bam, thank you, ma'am" school of seduction.

Probably Joe was willing to make a commitment to Rose when they married. But he was so determined to show the Protestant elite what the Irish Catholic boy could achieve, so determined to live like the Brahmins and be accepted by them, that family was secondary. He would take Rose to the suburbs, which, for a young woman who had been the acting first lady of a major city, was like tethering a racehorse in the backyard of a tract house.

John Fitzgerald did not worry about Rose's seeing Joe at social events for the young. The dances she attended had cards that were passed around, the boys signing their names so that the girls had to mix. And the private parties were always ones where the families of the youths were well-known.

What Rose's father did not know was that most of her social life was rigged. Many of the small parties she attended, given by close friends, were actually fronts. They were held solely so Joe could come and the two could be together.

When Rose attended the larger events, she would meet with Joe for the first dance, during which he would completely fill her card with false names. Their favorite was "Sam Shaw," and Sam often had enough dances with Rose to arouse her father's suspicions had he not been relieved to see by her card how little time she had spent with the Kennedy boy.

The romance became serious when Rose was sixteen, and suddenly John Fitzgerald became hostile to all that he had encouraged. She had attended Dorchester High School against her mother's wishes since the school was public, not parochial. And John had been enthusiastic about her attending Wellesley, a Protestant college, until he realized that she would have access to Joe. The answer was to consult with Archbishop O'Connell, a man who, ironically, Joe would use for his own ends in the future. The archbishop suggested a convent school where the nuns would see to it that Joe Kennedy did not come around. What Fitzgerald never expected was to break his daughter's spirit, hurting Rose in ways that altered how she lived her life and reared her children.

The schools chosen for Rose were the Sacred Heart convent colleges. Located in a number of cities throughout the world, she started in the college on Commonwealth Avenue in Boston. The nuns were well educated, but they believed that a woman's place was in the home.

Rose was also enrolled in the New England Conservatory of Music, a school she did enjoy. Joe was a lover of classical music, and Rose seemed to delight in the more popular tunes of the day. Piano playing was also considered a necessary skill for a proper woman of the day, so it fit her social position as well.

BG: WHEN I BEGAN WORKING for Mrs. Kennedy, she no longer played very frequently. But on those rare occasions when Rosemary was in Hyannis Port, she played for her daughter. Oddly, she had a limited repertoire. Despite her studies, she played a popular song of the day that I have long forgotten, and "Sweet Adeline." I'll never forget that one because she added all the trills and everything, as though it were a major concert piece.

Rosemary sat on the couch. There would be the single song while waiting to go to lunch. Sometimes Rosemary would be silent. Sometimes she would mutter, "Kathleen," her older sister's name. It was barely understandable, but there was no question whom she meant. It was just impossible to tell why.

I never did know why it was only one song and only at such odd times. But it was rare that Mrs. Kennedy played the piano other than those instances, if at all. Certainly in the ten years I was with her, I never heard anything else.

The American curriculum of the Sacred Heart convent college was meant to challenge a young woman's mind only so far as it could go without straying from a primary focus of marriage and family. Rose studied music, in addition to the intense piano studies she enjoyed at the Conservatory, French and German, which she failed to master to the degree her immersion in the languages would indicate, "domestic science," and the like.

BG: DURING MY YEARS WITH Mrs. Kennedy, she had a weekly ritual for trying to maintain her language skills. She would have a massage, and while her body was being pushed, pulled, and pummeled by the masseuse, she would play recordings of French literature and language. Some records had readings of novels such as the works of Flaubert. Other records had the voice of a teacher giving proper pronunciation and grammar.

The convent college was a place to make the transition from one man's daughter to another man's wife, never quite getting beyond the dependent-child state.

Rose left the Commonwealth Avenue school with her affections for young Joe unabated. The answer seemed to be to send her out of the country, so John Fitzgerald packed up both Rose and her younger sister Agnes and sent them to the Sacred Heart convent college in Blumenthal, Holland. It would prove the most defining, and perhaps the most emotionally devastating, experience of her young life.

In contrast to her life as a mayor's daughter, Rose's religious instruction taught a life of ascetic self-denial. As interpreted by the nuns at Blumenthal, the greatness of a woman in the eyes of God came from her enduring suffering, not the pleasures of life. Some of the nuns wore bracelets and other items designed to poke into the skin, giving them painful sensations with every movement. They were, in a simple way, sharing in the pain of Jesus crucified.

Oddly, Rose's competitive spirit came into play in the convent school. The ultimate achievement was to win the coveted honor of Child of Mary. This was achieved through the rigid adherence to all rules, regulations, and rituals within the school. At weekly ceremonies, the young women were honored with award cards, which were then put in a box. The best received *très biens*—"very goods." Next came *biens*. Some girls received nothing, of course, and not to be called forward was humiliating.

The girls' education lasted two years and was so rigid that most of their days were spent in silence when they were not in the classrooms. Their letters were censored whenever possible, and though many of the girls complained to their parents of the rigidity, the restrictions, and the unnatural world, such letters were opened by the nuns, then returned.

As a result, the letters from Rose that have been saved, many of which were used in her autobiography, *Times to Remember*, picture her as living a mindless existence. She talks of gifts received from home and shopping trips taken during breaks from school. She tells of her dedication to her classes, with such comments as, "We love Blumenthal very dearly." Even when requesting that her father free her from the school's rigidity, she does so in a way that will not offend the censorious nuns. For example, in one April letter written toward the end of the first year, she had learned that her father was considering running for mayor of Boston. While she knew full well that he was in perfect health, she wrote:

"It would be too much of a sacrifice for you and for us to remain away another year. If I did not *love* you all so *madly*, I might consider another

year or two. But I often think, how could I ever forgive myself if anything should ever happen to you or Papa while we are over here."

John Fitzgerald was not taken in by the deception. He knew that she
had secretly been corresponding with Joe Kennedy, whose picture she
kept at Blumenthal. She had to stay the entire two years, and her competitive spirit led her to strive for the status of Child of Mary.

Rose disciplined herself to gain the nuns' approval, arising fifteen
minutes earlier than necessary, and becoming so devoted to the rituals
of the convent school that she did ultimately achieve the title Child of
Mary, the highest honor a student could attain. The award was not for
academic achievement, nor was it for involving herself in the community. It was for mastering all the rituals of prayer and religious worship, a
mastery that was believed to result in piety. And once achieved, the
actions were to be continued in the outside world. A Child of Mary
becomes the vehicle for spreading the ideals of the Convent of the
Sacred Heart throughout the world.

Rose took quite seriously all the ideals as she understood them. In
hindsight, this adherence to the rigid teaching of suffering gained at
Blumenthal is the only logical reason for her tolerating what she would
one day be forced to endure. Joe would repeatedly cheat, including
bringing one of his mistresses to their home. His actions concerning
their sons and daughters would bring her intense pain. And she would
witness the unnatural deaths of four of her nine children, enduring all by
never deviating from the daily rituals that she mastered at Blumenthal.

If there was a valid criticism of her life, it was that Rose Kennedy
never sought the Christian community outside the walls of the churches
she attended. For all her rituals, she never concerned herself with the
issues of poverty, hunger, and education, which became especially acute
during the Depression years. Her idea of being right with God was to
perform all the rituals available to the laity, to do them longer, more
obediently, and with greater mastery than anyone else.

BG: Mrs. Kennedy's brand of religion was ritualistic. She attended daily
mass, sat in the front, usually alone, and daily put one dollar—
neither more nor less—in the collection plate. Joe had contributed
more, and of course that was always when he needed a favor from
the church leaders or when he wanted his family's name in the
paper.

When I worked for her, Mrs. Kennedy seemed to need to be seen there, perhaps to show what the goodness of being a Child of Mary could accomplish. In fact I remember one day when she dipped her fingers in some holy water, then sprayed it at my face. "People say I'm a saint," she told me, then wryly added, "so this is my blessing."

What troubled me was that immediately after mass, Mrs. Kennedy would return to the waiting car and start to complain about life and people. She would be angry about high costs for food and electricity, angry at people she disliked or felt had done something wrong. Whatever peace she had gained in church was not carried with her out the door.

The closest Rose came to rebellion was when she and other closely supervised students were allowed to go shopping for clothing. She loved the expensive stores, loved seeing and buying the latest fashions. In addition, she delighted in hearing the gossip about the various royal families of Europe, a love she would extend to the carryings-on in Hollywood and Washington, D.C., in the years to come.

Other teachings from those convent years also affected Rose's life and, quite probably, her relationship with her husband. Sex, according to the nuns, was for procreation, not recreation. A woman should not seek pleasure from an active sensual and sexual relationship. Joe, a crude man, was incapable of giving Rose a healthier perspective.

Prior to her experience in Holland, Rose Kennedy would probably have adapted herself to Joe's desires, providing he stayed monogamous. Afterward, she was so rigid in her thinking that she felt that even to casually kiss a man was wrong. Kissing was an act of betrothal: a single man and woman could not kiss unless they were engaged to be married. She certainly followed this belief with Joe, ignoring his lack of such restraints with his chorus girls.

Rose finished her education in 1910 while Joe was still at Harvard. He had his roommate invite her to the junior prom, but her father insisted she accompany him to Palm Beach, Florida, where he liked to vacation. When he went on a trade mission to Europe in the summer of 1911, he took Rose with him, primarily to keep her away from Kennedy. His excuse, as always, was that Josie did not want to be present. This was true, and Rose knew her father genuinely needed a sophisticated woman for socializing as the Boston Chamber of Commerce delegation traveled to Austria, Belgium, England, France, and Germany. Rose's education abroad made her an asset.

BG: MRS. KENNEDY TOLD ME that she also went regularly with her father to Palm Beach. Her mother accompanied them then, Honey Fitz liking to gamble.

Her father had an additional motive in inviting Rose to Europe. One of Rose's friends was a young man named Hugh Nawn, a graduate of Harvard and the son of millionaire Harry Nawn. The Nawns and the Fitzgeralds were so close, some evenings John preferred Harry's company to Josie's as he relaxed from a pressured day. Like a loving spouse, Harry would make Fitzgerald a peanut-butter sandwich along with a cup of either milk or cocoa, depending upon the time of year. This friendship added to Fitzgerald's hope for a marriage between Rose and Hugh.

Hugh Nawn was everything Joe Kennedy was not, and Fitzgerald hoped that if he could get his daughter alone with Nawn, a romance might start. The young man met the party in Ostend, traveling with them, dancing with Rose in the moonlight, but not exciting her passion in any way. Wherever she traveled, she kept Joe's picture with her. Nothing could deter her.

One other attempt would be made to get Rose interested in Hugh Nawn. On December 29, 1913, Fitzgerald arranged for a story to be placed in the newspaper. Next to a picture of Rose was a notice that she was planning to announce her engagement in January. But there was no way to embarrass Rose. She was too outraged over what had happened to her father earlier in the month.

After her trip to Europe, Rose was sent to New York's Manhattanville Convent of the Sacred Heart school. Most of the young women attending had previously attended one of the American Sacred Heart high schools. The girls were indoctrinated in a philosophy, a statement of which was read daily by the reverend mother. This statement is often quoted to show Rose's education:

The child of the Sacred Heart understands that her role is central to the design of creation. If she is not among those few called to the perfect life of religion, it will be her task to guide the souls of her own children. Her special influence depends upon her distinctively feminine qualities: tact, quiet courage, and the willingness to subordinate her will to another's gracefully and even gaily. Filled with the tranquillity of inner certitude, she does not disperse her energies in pointless curiosity, in capricious espousal of new theories, in the spirit of contention. Long years of silence, of attention to manners and forms, have instilled in her that self-control without which order and beauty are impossible. Her bearing is the outward shape of that perfect purity which is her greatest beauty, and which models itself on the ideal womanhood found in the Mother of God. She who can bear the small trials of daily discipline will not falter at those crises in life which require firmness and fortitude.

But the young women attending Manhattanville were elitist, both in their own minds and in the minds of the nuns who taught there. Part of this was spiritual. Part of this was social. Rose Kennedy, a Child of Mary, could attend daily mass, involve herself with the rituals of the Church, yet never personally get involved in the lives of people of different races or incomes.

Once Rose put school behind her, the religious activities diminished in favor of the glamorous life of being Boston's surrogate first lady. Her mother wanted nothing to do with the rough-and-tumble world of politics, with the endless social involvements that came with campaigning, with having to hear the snide attacks, mostly justified, concerning John Fitzgerald's moral character.

Rose, by contrast, loved the excitement, the intrigue, the glamorous trappings, and the way in which the mayor of Boston was greeted by his adoring supporters. She ignored the stories of her father's infidelities, either thinking them unfounded rumors or not fully understanding what they meant. Honey Fitz was good to her mother, good to her, a delightful little man who barreled through life in ways that made her feel a little like royalty probably felt when they let down their hair. And when he and her mother encouraged her to act as his hostess, greeter, and/or surrogate, she was thrilled.

Rose's social flings were as glamorous and raucous as the convent school had been sedate and colorless. For example, her society debut—a lavish coming-out party—was attended by slightly more than 450 people. Among the "Fitzgerald 450" attending were all the Boston City Council members, the Massachusetts governor, and two congressional representatives. The day was declared an official holiday in Rose's honor. The event was the talk of Irish Catholic society for weeks following, the Brahmins studiously ignoring the gaudy splendor.

Normally, in the weeks that followed an important coming-out party, the debutante was sought out for membership in one or more of the fashionable, almost exclusively Protestant women's clubs. Because she was Catholic and the daughter of a controversial politician, no organization contacted Rose. She understood the snub and was both hurt and angered by it. However, unlike Joe, who openly took his revenge when opportunities arose, Rose retreated to church and home even when her husband and children rose to greater power and influence than any other Irish Catholic families in the nation.

As her one act of retaliation, the strong-headed Rose founded her own exclusive social organization, the Ace of Clubs. This became even more restrictive than what the Brahmins enjoyed, Rose limiting the members to those who had gone to school abroad. Such young women were the daughters of the wealthy, and though they might have been less well educated than those who stayed at home to study at Wellesley and other schools, as Rose had wanted to do, they pictured themselves to be among the elite. The newspapers agreed, and among the times Rose's name was in the *Boston Herald* was just prior to her wedding in 1914 when she led the dancing party held by the Ace of Clubs at the expensive Somerset Hotel.

While Rose was making the rounds of social functions, working with her father, who would soon be facing stiff opposition in his campaign for reelection, Joe Kennedy was making his first move into finance. He had little practical understanding of the field, though he knew how to gain the knowledge he wanted. He obtained a job as a state bank examiner working in the eastern section of Massachusetts, a job that required only basic awareness of accounting and banking laws. Accounting methods were fairly simple, and being an examiner helped him understand how loans were made, how businesses were investigated for soundness, and where predictable, avoidable mistakes had been made. He was also able to judge the relative value of existing banks, and to see where a bank could be a vehicle for wealth for the owner. The work was a graduate-level course in business and finance.

BG: MRS. KENNEDY TOLD ME on a number of occasions, "Mr. Kennedy was
so lucky to have me because I had graduated from college and
traveled in Europe and met Sir Thomas Lipton [of Lipton-tea
fame.]"

Mrs. Kennedy believed that Lipton was one of her suitors. Many
writers think that was a fantasy on her part, that Lipton was after
Agnes. I've seen his picture, though, and to me he just looked like a
dirty old man!

One of Joe Kennedy's first good businesses was Old Colony Realty,
into which he placed a thousand dollars, becoming the treasurer. The
company, which had three partners, was dissolved during World War I,
Joe coming out with $25,000 in corporate assets. The profit was remark-
able, yet in all the writing about Joe Kennedy's life and early years, the
service he performed for the company is not known, if his role is even
mentioned. Likewise, near the end of Joe's life, he was involved with a
Hyannis Port financial institution whose main business, before it collapsed, seemed to be money laundering.

Old Colony revealed one other character trait—a lack of compassion.
The firm might be said to have specialized in evicting widows and
orphans, though the scenario was slightly less cruel. The company obtained workers' small homes when the laborers and other blue-collar
owners experienced short-term financial difficulty. Rather than helping
the owners with a short-term change in their payments so they could
keep what was probably both the first and only home they would ever
possess, the company took the properties and evicted the owners. Work
crews would rehabilitate the structures—usually two- and three-family
houses or small apartments—then the properties would be resold for a
substantial profit.

Whether the dispossessed owners had alternatives is not known.

Joe was successful at what seemed like a villain's role in a melodrama,
yet he wanted more prestige. He decided to become president of a bank,
though Columbia Trust, with approximately $200,000 in assets and co-
owned by P. J. Kennedy, was strictly small-time. Its only appeal was that
it was the lone bank in a working-class neighborhood that needed its
services, so a more aggressive bank could conceivably take it over.

First Ward National Bank had just such plans. However, First Ward was Protestant owned, with a policy of not letting any Irish rise beyond the lowest level of employment, regardless of their competence. Columbia Trust was owned and operated by and for the Irish. Stopping the takeover through stock manipulation, which Joe accomplished using a borrowed $45,000, would earn the gratitude of the community and might be an act he could parlay into power.

Joe Kennedy was twenty-five when he stopped the takeover, then demanded to be made president. He was not the youngest to hold such a position, a claim he and Rose would make the rest of their lives. Many other presidents of equally small, and sometimes larger, financial institutions, primarily in the Southwest, were the same age or younger. However, the brag certainly impressed Rose Fitzgerald, even if her father knew better.

The employees of Columbia Trust were less impressed with Joe's braggadocio. On one occasion he spoke of having to work sixteen hours a day at the bank. A high-level employee laughed and said that Joe must not have been competent as president because there was far too little work to warrant such hours. Joe, embarrassed, stopped using the story, which he had always known was nonsense.

Rose and Joe liked to think that Kennedy's increased social prominence influenced Honey Fitz's decision to agree to the couple's marriage. It didn't, because Joe would always be the lowest form of Irish to the respected mayor of Boston. However, an indiscretion of Fitzgerald's certainly helped assure Rose's willingness to challenge her father's hostility to Joe and to pursue her own dreams.

By 1907, Honey Fitz's administration was already notorious for its graft and corruption. Patronage jobs permeated every level of government. There was an official city dermatologist and official tea warmer. One man received a salary as the official rubber-boot repairman, and another was paid to climb trees.

Others had engaged in similar graft, though they were more circumspect. As a result, James M. Curley, another Irish politician who was as charming as Honey Fitz, as flamboyant except in his corruption, and equally politically knowledgeable, felt that he could mount a successful campaign for mayor. He decided to utilize Honey Fitz's corruption as the basis of his 1913–14 campaign.

No one was certain how much money Fitzgerald had either stolen for his own use or allowed to be taken by others as payoffs. Whatever the amount, it was greater than the public knew, and Fitzgerald was certain that full disclosure would lead to a backlash. Curley may or may not

39

have known the details of the dirty little secrets of his opponent. However, he gave the impression that all would be revealed, along with the Toodles scandal.

* * *

A *whiskey glass and Toodles' ass*
made a horse's ass out of
Honey Fitz.
—From a popular poem used by the
enemies of Boston mayor John
Fitzgerald

* * *

Elizabeth Ryan was a blond cigarette girl who worked at the popular Ferncroft Inn in Boston. Nicknamed Toodles, she had a reputation as a loose-moraled woman who would date the rich and powerful. Perhaps John Fitzgerald only liked to dance with her and flirt and kiss in public. Perhaps he was one of her lovers.

The mayor's female constituency would never have approved of his affair with Ryan. While some women in Boston found Honey Fitz's flirting endearing, most had been reared as Rose had, to consider Toodles an adulterer.

In a desperate and vicious act, Curley sent a black-bordered note to Josie Fitzgerald, which was read by both Josie and Rose, by then a young woman of twenty-three, the same age as Elizabeth "Toodles" Ryan. The note explained that Fitzgerald was having an adulterous relationship with a hooker named Toodles. Unless he withdrew from the mayoral race, the story would be spread throughout the city.

Many unknowns surround the family's reaction to the incident. The first is how much Josie knew before the letter arrived about her husband's philandering. Certainly she knew he was gregarious. He treated both men and women in a far friendlier manner than was socially acceptable for the average "high Irish" family man. But Josie stayed at home and avoided politics. She saw little, listened to less, and may have either not known what was taking place or deliberately avoided getting any details.

Josie had maintained her home almost totally devoid of politics. Men and women did not come by the house seeking help or favors. There were no meetings of political movers and shakers. Honey Fitz was seldom at home, but when he was, he was a family man, not a politician.

Adultery was a horrendous issue, but perhaps not so large as that Fitzgerald had allowed the rough-and-tumble politics of Boston to cross the threshold into Josie's home. Curley's letter had sullied what she valued most.

For Rose, the story of Toodles must have brought out many mixed emotions. She adored her father, was closer to him in many ways than the woman he married. She had seen him in campaign rallies. She had seen him at parties. She had watched him dance, watched him flirt, watched him act almost "naughty."

It is doubtful that Rose understood what adultery truly meant. The Kennedy girls joked about how naive their mother was concerning sex. Yet she did know that Honey Fitz had hurt Josie in ways that no man had any right to do. Certainly the letter was politics as usual. Boston was notorious for the viciousness of its political campaigns. The idea that James Curley would deliberately cause Josie, Rose, and Agnes embarrassment and pain to eliminate the mayor from running for another term was reprehensible. Yet in the odd morality of Boston politics, not to use such viciousness would have been a sign of weakness. Rose understood this. Rose also understood that her father's actions were coming home to haunt him. He might be innocent of Curley's charges concerning Toodles. He was not innocent of improperly spending time with her.

If Rose could find a positive side to all of this, it was in her own love life. Her father had been the moral arbiter of her personal relationships. She would not marry Joe Kennedy or any other man without her father's acceptance. He had objected to Kennedy primarily based on the youth's lack of integrity. But after his womanizing came home to Josie, Honey Fitz could no longer condemn the young son of his political rival. Rose would be allowed to marry the man of her dreams.

The marriage of Rose Fitzgerald and Joseph Kennedy on October 7, 1914, was a quiet affair, further proof of Honey Fitz's displeasure. He was still mayor of Boston, and the head of one of the most prominent Irish Catholic families in the state. He still saw social occasions as political opportunities, even if his own career had been derailed for what most political analysts thought was the short term. (Curley won the office after Honey Fitz withdrew from the race.)

Customarily, the wedding would be larger than the coming-out party. Everyone of importance should have been invited for this time of celebration and of giving and receiving favors. The father of the bride was expected to show off wealth, power, and position, the Toodles incident notwithstanding.

Instead, the ceremony, held in the private chapel of William Cardinal O'Connell, who officiated, was attended only by the closest family and friends. The wedding breakfast had just seventy-five in attendance.

The newspapers understood the importance of the event and the people who mattered. The small wedding was a public statement of Honey Fitz's displeasure with his new son-in-law, and the reporters understood the message. Posed photographs were taken by the press immediately after the ceremony. Some showed the wedding couple, but the picture in the *Post* showed Rose, her mother, and her father. Joe Kennedy was present in name only.

What happened next is uncertain. Interviews conducted by Larry Leamer, author of *The Kennedy Women*, indicate that during the reception Joe and Honey Fitz began arguing. Rose allegedly removed her wedding ring, setting it on the mantel before standing with her father. While the event may have occurred, like so many other Kennedy "facts," this may be family myth, used to show the earliest estrangement between two people who would rarely live "happily ever after." Certainly such an action would go against all Rose's training as a Child of Mary, and she never mentioned it in her autobiography.

After a two week honeymoon at the Greenbrier resort in White Sulphur Springs, West Virginia, the couple returned to take possession of their first home. The nine-room, wood-frame house in the suburban community of Brookline was located at 83 Beals Street, on the trolley line into Boston. The home was fully furnished, and Joe added a black Model T Ford. Although such purchases caused the couple to be financially strapped, they also established Joe and Rose as young people of growing importance.

3

Brookline

The house in Brookline was meant to be an unspoken message to the Protestant elite. After all, Brookline had long been considered the wealthiest suburb in the United States. Just as the upper-class Protestant Bostonians—the Brahmins—had once made the Back Bay area their home, by the time Joe and Rose were teenagers, Brookline was the "proper" address of the affluent families. The community was also convenient to Boston. It was the end of the line for the trolley, allowing a half-hour commute into town. In addition, the roads were good enough so cars could traverse the distance in relative ease.

When Joe and Rose Kennedy purchased their Beals Street home for $6,500, they did not understand that the fact that they could buy a house in Brookline meant that the "right people" had already moved on. They never understood that all the millions of dollars you acquired, where you were educated, or what job you held could not gain you entry into Protestant Boston society. The bigotry of old wealth erected barriers between people who would otherwise have been equals. The Kennedys were Irish Catholics, and by the time they moved to 83 Beals Street, only their families were impressed.

BG: Mrs. Kennedy would always hate the fact that the people she most wanted to impress dismissed her contemptuously as being *nouveau riche*. She tried desperately to impress them, including developing what I always called the "I'm rich. You're poor" look. She taught it to her daughters as well—the disapproving, intimidating look that parents learn to use with small children, and schoolteachers develop to control a classroom.

But the "I'm rich. You're poor" look only worked with those less wealthy than she was. She made the mistake of trying to act rich to the Brahmins, who only respected long-moneyed families with the sense to "dress down." For example, the Brahmins loved to buy large wood-sided station wagons—"woodies"—which they drove themselves. They wanted to pretend that they were just down-home, average suburbanites who happened to have more money than God. But Mrs. Kennedy didn't understand the subtlety of status games, so she and Joe bought a limousine and she had a chauffeur drive her everywhere. Only the people to whom she gave the "I'm rich. You're poor" look were impressed. Everyone else knew new money when they saw it and laughed at her efforts.

Rose did not understand the social order that continued to exclude her, though she did know that among the businessmen, the profession of banking was the most respected. The Brahmins needed bankers. Having made their money in earlier generations, they relied upon the banker to help them secure and increase their inherited wealth. Since Joe was a banker, Rose felt they were now on an equal footing with the elite. That his bank was the wrong type and wrong size to matter to the Protestants was something she never considered.

The Kennedys' new home was designed for wealth, and Rose was determined to live as graciously as she imagined the Brahmins did. She had a young Irish woman who was both cook and maid, and the house was designed for a nursemaid once she began having children. Dinners were formal, the maid wearing a black uniform with white apron, fine Limoges china and silver adorning the table.

They had an Ives and Pond grand piano, of course, which Rose enjoyed playing. Like the car, it was an important status symbol for upwardly mobile Irish Catholics. And it may have been for status as much as an awareness of Rose's interest in playing that led her two uncles to give the couple the piano for a wedding gift.

Even within the house, there was a reminder of Joe Kennedy's lower societal position, not just in the eyes of the Brahmins but also in the eyes of his high-Irish wife. The photographs that adorned the living-room wall were of the Fitzgeralds, with prominent pictures of Rose and her father. The choice was not personal. Rose was still deeply in love with her husband. Yet he had to be aware of the unintentional slight, especially after being excluded from some of the photo coverage of his own wedding.

Rose became pregnant fairly soon after the wedding. Their first child, a son named Joseph P. Kennedy Jr., was born on July 25, 1915. The pregnancy was not difficult, and the nursemaid began working in the house even before Joe junior's birth. But Rose was immensely lonely, greatly frustrated emotionally, as she made the transition from first lady of Boston to suburban housewife.

Rose frequently left the house during the nine months she was pregnant, going to meetings of the Ace of Clubs and regularly visiting her parents. Yet this life was quite limited compared with the excitement she had known. The family increasingly ignored the fact that Fitzgerald had dropped out of the mayor's race because his womanizing had been made public. They did not talk further about the letter alerting Josie to the affair with Toodles. Healing was easier if they thought of Honey Fitz as overworked and in need of a rest. Even Rose, who knew better, seemed to convince herself that her father's decision was based on his failing health.

Illness was a plausible explanation for Fitzgerald's withdrawal from the mayor's race. On December 2, 1913, a fire had broken out in the Arcadia, a South End flophouse run as a mission to detox alcoholics. Twenty-eight men died in the flames. Honey Fitz had immediately rushed to the area to see if he could help, them inspected the charred rubble for clues on how to prevent a recurrence. The mayor's concern was genuine, though Curley's men spread the false rumor that the mayor's brother had been one of the drunks killed in the flames.

Honey Fitz got little sleep over the next two days. He toured all the substandard housing in the South End. He climbed up and down stairs, checked each room, talked with as many residents as he could. He was constantly surrounded by the smell of smoke, burned flesh, alcohol, urine, excrement, and vomit. On December 4, while examining a rescue mission, he was overcome by the odor of coal gas and the normally foul smells that permeated the district. He collapsed, falling down some steps, and was hospitalized. The condition was not serious, though Curley increased his attacks while Honey Fitz was momentarily silenced. Curley implied that city officials, meaning Fitzgerald and those around him, were responsible for the conditions that had led to the many deaths.

But the withdrawal from the mayor's race had nothing to do with the fires, Honey Fitz's health, or anything similar. Everything stemmed from the Toodles affair, something both Rose and her father seemed to put from their thoughts as much as possible. In fact, Honey Fitz was later foolish enough to briefly consider challenging Curley, who won the mayor's race, during the next election in 1917.

John Fitzgerald "retired" to being an active player in backroom politics and running a weekly newspaper, *The Republic*, which he had purchased a few years earlier both to make money and serve as a political voice. In fact, while considering another run for mayor against incumbent Curley, Honey Fitz used his paper to attack the mayor for allowing an antiwar demonstration during the patriotic fever of the early days after America's entrance into the First World War.

Curley had allowed some socialists to speak their beliefs on the Boston Common. He silenced his rival by claiming that the personal attack by Honey Fitz using his newspaper's editorial page had not been personal at all. It was, claimed Curley, a means of "stifling free speech in general, as a measure of personal protection from the truth, which in its nakedness is sometimes hideous though necessary.

"I am preparing three addresses which, if necessary, I shall deliver in the fall, and which, if a certain individual had the right to restrict free speech, I would not be permitted to deliver.

"One of these addresses is entitled 'Graft, Ancient and Modern,' another, 'Great Lovers: From Cleopatra to Toodles,' and last, but not least interesting, 'Libertines: From Henry VIII to the Present Day.'"

Honey Fitz knew enough to shut up, not returning to politics as an active campaigner for almost two decades. And Rose Kennedy lost all chance at regaining the lifestyle she had enjoyed as daughter of the mayor. Even worse, Joe Kennedy, who had been a man of daring and excitement during courtship, was increasingly disinterested in Rose, the Brookline house, and his family.

Rose rented a beach house between Boston and the Cape in Hull, Nantasket, not far from where the Fitzgeralds annually leased a mansion on the sea. She planned to give birth there, following the advice of the various women's magazines of the day. The delivery would be painless through the use of anesthesia. Medical professionals would be present. And the beach house would be equipped to handle any emergency. It was the ideal situation for a modern woman, quite different from the days when a midwife would be present and the agony of labor a rite of passage.

At the first signs of labor, Joe called Dr. Frederick L. Good and his assistant/anesthetist, Dr. Edward J. O'Brien. Ether was used to prevent pain, though as was frequently typical with the doctors the Kennedys consulted over the years, the procedure was quite dangerous. Ether was known to complicate labor and, occasionally, to cause the death of babies. Fortunately Joseph P. Kennedy Jr. was a healthy ten-pound boy.

John Fitzgerald, ever the politician, upstaged his son-in-law the moment he was summoned from the beach to his daughter's birthing room in the cottage. He telephoned the press, the next day's *Boston Post* quoting him as saying of his first grandchild, "I'm sure he'd make a good man on the platform one day. Is he going into politics? Well, of course he is going to be president of the United States; his mother and father have already decided that he is going to Harvard, where he will play on the football and baseball teams and incidentally take all the scholastic honors. Then he's going to be a captain of industry until it's time for him to be president for two or three terms. Further than that has not been decided. He may act as mayor of Boston and governor of Massachusetts for a while on his way to the presidential chair."

Giving birth seemed to have been more memorable for Rose for its expense than for its pleasures. Although she expressed no emotion about seeing her first child, she did remember all costs—$125 for Dr. Good's prenatal care, postnatal care, and delivery; $25 for Dr. O'Brien; and $25 a week for the nurse who stayed with Rose during the last few days of the pregnancy. This did not include the $7 per week for the maid/cook, and $3 a week for the hospital-trained nursemaid who would be handling the majority of activities involving the baby. But they were long-term employees and thus a different concern.

Rose seemed to look upon motherhood as a job for the executive woman. Nursing a baby, playing with it, or sitting with it in one's arms were all for other women. Help changed the diapers. Help handled the feedings. Eventually there would be nine children, a number that easily justified having assistance. But Rose had two live-in helpers from before she gave birth to her first child. She could afford to distance herself from most of the care and nurturing right from the start, and she did so with gusto.

The appearance of being an upwardly mobile socialite may also have been a factor in her distance from her brood. The Brahmins' attitude was that children should be seen when desired but not heard. The hired help handled all the messy chores, the separate feedings, and the like. Only when a child was clean, properly dressed, and relatively subdued was he or she encouraged to be in the presence of the adults.

By contrast, immigrant families and the extremely poor were often forced to live in close contact with each other. Lax child labor laws meant many children worked in factories, but families had to interact in cramped tenements. Thus the ability to distance parents and children in a large house, ideally staffed with at least one to help, was a status symbol.

Rose was also frustrated over being forced to live in the suburbs with Joe frequently away from home. Within a few years, after Joe's philandering became too public for Rose to ignore, they avoided being in the house together at the same time. One would travel when the other was home, the children's nurturing being limited, both parents seemingly distant.

John Fitzgerald "Jack" Kennedy was the second child, born on May 29, 1917. He was not a healthy newborn, and he would always be sickly until the day he died, despite the public image the family tried to project.

Rose had other concerns when Jack was born. World War I began in April of 1917, and all of Joe Kennedy's former Harvard classmates eagerly enlisted over the next three months. They felt they had a duty to their country, and though men with college educations were almost certain to be placed in leadership positions away from the front lines, death was a possibility. They knew it, and some feared it, but the mood of the times was such that they felt risking their lives was a small sacrifice for the nation.

Among the men whose approval he had once sought, Joe Kennedy was alone in his refusal to enlist. Rose would later remember the time as one with honor, her husband doing important war work. She ignored that he was a *draft dodger*, avoiding active duty out of expedience and cowardice, not moral principles.

John Fitzgerald may have been disgraced by Toodles, but he was still a highly respected and powerful man in the back rooms of government. In 1914, Fitzgerald had convinced Charles Schwab, the head of Pennsylvania's Bethlehem Steel Corporation, to buy the Fore River Shipyard in Quincy, Massachusetts. Schwab knew that military conflict was likely in

Europe, and the coming of war would be highly profitable for any manufacturer who could fill military contracts. Fitzgerald knew that the new ownership of Fore River would assure jobs in the region. Many of the residents of Boston, nearby Quincy, and other communities were skilled shipbuilders who had been out of work. The plant's success, coupled with the coming war, meant employment. Even better, shipyard workers were exempt from the draft when it was created. Through the intervention of Honey Fitz, Schwab was willing to hire Joe Kennedy.

The situation was perfect for Joe, as he'd be draft exempt, and the public would think he was doing important war work. He knew nothing about shipbuilding, a fact that brought severe criticism from many of the management personnel and senior workers at Fore River. But he did know business, and everyone assumed he could handle the job. In addition, Honey Fitz had been paid back for the political favor of getting Schwab so profitable a company.

Joe Kennedy was never a leader of men. A loner, he had few close associates and even fewer friends. He may have been president of the Columbia Trust Company, but it had few employees, and he had few skills in managing people.

The Fore River workers had signed a contract guaranteeing that they would be paid the same wages as the men who worked in the nearby Boston Navy Yard. This meant a modest raise that would go into effect on October 15, 1917. When the 9,000 workers opened their pay envelopes two days later, they saw no increase. More than half the employees —5,000 workers—went on strike.

It is unclear who was at fault for failure to keep the agreement, but Joe Kennedy decided to prove his skills by taking a hard line against the workers. He would fire all strikers, replacing them with men who would be pleased to have draft-exempt jobs.

Kennedy's action was foolish and ill-conceived. Two issues overrode all others. The ships were critical for a nation at war and any delays could be disastrous. And the idea of firing, then replacing, workers was equally bad. The new employees would lack the skill of the former workers. They would need training. They would make more mistakes. And there would still be delays.

Kennedy did not budge, but Assistant Secretary of the Navy Franklin Roosevelt felt that false pride and tough talk were foolish. He contacted the union organizers with the appeal:

"There is probably no one plant in the Country whose continuous operation is more important to the success of this Country in the war, than that at Fore River. As a patriotic duty the Department urges both sides to sink all minor differences and to get together for the sake of the success of our Country in this war at once."

Roosevelt was on the side of the workers and made certain that the original contract was honored, ending the strike. Kennedy was demoted. For the rest of the war he would have little responsibility and no supervisory duties. He also lost his draft exemption, which he learned two months into his new job.

Joe Kennedy understood financial irregularities, profiteering, and corruption, even if he did not understand management. He had access to the shipyard books and apparently discovered war profiteering at the Fore River yard. War profiteering was a crime, and when Joe Kennedy learned of it, he used it for subtle blackmail. The threat of its exposure convinced Joseph Powell, vice president of Bethlehem Steel, to contact the Boston draft board to help keep Joe out of the military.

Powell's letter was not enough. Further pressure was brought to bear, and Powell cabled Washington on February 25, 1918, explaining that there were no more than a half dozen men in the yard whose importance could compare with Joe's. If that were true, it meant that the others were not particularly competent. Joe had failed at the level of responsibility at which he had been hired, and his demotion left him extremely expendable. However, the request was not closely scrutinized. Joe Kennedy was made draft exempt.

While working for Fore River, Kennedy had full access to personnel records. He learned the business of shipbuilding, and much about Bethlehem Steel. Ultimately he began buying stock in that company, as well as encouraging everyone he knew to also make purchases. In addition, he gained the competence and expertise that would help him in later life. That plus the fact that he was paid $20,000 per year ultimately made the war years rewarding.

Joe was rarely home before midnight during the week, to get whatever sleep he could, then return to Fore River. He had Sundays off, though other than fathering children, he seems to have spent little time with the family.

The separation was tolerable during wartime. Joe was safe at home each night, and though the hours were long, Rose retained a romantic image of her husband's war work. However, immediately after the war was over, in 1919, Joe went to work in the offices of Hayden, Stone and Company to learn to be a stockbroker. He took a cut in pay from his shipyard salary, knowing that working for the firm would lead to an understanding of how to manipulate stock in order to make high profits. An apt student, he soon headed the firm's stocks department, approaching his goal of making his first million by the age of thirty-five, and still keeping late hours.

Rose might have been isolated in the suburbs, but if she had ever been naive about philandering, her father's disgrace had changed all that. She realized that at least some of Joe's continued late hours had nothing to do with business. Only so many activities could keep a stockbroker legitimately involved at night. The rest of the time he was having affairs, which was brought to her attention by her friends and his enemies. She was convinced of the truth of the accusations. Even worse, the knowledge came to her after she gave birth to their third child, Rose Marie, in September of 1918, and was pregnant with their fourth child in the fall of the following year.

By January of 1920, Rose was fed up with her life. She had a husband in name only, a man who periodically dropped by to get her pregnant but was never involved with the family. She lived in a community she found stifling in its isolation. She realized that her father had been right, so she left the children with the hired help and moved into her parents' home, where she was completely ignored by Joe.

Ironically it was John Fitzgerald who made Rose return. She stayed three weeks, during which time he reminded her of her duties as a wife and mother. He made clear that she had made a choice that had changed her life forever. None of them could enjoy the times when they had dominated Boston. She had to honor the commitment she made when she married, regardless of Joe's actions. She returned home to find Jack sick with scarlet fever, then a frequently fatal childhood illness. She was also in time to give birth to Kathleen, the fourth child, on February 20, 1920. In the midst of her emotional turmoil she resigned herself to her status as wife and mother, and Eunice would be born the following year.

By 1922, Joe Kennedy had mastered banking and finance, business management, the stock market, and similar areas of investment. His income was extremely high, and he understood the emotional attitudes among investors that caused stock prices to fluctuate. He had become familiar with ways to pool his money with friends, then manipulate just enough quantities of stock to cause other investors to buy into businesses whose values were suddenly inflated. The prices soared, Kennedy sold his shares, and the members of the pool made large profits as they watched the value of the stock plunge.

Kennedy had also used inside information to make himself a millionaire. Years later this would be considered a felony offense for stockbrokers. For example, while working with stockbroker Galen Stone, Kennedy learned that Henry Ford was buying the Pond Creek Coal Company, which was then selling for $16 a share. Knowing that the price per share would rise when it became known that Ford was taking control, Kennedy borrowed enough money to purchase 15,000 shares. He waited until the stock had almost tripled in value, then sold, repaid his loan, and pocketed $210,000.

Joe continued to use insider information whenever possible to eliminate risk. But once on his own, Joe moved into the motion-picture industry, his first action being a partnership arrangement to buy thirty-one movie theaters throughout New England. The popularity of the theaters was so enormous that the profits were disproportionate to those from any similar investment he could make. It was one of the few purchases he made that he held for the rest of his life.

There were other deals, many of them legendary in financial circles. But more important for Rose was what was happening at home with their third child, Rose Marie.

4

Rosemary

She was the "dirty little secret" of the Kennedy family. Rose Marie, known throughout her life as Rosemary, was the first daughter, the third child, and the most beautiful of the Kennedy sisters. She was a debutante who met the queen of England when Joe became ambassador to the Court of St. James, then dropped out of sight from the family gatherings, the family pictures. Those who knew enough to question were told that she was a schoolteacher or that she was working with children. Whatever the specifics, the implication was that she had been called to a higher order of life, not as a nun but certainly pursuing good works.

The truth, which is rarely spoken, is that Joe Kennedy deliberately destroyed his daughter. He arranged for a surgical procedure that, though fairly new in the medical community, was so well understood that Joe was decisively told that it was not appropriate for Rosemary.

Joe had two principal concerns about Rosemary. She was not the competition-oriented ideal of Kennedy womanhood, and he thought her sexuality was too intense, untempered by the moral strictures to which the other daughters adhered. Joe destroyed a portion of her brain rather than risk what she might become if allowed to follow her own path in life.

The story most frequently told by Rose Kennedy was that Rosemary had probably been damaged by delayed birth. As usual, Dr. Good was the obstetrician scheduled to deliver the baby, and as usual, a nurse was present prior to the onset of labor. However, in 1918, millions were sick and thousands were dying of influenza. No treatment seemed to work, though companies promoted everything from breakfast cereal to toothpaste as being effective. Doctors were working overtime trying to ease the suffering of the sick, as was Dr. Good when he received the call that Rose was about to give birth.

The nurse could have delivered the baby on her own, as she was trained in childbirth and the process was simple. However, in those days, medical payment was based on services rendered. Dr. Good's high fee was paid only if he handled the delivery. As a result, the nurses who worked for him were ordered to keep the baby from coming out, if possible, until he arrived.

BG: Mrs. Kennedy told me that "the nurse held my legs together [to stop the birth until the doctor arrived], and we always thought that was the reason for Rosemary's retardation."

Eunice Kennedy Shriver, Rosemary's younger sister, was quoted by author Larry Leamer as saying that no one really knew what happened during that childbirth. The idea that the delivery was delayed was speculation. What was important was that Rosemary was born retarded. Or so it would be said many years later.

Rose and Joe Kennedy differed on many things when it came to the rearing of the family, but they did agree that the older children had to take an active role with the younger children. Thus Joe junior was to be the leader in the family. He was to teach his siblings sports and other activities after he had first mastered them. Often this led to rivalry, especially between the strong Joe and his rather sickly brother Jack. The boys frequently got into fistfights, which Jack usually lost.

Rosemary, as the first daughter, was expected to be both a follower of Joe and a leader of the younger girls. This caused no problems for the next girl in line, the vibrant Kathleen. She would grow up to be the most independent, vivacious, and strong-willed of all the Kennedy children. But the third sister, Eunice, was perhaps the brightest and certainly the most serious of the Kennedy girls. She was also the least attractive and seemingly jealous of the slower, yet quite beautiful, Rosemary. It was probably a painful irony that she would ultimately be given responsibility for Rosemary when they were both adults.

BG: I REMEMBER ONE of Rosemary's visits to Hyannis Port to see Mrs. Kennedy and others in the family. It was 1977, and Rosemary was escorted by Sister Juliane of St. Coletta's School in Jefferson, Wisconsin.

The nun had been watching the treatment of Rosemary by Eunice, who insisted upon bringing her retarded sister to the beach. Eunice made her get on one of the family's boats, pulling Rosemary despite Rosemary's protests. Sister Juliane said that Eunice was pushing her into the water to swim, then pulling her back in the boat, never thinking about Rosemary's preferences or limitations. Rosemary was a Kennedy sister, and Eunice was treating her as all the girls treated each other. But the other sisters were normal and could handle themselves. Rosemary could not, and the treatment angered Sister Juliane. I remember her commenting, "Eunice has no compassion for human weakness." She said that she could not wait to get Rosemary back to the Wisconsin convent where she could lead a normal life, everyone respecting her abilities and failings.

Rosemary had one other quality that made her a disturbing influence within the Kennedy family. Although Joe spent little time with his children, his desires for them were clear. He wanted them not only to be competitive with other youngsters, he wanted them to compete among themselves and to win at all costs. He expected them to be outgoing, aggressive, and unwilling to quit anything they tried.

Joe junior made every effort to comply with his father's wishes, as did Jack. Kathleen Kennedy was much the same, as Eunice would be. But Rosemary, the third of his nine children, simply did not care. Not the natural athlete that Joe junior was, not competitive, she refused to act how Rose and Joe thought a Kennedy should.

Rose was slow in developing compared with the older children, but she did not appear developmentally disabled. It would be more than twenty years before the field of early child development became a science and studied growing children to learn what was "normal." Only then would it be known how varied childhood development can be.

No one in the growing Kennedy family ever seemed to be concerned with Rosemary as an individual. No one studied her strengths and weaknesses, looking to see if she was developing in a way consistent with other children her age. Instead she was viewed by her parents as *a Kennedy*, a unique subspecies of children who were to have attitudes and abilities superior to others. While in church, their piety was to be greater than that of the children of other parishioners. They were to have a competitive spirit so great as to routinely drive them to victory in every contest presented to them in life. In the crude comment of one disapproving acquaintance, "Old Joe wanted the world to think that Kennedy shit don't smell."

Rosemary did not, could not, or would not live the life expected by Joe and Rose. She had her own pace, something Kathleen developed in a more aggressive way in her teenaged years. Rosemary had her own interests, her own values. But while Kathleen was outgoing, Rosemary was the quiet one. Beautiful and sensual in a manner distinct from her sisters, she would never be a typical Kennedy woman.

Rose Kennedy drove Rosemary incessantly. Rosemary was going to learn her mother's way if it killed them both.

BG: MANY A TIME Mrs. Kennedy lamented her daughter's tragedy, not because of the lobotomy Joe had ordered but because the retardation made the work her mother had put in a waste of time, something Kennedy women were never supposed to do. She would say to me, "Oh, I worked so hard with her to get her to read and write. The reason my handwriting looks as though it's partially printing was so that she could imitate it."

Every time Mrs. Kennedy and I had this conversation, she tried to justify the needless, destructive operation by saying, "But I was abroad when it happened."

Rosemary certainly hated her mother, though whether it was because of her mother's early pressures or because her mother abandoned her for twenty years, I never knew.

I remember the first time I drove to the airport to meet Rosemary and her escort, Sister Juliane. Rosemary was happy, comfortable, enjoying the surroundings. Then we arrived, and Rosemary was still calm. However, once inside, when Rose made her appearance, coming forward to embrace her daughter, Rosemary changed. She stared at her mother with hatred, screaming like an enraged child who knows she has been wronged. It was frightening in a way, but more tragic than frightening. As damaged as Rosemary had been, there was a depth of understanding of her past and an obvious inability to forgive the horrors that would haunt her until death.

Mrs. Kennedy did not show any emotion. She stepped aside and let the nun take Rosemary to the room where she would be staying. Then the cook, who had come out to see what was happening, Mrs. Kennedy, and I went into the kitchen together. Suddenly all the pain she must have been feeling overwhelmed her and Mrs. Kennedy collapsed in my arms.

It was then I realized that this was the real tragedy in the family. Two lives had been destroyed, and I had no idea how much the other children may have suffered as a result. I could never understand the family's hiding the truth for so many years, seemingly just to protect the image of old Joe. There were two victims, and no matter what else might be said of Mrs. Kennedy's involvement, she would pay the price until the day she died.

For the Kennedys, Rosemary was troublesome. That she had a learning disability is now unquestioned. Reading her diaries, which Rose was once eager to discard, analyzing her handwriting, and learning of the skills of the teachers in the British school where she thrived, it is almost certain that she was dyslexic. (The most recent analysis was done by a handwriting expert hired by the CBS program *American Journal* in September 1994 to confirm the truth of the problem. Ironically the highly respected program was aired on the same network employing Maria Shriver, whose mother, Eunice, was eventually made responsible for her sister's care. Eunice would also spread the family myth of early retardation.) Certainly Rose came to understand this probability after Nelson Rockefeller, then vice president of the United States, explained to the press that he had been dyslexic all his life. After reading what he went through, as well as what it had meant for him emotionally, Rose had

Barbara Gibson send him a note thanking him for coming forward. The implication at the time was that Rose had come to understand her daughter's original problem, as well as to realize that Rosemary was probably never either retarded or of lower than average intelligence.

None of the many stories about Rosemary's young life can be believed with any certainty. Rosemary's childhood history has been re-created in several different ways in "official" family versions, the first of which came out in 1939. That she was slow to learn in school goes without question. How slow, and the causes, are much more difficult to know. There have been stories of epilepticlike seizures, of fits of irrational violence, and similar "symptoms" of brain damage. Yet all these were mentioned only after family members and friends felt forced to justify the unnecessary, highly destructive prefrontal lobotomy.

* * *

In 1958, when Jack Kennedy had already been unofficially running for president for more than a year, Joseph Dinneen interviewed the Kennedys for a book entitled *The Kennedy Family*. He wrote:

"In large Catholic families, it is a commonplace that at least one child shall have a 'vocation,' a divine call to the priesthood, the Christian Brothers, or a women's religious order. All of the Kennedy children loved rough-and-tumble sports except Rosemary. She cringed and shuddered at violence of any kind; she was a spectator, but never a participant. Unlike her siblings, she shunned the limelight and was shy and retiring. It was inevitable, perhaps, that she should study at the Merrymount [*sic*] Convent in Tarrytown, New York, and devote her life to the sick and afflicted an particularly to backward and handicapped children.

"She is the least publicized of all the Kennedys. She prefers it that way and her wishes are respected."

In 1939, when the Kennedys were interviewed by members of the British press, one reporter came away with this story: "She [Rosemary] is the quieter of the older girls, and although she has an interest in social welfare work, she is said to harbor a secret longing to go on the stage."

When the *Saturday Evening Post* ran an article entitled "The Senate's Gay Young Bachelor" in mid-June 1953, Rosemary was described as a "schoolteacher in Wisconsin."

A 1976 Associated Press story by Mary Voboril published when Rosemary briefly wandered away from St. Peter's Church in Chicago, getting lost, stated that Rosemary was first hospitalized in 1941. She then quoted Eunice Shriver's writing:

"Rosemary was not making progress but seemed instead to be going backward. At twenty-two she was becoming increasingly irritable and difficult . . . her memory and concentration and her judgment were declining.

"She has found peace in a new home where there is no need for 'keeping up' or brooding over why she can't join in activities as others do. This . . . makes life agreeable for her."

Look magazine for October 11, 1960, in an article titled "The Kennedy Women," has a caption under a family photograph that identifies Rosemary as "a victim of spinal meningitis, now in a Wisconsin nursing home."

Doris Kearns Goodwin, in her book *The Fitzgeralds and the Kennedys*, stated that Rose did not know Rosemary had had a prefrontal lobotomy until after Joe's stroke in 1961. That was also the first time she was said to have visited St. Coletta's, where Rosemary had been living for twenty years.

Rita Dallas, Joe Kennedy's nurse in the final months of his life, was told of Rosemary's slow deterioration, culminating in the family's decision to put her in the extended-care facility in 1948.

The *Palm Beach Daily News* published an article by Chris Romoser on Sunday, July 22, 1990, reviewing Rose Kennedy's first one hundred years. The article included the paragraph: "As the children matured, it became apparent that Rosemary was different from the rest. When she was diagnosed as mentally retarded, Joe Sr. decided to send her to a special boarding school near Milwaukee. Mrs. Kennedy was said to have been crushed when her oldest daughter went away. To the public, however, no disappointment or despair ever was voiced."

*   *   *

The stories about Rosemary were endless. Each reflected whatever reality the family thought could be handled by the public without a political backlash.

Perhaps no one will ever know the truth about Rose and her oldest daughter. The authors of this book have spent several years trying to discover what really took place in Rosemary's life. We located the Boston doctor who refused to allow Joe Kennedy to give his daughter a prefrontal lobotomy in the area's hospitals because she in no way matched the necessary protocol of the times. We also learned about the technique used in St. Elizabeth's Hospital in Washington, D.C., where far more lax ethical standards allowed for the operation.

Barbara Gibson obtained Rosemary's personal diaries after Rose ordered them placed in the trash. We examined all the family quotes concerning Rosemary that we could find. In addition, Barbara Gibson met the now severely retarded (as a result of the operation) Rosemary and "talked" with her. (Rosemary's communication skills are extremely crude. In a seeming verbal parody of her dyslexia, she called Barbara "Arbarb.") Barbara Gibson talked with Rose about her daughter and observed Rose's anguish because Rosemary, now a woman in her seventies, is partially paralyzed on her left side and communicates ineffectually. She walks with a limp, and her arm is bent, with her left hand held in front of her at all times.

When it comes to Kennedy family friends, references to Rosemary Kennedy are always made with hindsight. Horror over the tragedy that has befallen her, compassion for a family that has had four children die violently, and a belief that the "truth" of myth is easier to accept than the facts of her life have all helped perpetuate the most easily acceptable story. Rosemary was born retarded, her intelligence well below average on the tests of the day.

Family members, friends, and historians like to tell the stories of the childhoods of Joe junior, Jack, and Kathleen, or of the younger family members, such as Eunice, Bobby, Teddy, Jean, and Patricia. But the family's first daughter is like the tragic heroine of a Victorian novel, a daughter destined for misfortune, who might have been named Poor Rosemary, a sigh of sadness escaping the lips of anyone so much as whispering her name.

Writing in her memoirs, *Times to Remember* (New York: Bantam Books, 1975), Rose gave two clues to a hidden secret to the story of Rosemary. First, in a description of Rosemary's childhood Rose commented: "When she was old enough to learn a little reading and writing, the letters and words were extremely difficult for her, and instead of writing from left to right on a page she wrote in the opposite direction."

This is a description of a common learning disability then called mirror writing, caused by what is now called dyslexia.

The memoir hinted that Rosemary's abilities were limited, showing numerous misspellings in her writing when she was of an age to have a better grasp of the English language. At seventeen, for example, she was supposedly writing "papper" for *paper*, and "diddn't" for *didn't*. What went unsaid was that her brother Jack was a notoriously bad speller despite being the voracious reader of the family. Had Jack Kennedy's writing been compared with that of his sister, and had he not grown to mythic proportions through the family's public relations efforts that made him president, the average person would conclude that spelling was not a Kennedy strong point. A comparison of Rosemary's and Jack's mastery of the English language would have raised questions about both of their abilities, despite Jack's Harvard education.

The second clue inconsistent with the myth that Rosemary was retarded is Rose's story of how Rosemary and Eunice traveled throughout Switzerland together when Rosemary was nineteen and Eunice was sixteen. There was no chaperon, no one to look out for the girls. Yet this was a family where the younger children were taught to always obey the older, where Rose supposedly worried about her oldest child's sexual coming of age, and when having a paid escort, if necessary, would have been readily affordable. If Rosemary was retarded, would she and her younger sister have taken such a trip? Of course not.

With the daughters, Rose also worried about their becoming seriously involved with boys before marriage. Both Rosemary and Kathleen delighted in male attention. There was nothing abnormal about any of this, and Rose admitted that the only one she did not worry about was Eunice, who began dating later than the others. Rose assumed that Eunice was slow in developing, though the truth was that Rosemary was the most attractive of the older daughters, and Kathleen the most vivacious. Eunice, by contrast, seemed rather horsey and uninteresting in both appearance and personality during her teenaged years. Given the moral standards at that time for Irish Catholic young women, to which Rose strictly adhered, there is no way a "retarded" young woman and her younger teenage sister would have been allowed to travel to Switzerland unaccompanied by a responsible adult. Nineteen-year-old Rosemary, *learning disabled rather than retarded*, would have been allowed to take sixteen-year-old Eunice. But in those days Eu-

nice would not have been expected to be responsible for an older, retarded sibling.

Barbara Gibson discovered Rosemary's diaries in the 1970s. By this
time the myth of Rosemary's retardation was accepted by everyone except for several of the nuns who cared for her in a special home in
Wisconsin and had learned the truth about her childhood. *Times to
Remember* was being prepared for publication, and Rose wanted it to
serve as the official family story. The Kennedy Library was in development to honor the late president and to house the bulk of the family's
historical records. But while too many knew the truth about Joe's philandering and bootlegging to cover it up completely (despite this, boxes
of records about the period when some of those activities took place
were conveniently "lost" in shipping from New York offices to the Kennedy Library), Rosemary could remain the family's secret.

Barbara was told to throw away the diaries.

Fortunately for history, Barbara did not discard the books. First she
took them to the man who headed the Kennedy Library and offered
them for the collection. The books were a part of the family record. The
information they contained, and the facts revealed about the normal,
healthy young woman who had been Rosemary Kennedy, would add
extra depth to the family story. Thus they seemed to belong in the
archives, even if sealed from the public as with other potentially embarrassing material.

The Kennedy Library officials did not want the diaries. They agreed
with Rose that the papers should be discarded. Yet since Barbara Gibson, formerly a clerical employee of the FBI, knew that an item in the
trash may be taken by anyone and owned with clear title, just as if it
were a gift or a purchase, she took the diaries home with her.

Among the diaries were records from the London trip Rosemary took
in the spring of 1938. She talked of shopping and clothes, of movies
seen, and the diet she was trying based on tips from Gloria Swanson.
They are not the writings of a retarded woman.

If anything, the diaries are fascinating for their ordinariness. She de-
tailed the activities of each day, from when she arose through afternoon
tea and bed. She mentions the courses she was taking from some nuns,
her athletic activities, which, contrary to the image of uncoordination
her mother tried to convey, appeared to have been successful. Games of
tennis against school friends, casual swimming with friends (versus the
competitive style she faced with her siblings), trips to Buckingham Pal-

ace, and the like are all part of the writing. There is no depth to what is there, no details concerning what she saw, but that superficiality just made her diary similar to those kept by the rest of the family. The diaries were a discipline, not a creative tool.

For example, there might be: "Have a fitting at 10:15 Elizabeth Ardens. Appointment dress fitting again. Home for lunch. Royal tournament in the afternoon." Or, while traveling on board the ship, she might detail: "Up too late for breakfast. Had it on deck. Played Ping-Pong with Ralph's sister, also with another man. Had lunch at 1:15. Walked with Peggy. Also went to horse races with her, and bet and won a dollar and a half. Went to the English Movie at five. Had dinner at 8:45. Went to the lounge with Miss Cahill and Eunice and retired early."

The only time the diaries had more detail was when she was interested in something she was seeing. For example, an entry on July 22, 1936, made while staying at the Grand Hotel, told of viewing the dungeons and torture chambers at the palace. She also described the fortified town she was visiting.

Unrelated to the British trip, Rosemary described being an active part of the family. On January 20, 1937, for example, she told of going to the White House, meeting with President Roosevelt, his son James, and various diplomats. "Went to luncheon in the ballroom in the White House. James Roosevelt took us in to see his father, President Roosevelt. He said, 'It's about time you came. How can I put my arm around all of you? Which is the oldest? You are all so big.'" Later she wrote that she talked with Betsy Roosevelt and attended the reception for Postmaster General Farley.

All through the pages there are the notes of a girl entering womanhood, engaging in ordinary and extraordinary activities, the latter the result of her father's political prominence. She wrote of attending concerts, of seeing Leopold Stokowski, Lawrence Tibbett, Ezio Pinza, and numerous other greats of the symphony and the opera. Yet while Rose implied that her daughter was carefully controlled and retarded enough that she had to be rehearsed for special events, such as meeting the Queen, the diaries only occasionally confirm such preparation. She was rehearsed before meeting the Queen, but so were Rose and the other children present. By contrast, when meeting with President Franklin Roosevelt and his family, no such preparation is indicated. No "tight leash" kept her from embarrassing herself or others. In fact, there was no need for such measures. Rosemary was not retarded.

BG: THE RELATIONSHIP BETWEEN Rosemary and her mother seemed to have always been bad. At times when I watched Rosemary walking through the halls of the house when visiting Rose, she seemed to have gone back to her earliest years. Her facial expression never changed, but she would mumble, replaying old dialogue. When she was most articulate, the words sounded as though they were forced through thick wads of cotton. At other times they were incomprehensible. But Rosemary had one internal conversation where all of us who heard it thought she was saying the same words: "Damn that baby. Damn that baby." It was the scolding litany of a mother to her child, and so far as we could tell, she was parroting something Rose had repeatedly said to all the children. Rosemary had heard it when she was small and her younger siblings were growing up. It was a sad memory to retain when so many happy times were apparently erased from her mind.

In addition to the myth of retardation, there were also stories of Rosemary's temper tantrums and violent outbursts over the years. Mentioning such violence was necessary to imply that Rosemary fit into a category of brain-damaged individuals for whom surgery was sometimes used. Again in *Times to Remember*, Rose quoted Mary O'Connell Ryan, whom she said was one of her closest friends. Mary Ryan mentioned that Rosemary seemed rather shy, yet that those who knew the family recognized that Rosemary's younger sister Kathleen ("Kick") was so outgoing and vibrant that it was natural for Rosemary to be uncomfortable. Mary Ryan said, "So that's the way it was, nothing to indicate that Rosemary had any special problem, because I'm sure lots of little girls could feel inhibited by an especially beautiful baby sister. And on Rose's part, nothing, nothing at all. Nothing was ever said even to very close friends. No one outside that family—except I suppose some doctors—knew or suspected that Rosemary's condition was that unusual." Mary Ryan then said that the first she knew that Rosemary was retarded was when Joe Kennedy mentioned that "fact" during an interview he gave in 1960.

Doris Kearns Goodwin quoted Ann Gargan as saying of Rosemary prior to the surgery, "She was the most beautiful of all the Kennedys.

She had the body of a twenty-one-year-old yearning for fulfillment with the mentality of a four-year-old."

The statement is patently ridiculous, assuming the quote is accurate. The diaries and well-documented activities of Rosemary in England are proof that her mentality was not that of a child. This was not a beautiful yet severely retarded victim waiting to be raped. Her judgment may not have been ideal for her position and the times in which she lived, but no one with the "mentality of a four-year-old" could have enjoyed the activities she writes about.

Another side to Rosemary may have been troubling to both parents. The dyslexia was frustrating for her. Joe and Rose thought they were helping her by demanding that she do what the other children were doing. They seemed to feel that with the right encouragement, she would either succeed or feel better about herself. Yet the pressures were so intense that she was becoming increasingly angry and rebellious. She would verbally and physically lash out in frustration. She was not dangerous to herself or others, the tantrums being a sign of immaturity and overwhelming stress rather than declining mental health.

Rosemary Kennedy might have led a normal life had she been allowed to stay in England where she was living and going to school just prior to World War II. She had accompanied her family to London when her father was named ambassador to the Court of St. James, and there she had begun attending a school where the staff understood learning disorders. She had thrived in that environment, but Joe Kennedy did not want Rosemary remaining in England during the war with Germany. He brought her home, and by 1941, he was determined to correct her problems.

Exactly what happened next is uncertain. There were reports of rages where Rosemary violently smashed whatever was within reach. Allegedly, Rosemary kicked her grandfather John Fitzgerald as the man sat on the porch in Hyannis, Massachusetts, during the summer of 1941. If the incident occurred, no one discussing it knew the details. Certainly the idea of a powerful young woman beating a frail old man is a horrible one. But did it happen? And if it did, what were the reasons for the loss of control? Why isn't more of the story known?

Likewise, it is uncertain when Joe Kennedy decided to stop his daughter once and for all, or who knew about it. Kathleen Kennedy was working for a newspaper in Washington, D.C., at the time of Rosemary's operation, and her closest friend was John White, a fellow writer who was doing a series of articles on the mentally ill. He was covering prefrontal lobotomies, a surgical technique to control extreme mental illness, and Kathleen discussed this with him in detail.

The people truly in the know—Kathleen Kennedy and her father—are dead. John White only knows what Kathleen discussed with him, not all the reasons why. And the other family members, including Rose Kennedy, were deliberately kept unaware of what was taking place.

It is quite possible that Joe Kennedy used Kathleen as a confidante before the operation, that she knew what was going to take place. It is also possible that she was seeking information on her own, but that Joe explained what he had done following the procedure. Whatever the case, Joe Kennedy, supposedly without discussion with his wife and without her approval, arranged for Rosemary Kennedy, his oldest daughter, to have a prefrontal lobotomy at St. Elizabeth's Hospital in Washington, D.C.

Or did Joe act alone?

Rose Kennedy presented two stories to the world. In one, she and Joe jointly made the decision to give Rose the operation. In the other, Joe made the decision when Rose was out of town. It is known that Rose was away when Rosemary entered the hospital. Yet Rose had a history of noninvolvement with her children. She probably spent more time with Rosemary than with the others, yet this was limited by the standards of most families. She was also not the type to feel the need to provide support prior to the surgery. In fact, she may even have felt that the operation was minor, that nothing bad could happen, and she would talk with Rosemary when her daughter returned home.

Rose Kennedy also believed in the infallibility of modern medicine. She claimed she allowed the nurse to keep her from giving birth to Rosemary until the doctor could come. She would certainly have trusted a doctor if he told her that a procedure was minor, which this was in terms of the risk of death. But it was major in that it could destroy the patient's mind, something no one anticipated.

BG: MRS. KENNEDY WAS SITTING at her desk one day, discussing Rosemary. She commented, "I was so disgusted [by the doctor destroying Rosemary's mind]. After all my work to develop her to write and read and attend parties and dances. She was even presented at court."

Rose also had another worry that could have clouded her judgment. Rosemary had not been influenced by the convent schools in the same manner as Rose. She was pretty, sensual, and delighting in the interest of males who saw her. In many ways Rose may have seen Rosemary as almost a mirror of herself. She might have felt that the prefrontal lobotomy would keep Rosemary from losing her virginity.

It is somehow more comforting to think that a man so ruthless as Joe Kennedy acted alone. In that way both Rose and their daughter can be seen as victims. Yet the destruction of Rosemary caused no estrangement between Joe and Rose. If anything, they seemed united in not telling their children the truth, in creating cover-up stories. There was no anger, no resentment.

BG: THERE WAS ONE INCIDENT that I witnessed when Mrs. Kennedy arranged for one of the infrequent visits to Hyannis Port by Rosemary. Joe Kennedy would never allow such visits, but he was dead.

Mrs. Kennedy and I were working in her bedroom. She was obviously uncomfortable as she dictated to me. She would periodically walk to the window and look out, trying to spot her daughter, who was always accompanied by nuns from the institution where she lived. Mrs. Kennedy would say, "Where is Rosemary? The poor little thing."

There was much sadness, and it seemed to increase with each passing day of the visit. Then, one afternoon, Mrs. Kennedy and I were swimming in the pool, as we did regularly. The pool, Olympic size, was in a glass enclosure for year-round use.

The nuns brought Rosemary to the pool, but she was not interested in swimming. They sat her on a straight-backed chair facing sideways so that she wouldn't be directly facing her mother in the pool. Then she sat there, facing straight ahead, like a dutiful child who has been punished for misbehavior so often that she has vowed to behave perfectly.

We were just paddling around, and Mrs. Kennedy, staring sadly at her daughter, said, "Oh, Rosie, what did we do to you?"

Before tranquilizers, antipsychotics, and other pharmaceuticals were invented after World War II, psychiatrists relied upon physical restraints and shock therapy to keep violent patients from hurting themselves or others. A straitjacket, padded cell, and/or leather cuffs for wrists and ankles were all used by hospital staff acting as caretakers. Anything, including a prefrontal lobotomy, that could enable someone locked away for life on the back ward of a hospital to suddenly be able to live independently was considered valuable. Yet even in the early 1940s, only the most extreme patients warranted the prefrontal lobotomy. Even if Rosemary had had problems so severe as Kennedy myth alleged, she would not have been a candidate for this procedure. The only conclusions that can be made, knowing the state of understanding of the medical profession of the day, are that the Kennedys either came upon a disreputable surgeon or that they encouraged a surgeon to act improperly.

Efforts, generally fruitless, were made to learn with whom Joe Kennedy first consulted when he tried to have his daughter operated on in Boston and other nearby, larger cities. Dr. Robert Eiben, now retired, who remembered the case from when he first started medical practice in Massachusetts, recalled that she did not fit the standards. But whether Joe actively sought the procedure or simply wanted information concerning his daughter's condition is unknown. Even in those days of limited options, no surgeon following generally accepted standards for patient selection would perform the procedure on the young woman.

Doctors at St. Elizabeth's Hospital in Washington, D.C., where Rosemary's procedure is believed to have taken place, and at George Washington School of Medicine, often had somewhat lower standards for prefrontal-lobotomy patient selection.

(Readers should keep in mind that all of this occurred more than a half century ago. Many highly respected medical institutions were involved in similar activities that today are controversial at best, reprehensible at worst. But at the time, everyone involved thought they were providing state-of-the-art medical care. Once there were better methods, almost everyone abandoned the surgical procedure.)

A prefrontal lobotomy was also the method of choice for dealing with misfits in society. Frances Farmer, a Hollywood actress who gained great notoriety for her outrageous public behavior, was declared mentally ill and eventually forced to undergo a prefrontal lobotomy. The operation was supposed to "cure" her insubordinate behavior. Such was the thinking back then.

Some hospitals or communities had strict standards that limited the use of the lobotomy to people incapable of functioning in much more than a catatonic state. Others allowed the prefrontal lobotomy on those with "unacceptable" behavior, such as Frances Farmer. And some seemed willing to perform the operation on demand when a family member wanted to alter behavior without medication or counseling. The latter situation seemed to be the case with St. Elizabeth's Hospital.

The more liberal attitude in Washington, D.C., was because the St. Elizabeth staff included Dr. Walter Freeman, who, along with Dr. James Watts, was among the first physicians to try the technique. Freeman thought the procedure could be done without obvious scarring or disfigurement of the patient. Standard surgical technique involved separating the anterior part of the frontal lobe from the rest of the nervous system by cutting through just the white commissural pathways, the ones that run back and forth in the brain, essentially isolating the frontal lobe, according to Dr. Robert Eiben, who helped develop appropriate protocols for utilization of the pioneering work at the time. He noted, "That's the area of the nervous system that is not developed in the newborn, and all of the growth that takes place in the first year or two years of life is the growth of the anterior portion of the frontal lobes, and the anterior portion of the temporal lobes. The anterior portion of the temporal lobes [is involved] more in retentive memory, and the anterior portion of the frontal lobes [has] a lot of relationship with learned motor activities, and the development of a lot of the behavioral patterns that evolve, that newborns, toddlers, and so forth are just not capable of. These areas mature and these connections are made, and the attempt is made to sever these connections; they obviously will not be so graceful in their ambulatory efforts and are just dull in their social adaptive responsiveness."

The surgeons were remarkably precise, the complications almost all coming from infection and problems with the myriad blood vessels in the area. Except when Dr. Freeman operated.

Determined to find a method that would not be so disfiguring, Dr. Freeman studied the anatomy of the skull and found that entry could be made through the upper portion of the eye socket. This sounds terrible, though the reality was neither painful nor dangerous to the person's sight. The location was far enough away from the eye so there was no risk of blindness. And because the brain cannot experience pain, recovery was both rapid and without discomfort. However, his efforts were not exact. He used a gold-plated ice pick that was sterilized before each use, and he struck in a dangerously wide arc. Although he performed more than four thousand procedures with his ice pick, the end results were never so predictable as in Boston and other more conservative medical communities.

What did Joe Kennedy expect would be the results of the procedure? Again no one knows. Based on the literature of the time, he most likely expected a passive child, a daughter who would be more like an obedient staff person than a vibrant, aggressive Kennedy. She would have no extreme mood swings. She would not be much help in fulfilling the plans he had for putting his sons in high office, as the other girls would be, but she would also cause him no embarrassment.

Instead, the unnecessary, unwarranted procedure was a disaster.

BG: YEARS LATER THE NUNS who cared for her commented that based on what they had learned about the case, the worst that would have occurred was that Rosemary would have been mildly retarded had the surgeon just left her alone. St. Coletta's nuns, all well trained when I knew them in the late 1970s, were both appalled and saddened by what had needlessly taken place.

Joe Kennedy had waited until Rose was out of town before putting his plans into action. Rosemary entered the hospital, had the procedure, and it was an instant failure. She went from being an attractive young woman to being a perpetual five-year-old child in a woman's body. Joe Kennedy had orchestrated what proved to be the destruction of his oldest daughter's mind.

The cover-up was swift and brutal. Allegedly on the recommendation of Archbishop Richard Cushing, Rosemary was sent to St. Coletta's School in Jefferson, Wisconsin. She was not allowed to return home. Rose was not made a party to that particular decision, regardless of what else she may have known. It was as though Rosemary had to be thrown away after failing to come through the operation in the manner her father had desired.

The children were not allowed to ask what happened to their sister, though Kathleen, Joe's favorite daughter, apparently knew. Rose allegedly did not learn the full truth until 1961, though she could have known had she bothered to ask. She did not try to see her now retarded daughter for more than twenty years, as Eunice oversaw Rosemary's care as necessary. Yet Rosemary, during her periodic visits to the Kennedy family home after Joe Kennedy died, reacted to Eunice as if she were to be feared. As for the father, Joe Kennedy refused to see Rosemary ever again, making certain that only lies would be printed.

BG: THERE ARE MANY stories about where Rosemary lived over the years, but Mrs. Kennedy stressed to me that she had been at St. Coletta's from the time she left the hospital in 1941. Mrs. Kennedy also claimed to have visited Rosemary every year, though it was always my understanding that these visits did not occur until after Jack was elected president.

I did know that Mrs. Kennedy wanted Rosemary to come home for a visit and that Joe thought it would be too upsetting for everyone. Oddly, Joe was dead five years before Mrs. Kennedy had Rosemary come to the Cape in August 1974. That was when I met her, a woman who looked much younger than her fifty plus years. Only a few strands of her short, curly hair had turned gray, and though she had put on some weight, she was still the prettiest of the Kennedy sisters.

Rosemary was also the one most comfortable with people, a truly agreeable child/woman. It was heart wrenching because she was so young mentally.

I remember one time when Mrs. Kennedy was in one of her cheap moods. Rosemary was flying to Boston to see her mother, and in the past two nuns would accompany her. Mrs. Kennedy did not want to go to that expense, though, so she insisted upon a single nun/companion.

My daughter Kathleen and I drove to the Boston airport to greet them. We all walked to the carousel where the luggage would come in. As the luggage was unloaded, the three of us became momentarily engrossed in removing the bags. Suddenly Kathleen looked up and asked where Rosemary had gone.

The nun was extremely upset. The reason for having two companions was so that one would never take her eyes from Rosemary. As it turned out, Rosemary had seen a boy she thought was just her age—five years old—and followed him down the hall, out the door, and into the parking lot. She wanted to play with him. Fortunately we managed to retrieve her before she could get hit by a car or arrested for bothering the child since, standing still, she looked normal at the time and might have been mistaken for a molester.

The whole thing was heart wrenching and so needlessly tragic.

What also went unsaid, what has gone unsaid to this day, is the way the surgery affected Teddy. How did the nine-year-old youngest son feel when his oldest sister was suddenly discarded? The Kennedy family must have seemed like a tragic game of musical chairs, where no one had a permanent place, or a room of one's own.

The only permanent child's room was the nursery, and the oldest children came to joke that, after they had been away for a while, it was important to check if anyone new had been born. But everyone else stayed in whatever room was empty.

BG: THE FAMILY'S NOMADIC LIFE created other problems. Jean Kennedy Smith, Mrs. Kennedy, and I were swimming in the pool one day. Mother and daughter started talking about the night before at the dinner table when they had been discussing the grandchildren and the different schools they were attending. The two were referring to what Teddy had said about the problems with his education when I asked, "Did the senator go to a lot of different schools?"

Jean said, "Yes, he went to fifteen."

And I said, "Fifteen?"

Jean replied, "Well, I went to twelve and that's why I'm still trying to get my head screwed on."

And then Mrs. Kennedy got upset with her daughter and the conversation. She got out of the pool and stomped into the house muttering, "Well, what was I to do? Mr. Kennedy was always away. I was left alone with you children."

I stared in amazement, her comments having nothing to do with the turmoil she and Joe had created for the children. But Mrs. Kennedy wasn't finished with her tirade. She ran into one of her nephews and complained, "And I had to take care of you." Then she proceeded into the house.

The disappearance of Rosemary, when combined with the pressures his parents placed on him, was probably the major factor in forcing Teddy to sublimate all personal desires. Teddy, desperate for stability, for parental approval, and for love he probably seldom felt he experienced, witnessed his oldest sister, a sweet, gentle girl as he remembered her, seemingly rebel against their father. She did not behave the way Joe Kennedy wanted a Kennedy to behave, and one day she went away, never to come back. Teddy was not allowed to ask what had happened to her, where she was, or what might be happening.

The message was clear. Disobey Joe and Rose Kennedy and you will cease to exist. From that time forward, Teddy Kennedy placed his own emotions on hold, never letting himself become too close to anyone, carrying anger, fear, and guilt trapped inside his troubled heart. The destruction of Rosemary, along with the reinforcing negative factors in his life, ultimately led the surviving male child to become a drunk, a womanizer, and a bloated figure, ironically while achieving more genuine long-term political power and influence than any of his favored older brothers.

Many years later, the family members obviously knew what had happened to Rosemary. The brothers and sisters, the second and third generations, had apparently been gossiping.

David Kennedy, one of Bob's sons, a troubled youth who eventually died of a drug overdose, talked about his Aunt Rosemary. He had been having trouble in school, trouble with the family, trouble with the law. His mother spent little time with him, sending him to schools, camps, relatives—anywhere she would not have to work closely with her son. His brushes with the law were periodically reported in the newspapers, which resulted in regular family conferences and private talks with Ted, his aunts, and trusted friends or retainers.

David felt he was fortunate to be a problem Kennedy after Joe was dead. He said that if his grandfather were still alive, the same thing that had happened to Aunt Rosemary could happen to him. He said reflectively, "She was an embarrassment. I am an embarrassment. She was a hindrance. I am a hindrance."

Tragically, David was probably correct in his thinking.

5

Mobsters, Moguls, and Movie Stars

Rose Kennedy may have been naive in some matters, including human sexuality, but she was extremely sophisticated in others. Honey Fitz had seen to it that his daughter was both worldly and streetwise. She was reared in the midst of cutthroat politics. She witnessed smear campaigns, corrupt voting, and the manipulation of a city. She understood power at least as well as Joe did and early in their marriage might have been the ideal partner for his dealings. Whatever morality she had learned as a Child of Mary, it applied solely to home and family, not business and politics.

Joe Kennedy never considered Rose as a possible partner in his ventures. He needed to be in control, to dominate in business and in life. He had to be able to take decisive action without anyone's counsel, bragging about those bold decisions that worked and hiding the results when he failed. That was why he was comfortable ordering Rosemary's prefrontal lobotomy, and that was why he was equally comfortable sending her to a convent for care the moment he learned the operation destroyed her mind. He ordered Rose not to see her. He ordered the children not to contact her. And he himself refused either to face his broken child or to visit her literally from the moment she awakened from the anesthetic.

Joe decided where the family would live and how their lives would be conducted. And he was willing to cheat anyone for his own ends.

What Joe Kennedy would not do was work with a woman who insisted upon being his equal, not his ever-faithful subordinate.

The man with whom Joe worked most closely, the person he allowed intimately into the world from which he excluded Rose, was Eddie Moore. Ironically, Joe hired him from the staff of his father-in-law, whom Eddie had served when Honey Fitz was mayor. So close did the two men become that Joe and Rose named their youngest son—Edward Moore "Ted" Kennedy—for him.

Eddie Moore had mastered the amorality of backroom politics. He was astute enough never to take credit for original ideas of his own once such ideas were embraced by the men for whom he worked. He knew to let Honey Fitz and later the ex-mayor's son-in-law provide leadership or keep the appearance of being in charge. He used his creativity and business skills in carrying out his assignments. He could be trusted to do anything he was asked, and in a manner where neither he nor his employer would ever get in trouble.

Rose would not have wanted to assume Eddie Moore's role. She had been the de facto first lady of Boston. Anything less than an equal partnership with her husband would have seemed demeaning. Yet had Joe but asked, she could probably have been convinced to let the staff rear the growing family while she worked in Joe's business empire. She already considered herself an executive in her home, following a women's magazine idea to make a card file on each child for effective record keeping of illnesses, inoculations, and other important data. A Child of Mary could be a leader in both business and the home, provided that the business also involved her husband.

But Joe held no such respect for women. He had no intention of ever being faithful to Rose. He seemed unable to emotionally commit to anyone, a trait that was most blatant in Jack, though seemingly shared by all of his sons. The closest he ever came was to actress Gloria Swanson, yet even that affair ended with her discovering that the most lavish gifts he had bestowed upon her were paid for with her own money.

The end result was that Joe and Rose increasingly led two distinct lives. Joe's world was known to Rose only to the degree he wanted her to be aware of it. And since Rose was the family chronicler, the source for information passed on to the children, parts of Joe's world were lost to the family. They could only be discovered through business records, diaries, memoirs, and interviews with others, many of whom were involved with organized crime.

It should not be surprising that the large sums of money that helped

Joe Kennedy with his business dealings initially came from bootleg liquor. Some people have said that this was because he never stopped thinking like the son of a barkeep, but that is unfair. Joe Kennedy was attracted to service businesses for which there was seemingly unlimited public demand.

Prohibition was yet another opportunity to make money, and while Joe always craved acceptance from the Brahmins, he was not against going into partnership with the rogue members of other immigrant groups.

The one semipublic acknowledgment of Joe's activities came when he was the official supplier of high-quality, illegal liquor to his Harvard class's tenth year reunion. He may also have bootlegged liquor in the Hyannis Port area of Cape Cod, where he and his family would eventually buy a home. Because of its fishing industry and its many coves, Cape Cod was ideal for smuggling liquor.

BG: Mrs. KENNEDY NEVER DRANK and never understood how much her daughters did. Only when she read newspaper stories about Pat's and Jean's overindulgence did she become at all concerned.

Joe used to be upset that his wife wouldn't drink because the family's wealth was initially based on the liquor business. "I think it's stupid," Mrs. Kennedy told me. "My husband used to say I was terrible because he made a lot of money from liquor and I never drank any."

Ironically, Mrs. Kennedy was most worried about the staff drinking any liquor that might be kept in the house. She did not realize that her ban against it only affected her children, who used to have to bring their own bottles.

Joe Kennedy was not alone in his bootlegging. A number of business leaders, during the course of their careers, became involved with such groups as the Irish Mafia, the Bugs and Meyer Gang, La Cosa Nostra, the Purple Gang, the Cleveland Gang, the Jewish Combination, and numerous others. Chicago's notorious gangster Frank Costello was one of Joe's earliest partners in the illegal liquor business, the same man who would be Joe's partner in the purchase of Hialeah Race Track in the 1940s.

Rose Kennedy and Her Family

This is not to say that Joe Kennedy was an active participant in organized crime. He was simply one of many businessmen who were willing to enter into a venture with the devil if a profit could be made. However, such a history would not look right in the family background of a president, and as Jack rose in politics, those in the family who knew the truth about Joe's illegal ventures worked to keep them from becoming public knowledge.

Rose was oblivious to all this history and focused on the end results of Joe's work. She traveled first-class. Her children went to private schools. Chauffeurs, maids, cooks, and other help allowed her to focus on whatever activities she desired to pursue. The staff handled anything she found unpleasant, including being the primary nurturer of her growing children. If Joe was in partnership with criminals so she could dance with royalty, then so be it.

In contrast to his illegal activities, the unethical dealings of Joe Kennedy were not secrets. Since he was breaking no laws, though laws were later passed to keep others from emulating his actions, he bragged about his successes.

The Kennedy family was constantly growing during the early years of Joe's business ventures. By the time Joe junior, Jack, Rosemary, and Kathleen were born, the family obviously needed a bigger house. Brookline was still the most desirable neighborhood in their minds, so they moved in 1921 to a larger house just a five-minute walk away at 131 Naples, hiring more servants just prior to Eunice's birth.

The move did not help the couple's relationship, however, and their separations were becoming more frequent. For example, Rose Kennedy's diary notes on January 16, 1923: "Joe left on 5 o'clock for Palm Beach with Bill Spargo, Eddie & Ted O'Leary. They joined him in N.Y. & left there about 5 o'clock Wed." The next day Rose took her oldest daughters, Rosemary and Kathleen, and went to the community of Poland Springs with Mary Moore, Eddie Moore's wife. They returned on January 27, the staff having cared for the two older boys. A little over a week later, on February 8, Joe returned to the family. Then, after a few weeks with the family, Rose again packed her bags and took the train to California, traveling with her sister Agnes. It was April 4, and Jack was outraged. Rose's diary entry from the previous day states, "Jack said, 'Gee, you're a great mother to go away and leave your children all alone.'"

Later Rose would dismiss the incident. She claimed to have been troubled at first, but then she had to return for something she had forgotten. She expected to find her son still moping about being sad. Instead, just five minutes after the tearful parting, he was happily playing, seemingly oblivious to her departure. Yet over the years Jack would lament to friends that his mother had been cold to the children, never hugging them, never being present when he felt they needed her. He needed nurturing his mother was incapable of providing, and his father was so rarely home, he was little more than a distant authority figure to be obeyed without really being known.

Friends of Kathleen's later said that she felt that both she and Jack were similar to their mother in not being emotionally committed to anyone. Interviews with some of the women Jack dated both before and after his marriage said that he was not physical outside of sex. If there was warmth in him, it was reserved for his children, whom he would know far too briefly.

Rose's attitudes toward her husband and children were odd. She regularly explained that Joe was being a good provider, working long hours for the family to be comfortable. Since he spent lavishly on them, she may actually have believed all this. She certainly did not look too closely at what he did on vacation without wife or children, even though he could well have afforded to take them with him.

Likewise, as her children entered adulthood, Rose seemed to believe that she had devoted herself to their well-being. Her influence on them was enormous, and they feared her wrath their entire lives. Yet her prolonged absences, beginning when her oldest children were barely of school age, seem rather cruel.

What seems most likely is that the children were always desperate for the approval of both their parents. They would do anything to try to win their love. The frequent absences may even have seemed like punishments for some wrongdoing, causing the children to strive even harder to please. All that is certain is that both parents, not just Joe, were frequently absent.

In the midst of his rapidly growing family and moves to ever larger homes, Joe Kennedy first became aware of the movies. At first he looked at the popularity of the movies as just another way to make money. Although he kept the truth from Rose, and his children would have only limited awareness, the family fortune was jump-started by Joe's willingness to enter any venture where large profits could be made. Bootleg

79

whiskey was already making him wealthy. Then he began seeing movies differently, gradually coming to recognize the power of the new industry. Projected in the dark, on the flickering screen, a movie could shape public opinion. Though it could be fantasy, the viewer, seeing it with his or her own eyes, believed it.

Joe's first partnership was with Galen Stone and Guy Currier, a former Harvard classmate, with whom he bought a chain of thirty-one movie houses called the Maine–New Hampshire Theaters. In addition, he gained the franchise for the Universal Pictures films to be shown in the area. By 1923 he'd added a movie house in Stoneham, Massachusetts, just north of Boston. And he also bought the rights to several British pictures, which he could then offer exclusively in his small territory.

The film industry in the 1920s was not a respected one. The Catholic Church was quite hostile, and some states, including Massachusetts, were exploring the issue of a state censorship code. Joe's involvement with the film industry was a moral dilemma for Rose, though she found that she delighted in the glamour of the business. She and her children were well aware of the emerging fan magazines that made actors and actresses appear as sophisticated as royalty. Rose found it exciting that her husband was connected with all of this, though the moral issues were still serious concerns.

Rose took advantage of a California trip in April 1923 to travel to Hollywood. Despite her misgivings about the industry, she was irresistibly drawn to the glamour. Her diary from the trip records her pleasure at seeing the most famous young female star of the day—Gloria Swanson. Neither woman had any idea that Swanson would eventually become Joe's mistress.

Eventually Rose handled the moral issue the way she handled most concerns that might have brought her into conflict with Joe. She ignored it.

Joe Kennedy's Hollywood years were lonely ones for Rose. She either stayed at home with the staff and the children or traveled to shop. She was settling into the life of the rich matron whose existence is circumscribed by the swimming pool, the golf course, and the most exclusive specialty stores. It was like a period of hibernation when the actions of others would ultimately determine how drastically her life would change, and how dramatically the future would unfold.

Joe cultivated a friendship with Will Hays, the former Indiana lawyer and cabinet appointee under President Warren G. Harding, who was hired to establish and enforce standards of decency for the new Motion Picture Producers and Distributors of America (MPPDA). Hays felt that Joe, a strong family man, a businessman, and someone untainted by the scandals of Hollywood, should work in films. As a result, Rose was certain everything would work out and she chose not to talk further about her moral concerns. Hays hoped Joe Kennedy could bring fair financing methods to the industry.

Kennedy decided to work briefly in New York as an assistant to producer Jesse Lasky. Lasky was part of Famous Players–Lasky, whose chairman of the board was Adolph Zukor. Lasky was in his final few years of power, being pushed out of the business in 1936. But this was a decade earlier, and Lasky was considered one of the most knowledgeable men in the business.

Kennedy learned the best way to make money in the film industry was to focus on action pictures, often westerns, that involved a lot of dangerous stunts. They were relatively short, could be made quickly, then had to be moved from town to town. Though popular with children and adults, their appeal was short-lived. Most of the films were in a community's movie theater only three or four days before audiences demanded something different. However, there was no censorship problem. Catholic Church leaders felt that such films were proper family entertainment.

Guy Currier agreed to use his law office and political connections to put together a financial package for Joe's planned productions. Currier's wife, Marie Burroughs, was a Shakespearean actress, and the two of them had a strong appreciation for all the arts, including film.

The vehicle for Joe's work was to be FBO, a small, heavily indebted production company. Originally called the Robertson-Cole Company, it was created in 1918 as a means of H. F. Robertson to expand beyond his vaudeville business. The company, which Robertson ran in conjunction with Rufus S. Cole, had its studio at 780 Gower Street in Hollywood. Ironically for a studio in jeopardy of "dying" because of excessive debt, the land had been purchased from the Hollywood Cemetery.

Robertson-Cole bought the Triangle Studio along with its Santa Monica ranch production facility for westerns. The company was well-known for such pictures, its biggest and highest-paid star being Fred Thompson. The actor was so successful that he used a custom-built Packard just for transporting his horse. More important, the purchase was for a token fee of a dollar. The owners thought that they could not miss becoming a major player, constantly trying new mergers and, eventually, new names. Unfortunately, by the time the company became the Film Booking Office of America, or FBO, it was thoroughly mismanaged. There was massive debt, most of it to Graham's Trading Company and Lloyd's of London, both in England.

Joe Kennedy began negotiating with FBO's creditors to buy the movie company for $1 million, a third of the debt that existed in 1925. The price was considered too low, so Joe bided his time, spending the winter working on some Florida land deals. In the meantime the FBO debts kept mounting, and it was obvious that nothing would ever be paid back. Getting a little less than a third of what was then owed seemed a better deal than getting nothing. In February 1926, as Joe left New York's Harvard Club in preparation for a Florida vacation, a telephone call came in from England. with the help of an investment consortium of businessmen put together by Currier, the deal was made.

Rose Kennedy was uncertain what any of this would mean at first, but her father knew. He had even taken a small stake in the Currier package. Though only a minor investor, he immediately went to the Boston papers, touting his almost nonexistent role in the deal and raising the supposed price paid to $10 million. The headline in the *Boston Post* was "Fitzgerald Film Magnate."

The other newspapers seemed to know that the ex-mayor was probably not a major force in the deal. But he was part owner, he was high Irish, and Joe remained "the son of Pat the barkeeper" in their eyes. The incident was yet another reason for Joe's anger toward the world of the Boston Brahmins, who seemed determined never to give him credit for any success he might have.

FBO would be headquartered in Manhattan, and Joe planned to move Rose and his children to New York. (There were seven children by then, Robert having been born in 1925. Jean would follow in 1928, and Edward Moore "Ted" Kennedy in 1932.) Joe hated Massachusetts by then and was looking for a property to buy when Rose refused to move. She felt the children's lives shouldn't be disrupted every time Joe went into a new business. They needed consistency, the schools they attended were good, and she felt that Joe could commute. Many of the Brookline men had offices in New York, commuting by train daily or weekly. Joe might have to stay overnight at times during the week, but he was a member of the Harvard Club and he could stay there. Joe would honor her decision, though only for the short term.

Joe approached FBO as a businessman, hiring mentor Lasky's most trusted New York production chief, William Le Baron, to work the same job at FBO. Le Baron was to increase the number of FBO's pictures to one per week. He was told to make action-type pictures, known to make money.

Joe cut pay wherever possible, made film stars out of popular heroes of the day, such as football great Harold "Red" Grange, and ended weekly salaries. Pay was for each day worked.

BG: MRS. KENNEDY FOLLOWED this type of thinking to the detriment of her staff. She had a rule that anyone paid by the hour would receive no money when she wasn't in the residence where that person worked. The maid in Hyannis Port had no Kennedy income when Mrs. Kennedy traveled to Europe or down to Palm Beach for a prolonged stay. The maid in Palm Beach faced the same problem. Since most of the staff were paid by the hour, Mrs. Kennedy always had high staff turnover. Joe was not stingy and paid the staff no matter where he and Rose were traveling. But when he died, she applied his management practices from Hollywood to the homes she kept, much to the regret of the staff.

Hollywood half-welcomed Kennedy at first, which was greater enthusiasm than had greeted him when he first entered other businesses. The studio heads ultimately came to loathe most aspects of the Kennedy years because they felt that the quality of films suffered under banker-financed pictures. They liked making a movie any way they wanted, then using most of the profits to make their next film. They wanted to both lead the cultural tastes of their audience and be audience driven in some of their films, taking risks, experimenting with new forms of comedy and drama. True, many of the stories involved gangsters and violence, but with Prohibition many cities were then living under the domination of organized crime. And while some members of the Mafia ultimately entered the glamour industry, Joe Kennedy was the rare studio executive involved with both Hollywood and the violent side of bootlegging.

The Los Angeles press was the most delighted with the Eastern businessman. Having reported a series of scandals, they liked the image of a casual, youthful, freckle-faced, supposedly dedicated family man who would restore something special to the industry. And no one complained about the movies he ultimately made because they were innocuous fare, a combination of melodramas and westerns starring both established favorites like Thompson and men such as Red Grange who were popular with kids but had little acting ability. The nickels of those kids in the box office, though, eventually produced excellent profits.

By 1927, the successful film mogul Joe Kennedy could no longer tolerate living in Massachusetts. He knew that despite his success and his respect in Hollywood, a family of Irish Catholic descent would never gain respect in the state where he was born. His daughters would never be asked to join the social clubs their wealth should have allowed them to join. He would never be a part of the business elite, even though he was amassing a fortune that was greater than many of theirs.

Rose Kennedy had fewer frustrations than her husband. She was forced into a world of isolation because of his travels, but she was still the ex-mayor's daughter. She still was the more respected of the couple, the person who had many friends in such groups as the Ace of Clubs, which she founded.

Rose was also close to her father, and being physically near the man she still adored despite the Toodles incident was important to her. The children were all right, and because of the way they were being reared, they were not a serious concern. The Kennedys were expected to be their own best friends, and to be intensely competitive among themselves and when challenging or challenged by others. Yet Rose often treated the family as a burden she needed to escape. Over time it seemed to become a respite from her other activities, which involved much socializing.

Fed-up and not caring what Rose thought, Joe acted independently. He first bought the Hyannis Port house the family began renting in 1926 for summer getaways. The price reportedly was $25,000, but Joe Kennedy immediately brought in the architect who had designed the house in 1903. He wanted the place doubled in size, and he wanted to add a room where he and his family could watch movies, including what were called the talkies. The price for the projection equipment alone would be $15,000, higher than the price of many of the homes in the area.

Separately, Joe had Eddie Moore locate a mansion for the family just outside Manhattan. He found one in Bronxville in Westchester County, just a seventeen-mile commute from the city. The county was both wealthy and Protestant. The family moved on September 26, 1927. There were twenty rooms, cottages for the chauffeur and gardener, and five acres of wooded land. A private railroad car transported the family, their servants, and their possessions.

At the same time, Joe Kennedy rented a mansion on Rodeo Drive, the luxury center of Beverly Hills, the most expensive real estate in southern California at the time. There was a swimming pool and tennis courts, in fact everything that was needed to delight his growing family. All that his California residence lacked were his wife and children. Rose had no place in what Joe considered the "good life." All he needed were starlets for sex, and those he had in abundance.

During his Hollywood years, Joe Kennedy essentially divorced himself from his family. The luxury trains on which he traveled from coast to coast took four to five days in each direction, time spent out of contact with his growing businesses. Whatever his relationship with his wife, he had the money and the power to attract every beautiful woman who thought that having sex with the tall, skinny producer would be the way to a starring role. He seldom traveled unescorted, even taking women to many of his business-dinner meetings. And he knew that, because of the way she was reared, he could always return to his wife's bed and enjoy her favors whenever he bothered to return to the family home.

Yet the women Joe Kennedy was known to be dating were using their bodies, not their brains, seeking to benefit from a man's weakness, not meeting him head-on as a strong equal. Not until Gloria Swanson.

If Rose Kennedy had not been rigidly molded by the Catholic Church, and if she had pursued the lifestyle she enjoyed when acting as her father's representative during his time as mayor, she would likely have been the emotional twin of Gloria Swanson. Both women were bright, aggressive, eager for all the experiences of life. But Gloria had been reared without moral constraints, was given limited formal education, and, sexually liberated, was comfortable experiencing whatever the man in her life desired. Married or single, she made her choices and let the man make his. Convention was for others.

The biggest difference between the two women was their physical appearance. Gloria entered womanhood as a fairly flat-chested, almost stick-legged girl with an overly wide mouth, large blue eyes, and pixie nose who took several years to grow into a genuine beauty. The young Rose was the far more attractive of the two women, though the frustrations of a bad marriage, the frequent childbirths, and her tendency to withdraw into Church ritual led her to frequently appear somewhat dowdy as she got older. Both women learned to use makeup and clothing to enhance their appearance, but by the time Joe Kennedy met Gloria Swanson, she was flaunting her beauty for the men in her life while his wife was seldom trying to please him.

Much has been made of the meeting between the banker and the actress, somehow implying that each was instantly taken with the other's looks. While Joe Kennedy may have been impressed with Gloria Swanson, who, at five feet one, was close in height to his wife, she later said of him, "With his spectacles and prominent chin, he looked like an average working-class person's uncle."

The couple met in November of 1927 in New York City at the luxury Savoy Plaza Hotel on Fifth Avenue, where she was staying, meeting with the sales and distribution personnel for United Artists. Her debts were greater than the average middle-class family could hope to earn in fifty years of hard work. Numerous lawsuits had been brought against her for not paying her bills. Yet she understood image and alerted the maître d' to put the cost of the lunch with Joe Kennedy on her bill. Should there be any problem, should Joe Kennedy become insistent, then the maître d' was to say that the couple were the guests of the hotel. Either way she would cover it.

Gloria Swanson knew that though she was broke, she had to appear every inch the star—glamorous, rich, in total control. In truth she was facing financial ruin for the lavish lifestyle she had no intention of ending. The most famous movie star of her day, she received an average of ten thousand fan letters each week. At twenty-eight, she represented the modern American woman, her hairstyle, clothing, even her mole being imitated by young women throughout the nation.

Joe was intrigued by many aspects of that lunch. There was no magic in their relationship, no lust. He had told Rose and the children he would be dining with her, and all of them were impressed. Kathleen was an avid fan, and her esteem for her frequently absent father rose greatly. However, what impressed Joe was the way the other diners looked at them. He was important with Gloria at his table. He was special. Why else would Gloria Swanson sit with him? He was a man to be envied. It was a feeling Joe had never experienced in Boston.

Gloria needed money, which Joe knew before meeting her. She wanted a loan to cover cash-flow problems and to finance her next picture. She brought the financing proposals made by both the Bank of

America, one of the few California banks willing to provide fair loans for movies, and United Artists. She hoped Joe could look at the papers and decide which deal was better. She also hoped he might make a third proposal, a better deal.

Gloria had an accountant for her business, a supposedly competent man who had not been able to restrain Gloria's spendthrift ways. She also had a friend in Robert Kane of First National Pictures, a man who also knew Joe Kennedy. He had alerted Kennedy to Gloria's circumstances and suggested that Joe might wish to take over Gloria Swanson Productions. Large sums of money could be made once the unnecessary spending was ended.

If anything came from that first meeting, it was that they realized that both of them had an excellent grasp of motion pictures as a business. He enjoyed the gossip of the industry, including the way she had gained the rights to the Maugham property, but his grasp of the intricacies of foreign sales, various rights, accounting procedures within the industry, and all the other details of production that could ensure success exceeded her own. But she was not a pretty face capitalizing on her beauty. She knew production, distribution, and the roles of all the people needed to assure the success of a movie.

By December of 1927, Joe Kennedy and his staff, working from their rented home in Beverly Hills, had completely changed Gloria Swanson's finances. He analyzed her income-tax deductions, the money she was paying for staff, the ways in which she made movies, and everything else related to her business. He realized that she was in complete control of every aspect of her life except its finances. She not only had no comprehensive business sense, she had no interest in either the tiniest of details on the sets or the overall financial framework in which every movie had to be made. Yet awareness and involvement were critical for maximum success.

Finance was Swanson's only weak point, though. Of limited education, without adequate guidance, and with a series of crises women with twice her years might not have handled effectively, still she triumphed. She learned from life, from both mistakes and successes. Quite beautiful, she had conducted her personal life prior to marrying Henri de la Falaise de la Coudraye in a way that meant she might see sex as Joe did —recreation frequently unrelated to love.

Just when Joe Kennedy decided to have an affair with Gloria Swanson is uncertain, though it is known that his closest associates helped him. Joe, his personal business staff, Gloria, and Henri were in Palm Beach,

Florida, in January 1928, working on her business affairs. The rest of the Kennedys were up north, Joe making certain he would not be disturbed by such nuisances as wife and family. Perhaps he carefully plotted that first day's sexual escapades. Perhaps he concluded that the timing couldn't be better. However it happened, when Eddie Moore convinced Henri to go deep-sea fishing, initially everyone was going. But then Gloria convinced her husband that she was afraid of small boats and needed to do some shopping. Kennedy, seemingly always under business pressures so intense his stomach constantly troubled him, had important business calls to make.

Swanson did go shopping, then returned to the hotel where she and her husband were living. She was in a kimono, lying on the bed, talking to the hotel florist when Joe entered the room, having come into the suite as the maid was leaving. As she later wrote in her autobiography:

"He wasn't listening. He just stood there, in his white flannels and his argyle sweater and his two-toned shoes, staring at me for a full minute or more, before he entered the room and closed the door behind him. He moved so quickly that his mouth was on mine before either of us could speak. With one hand he held the back of my head, with the other he stroked my body and pulled at my kimono. He kept insisting in a drawn-out moan, 'No longer, no longer. Now.' He was like a roped horse, rough, arduous, racing to be free. After a hasty climax he lay beside me, stroking my hair. Apart from his guilty, passionate mutterings, he had still said nothing cogent."

Gloria Swanson had no illusions about the relationship, nor any wish to end it. Joe Kennedy was a staunch Catholic, married to a woman for whom the teachings of the Church were to be followed so rigidly, it would not matter if her personal life was in tatters. Gloria was married to a nice man with little ambition, great kindness, and a desire to help his wife succeed without trying to live off her career. She had no interest in divorcing Henri and knew that Joe Kennedy would not leave Rose for her. Still, she also knew she would yield to whatever he desired from her for so long as he sought her favors and/or her companionship.

The relationship between the two lovers was brief, stormy, and well-known. Even today, at such Hollywood insider haunts as Musso and Frank's Grill on Hollywood Boulevard, one can see photographs of the couple obviously more intimate than business partners. However, each had the good fortune to be married at the time. With all the morality codes, no one felt pressured to break up an adulterous couple so long as they were reasonably discreet, not living together or having parties for the press, and could trot out their respective spouses when needed.

Because of this, the relationship took on a rather outrageous nature when Joe Kennedy, who had just made his mergers with RKO and RCA, agreed to produce Gloria Swanson's first all-talking picture. The film, called *The Trespasser*, contained the song "Love, Your Magic Spell Is Everywhere," which would show that Swanson could effectively carry a tune. It would premiere in London, England, where she was popular, and the opening would be attended by both Henri, who would travel from France, and Rose, who would travel from America with Joe, Gloria, a woman friend of Gloria's, Virginia Bowker, and Joe's sister.

Before the trip, Gloria and her daughter traveled to Kennedy's Hyannis Port residence. In addition to its spacious movie theater, the twenty-room house featured the doll room. Rose collected dolls from every country in the world. Special glass-covered shelving lined the walls so the dolls could be simultaneously protected and displayed. The high-ceilinged attic was largely ignored, though it contained invaluable treasures, as well as massive cedar-lined closets and drawers where Joe kept his clothing. Steel cabinets held files, and the numerous antiques were so varied that they might have been the holdings of a store catering to collectors with widely differing tastes. For example, there were two plates used by George Washington, each accompanied by a lock of his hair, mounted in shadow boxes. They were hidden away in the cedar closet, Mrs. Kennedy having forgotten about them until Barbara Gibson discovered them around 1975. In another case was a baton once used by famed conductor Arturo Toscanini.

There were other unusual holdings as well. When Joe was in New Hampshire, he bought the Shea family collection of antiques. They had an entire room filled with valuable furniture, cranberry glass, hand-carved duck decoys, silver hollowware, and numerous other items. Joe wanted completeness, so he even had the floorboards of the room where the Shea family had had the collection taken up, then laid down in the sunroom. The fireplace mantel and other items were added as well. The holdings became a room within a room, like a historical museum display that tries to re-create the cabins of early settlers inside the larger building.

Joe and Rose liked best that the grounds could be used for the standard competitions among their children and other family members, whether that meant sailboat races, baseball, or football.

BG: Joe Kennedy enjoyed lavish surroundings that Mrs. Kennedy seemed not to care about. Just as the Hyannis Port home showed his taste and interests, so did the home the couple owned in Palm Beach.

By the time I first saw the Palm Beach house, everything was at least a generation out-of-date. The property, seemingly indistinguishable from other wealthy family homes along North Ocean Boulevard, had a big red door complete with iron straps and large circular handles. The Spanish-style house had a red-tile roof and a white stucco interior. There was also a white stucco wall with wooden gate that was generally kept unlocked.

The house was most desirable because it was designed by Addison Mizner back in the 1920s. Mizner was the Florida architect of choice for the wealthy, and in this case the client had been the Wanamaker family of Philadelphia. They had wanted to entertain, and the design showed that. For example, the kitchen comprised several rooms meant for different uses. One high-ceilinged room had a big metal table and three restaurant-type freezers. The primary part of the kitchen had two stoves, a refrigerator, and endless built-in cabinets. The butler's pantry, larger than most people's kitchens, had glass-fronted cupboards with dishes and glassware.

The entry foyer led to a living room on the right and a massive dining room on the left, both rooms having expansive views of the ocean and front lawn. There were ten bedrooms, including four small ones for live-in domestics. There was a tennis court, swimming pool, dressing rooms with showers, and even a private beach entrance in the sea wall for those who wanted to swim in the ocean. Naturally that entrance had additional dressing rooms.

By the time I was at the house, everything had changed for the family. Joe was dead and Mrs. Kennedy was too cheap to maintain the place properly. The beautiful red-tile roof was falling apart. Wooden window frames were rotting. The outdoor glass patio tables were frequently cracked by coconuts that had fallen from the trees. And some of the stone that surrounded the swimming pool had been so rust stained, it looked as though a murder had taken place, the blood not completely washed away.

Inside was as bad, with threadbare curtains, greasy old linoleum, and peeling paint. Joe liked luxury. Mrs. Kennedy had no interest in the upkeep once he died.

Gloria found that Joe was different at home from how he had been in Hollywood. He was always a fantasy figure for his children, the one person who both seemed to care for them and who was forever traveling somewhere else. Rose, in her pain, withdrew from the children and traveled as much as she could. For example, she made seventeen European shopping trips in the six years following the stock market crash. But the children considered her someone to be ignored, accepted, and/ or feared in contrast to the way they treasured their frequently absent father. The children were determined to take advantage of him, to play with him, to show off for him, to win his approval one way or another, whatever that took. It was almost as though they felt responsible for his frequent absences, determined to do everything right so he wouldn't leave them again.

Instead of the wealthy playboy and business genius, Gloria saw a proud, seemingly loving father. He was also intensely stern, setting the highest possible standards so he would not "overwhelm" them with love.

It is impossible to know what Rose saw this August 1929, when the summer people were visiting Hyannis Port in large numbers. Joe regularly introduced Gloria Swanson as his most important business associate. He referred to her as Rose's friend, though Rose did not know the movie star. As for the community, most people viewed movie stars as magical. Gloria had somehow been dropped into their midst, and they delighted in her presence, gossiping about her, observing her, becoming almost giddy with each new contact. Many local children had trouble believing that the girl playing with Pat Kennedy and going to school with her was really Gloria's daughter.

Kathleen was delighted by Gloria's presence. She, her sisters, and her friends were using a room above the garage as a clubhouse. It was decorated with movie posters, and they all read such fan magazines as *Photoplay*, learning about the stars. They were thrilled that Gloria Swanson visited their hideaway and overwhelmed when she signed her name on the wall. Ironically, after Kathleen learned that her father was intimately involved with the actress, she never removed the autograph. However, she did become totally devoted to Constance Bennett, a glamorous rival of Gloria Swanson's. So abrupt was her intense reversal that her friends, who knew nothing of the affair, were still afraid to ask why.

Rose had long tried to comfort herself with the stories in *Photoplay*, *Motion Picture World*, and similar publications that stressed the home life of Joe Kennedy. They ran photographs of Joe, Rose, and their seven children. He was portrayed as a devoted husband and father because the industry wanted the public to have such an image of the man.

But Rose did understand what was happening, though she publicly denied it. Honey Fitz was outraged by Joe's cheating, though he had rarely been faithful to his wife. Josie Fitzgerald told Rose that she could finally see what all men were like, that Rose's precious Joe Kennedy was no different.

Yet Rose never acknowledged the pain. The act fooled no one, and many years later her daughters were quoted as saying that they would not have put up with what their mother had. And in their own ways, that was true. Pat Kennedy eventually divorced womanizing Peter Lawford. Joan Kennedy, a Kennedy by marriage, eventually divorced Ted Kennedy.

BG: I WAS WITH Mrs. Kennedy when Teddy called to tell her he was getting a divorce. Nellie, the cook, Mrs. Kennedy, and I were in the maid's dining room when the telephone rang. Mrs. Kennedy went to the telephone and we overheard the conversation.

"Yes, dear," she said after hearing the news. Her voice was calm, no different from that of someone suggesting a lunch appointment. "Is there someone else?"

All I could think was, of course, like fifty-six other women.

Mrs. Kennedy did not say anything to Nellie or me, but she had talked enough about the couple in the past so I knew there was no surprise. She had told me about staying in Ted and Joan's house, discovering that they did not sleep in the same bedroom. She had also found that Joan slept in in the morning so as not to have to deal with her husband.

Teddy also brought other women to dinner and lunch at his mother's home. I don't know if he was affectionate toward them, but he wasn't affectionate with anybody. Besides, just their presence instead of his wife's told Mrs. Kennedy anything she might want to know.

Rose continued her usual routine during the Swanson visit, including mass at St. Francis Xavier Church each morning, then breakfast with her older children. Joe had time alone with his girlfriend, but not nearly enough. He decided to take her on a sailboat he had purchased in 1927, a vessel ironically named the *Rose Elizabeth* by his oldest sons.

The *Rose Elizabeth* had a hold large enough to a hide a twelve-year-old boy, and Jack hid there when his father and Gloria Swanson went sailing. She was unable to swim, but Joe was good in the water and skilled with the boat. He had not asked any of his children along, so Jack decided to surprise his father. Jack sneaked up on deck, discovered his father and Gloria in a more intimate fashion than "friends" or "business associates," and, shocked by what he saw, leaped over the side of the boat, swimming away from land.

Joe, not knowing what was in his son's mind, yet realizing that Jack was a sickly youth, not strong enough to save himself, leaped into the water. While he saved his son's life, that incident seemed to have been an emotional turning point for the future president. Many of his cavalier attitudes toward women as sexual objects, especially his relationship with Marilyn Monroe, seem to have stemmed from his shocked disillusionment with his father. In the future Jack would have only one serious relationship, with Inga Arvad, a woman he met at the start of World War II.

Rose Kennedy spent the entire ocean voyage to London in 1929, to see the opening of Gloria Swanson's film *The Trespasser*, playing the naive wife. She talked delightedly with Gloria, sharing stories of their respective children (Rose's eight and Gloria's two, at that time). The only other subject that seemed to hold interest for Rose was the Church.

Joe's only effort to be discreet was to spend nights with his wife. He frequently ignored everyone except Gloria and once threatened to start a fight with a man dining at the next table who was (in Joe's mind) excessively eyeing the movie star. Gloria was both embarrassed and certain Rose would be irate. Instead Rose expressed compassion for Gloria's endless lack of privacy and need of protection from strangers.

After the London premiere and before the return to New York for the U.S. opening of *The Trespasser*, the stock market crashed. Much to Joe's delight, the movie business boomed during the Great Depression. Joe, who had sold his various holdings long before the crash, was sitting back, waiting for the economy to strike bottom, so he could buy the companies shattered through the misjudgments of old friends and foes alike.

Near the end of 1929, according to an unconfirmed and controversial allegation by Gloria Swanson, Boston's Cardinal O'Connell came to New York to visit the actress prior to her return to the West Coast for the holidays. He wanted to talk about her association with Joe Kennedy, and while they both avoided being specific at first, Gloria knew he meant the personal, not the business relationship.

According to Swanson, Joe Kennedy knew that he could never divorce Rose to marry Gloria. The Catholic Church would not permit it, and though he never said so, it was doubtful that Joe wanted a divorce. Love was one thing. Divorcing a woman with eight children was another. Joe was too greedy, too frightened of losing even a portion of his wealth, to consider divorce even if he had been a Protestant. What he sought, ostensibly because he was a Catholic, was the right to live apart from Rose and maintain a separate home with Gloria.

The cardinal explained that Gloria had become an "occasion for sin" every time she and Joe were together. Joe's public appearances were closely scrutinized since he was supposedly one of the most prominent Catholic laymen in America. The latter was probably an exaggeration because Joe distanced himself from the Church as much as possible except when its leadership or its members could be used for his own ends. However, the potential for scandal was there.

Gloria was irate. She informed the cardinal that what he was discussing was Joe's problem. If he was not at peace with his faith, then he would have to take some action. She told Cardinal O'Connell to talk with Kennedy, not her.

Some have tried to dispute the story, to say that O'Connell did not make the contact or that he did not make it when claimed. More likely the story is true and that the source of the information concerning Joe was Rose. Sending the cardinal may have been what she felt was a last chance to stop her husband's public mockery of his marriage vows. All relationships before and after Gloria were adequately discreet. Gloria, by contrast, was no different from Honey Fitz's Toodles, the "wench" flaunted to such an extreme that Rose's mother became the object of either pity or derision.

Henri was not willing to play the role of silent martyr. Early in 1930 he sent his wife a letter saying they should plan a formal separation. Then, in whatever way Gloria chose to announce it, she could file for divorce. Joe Kennedy was never mentioned. Henri, too, could be "civilized," though unlike Rose, he had no intention of being in the midst of the lie.

Joe Kennedy's film production career was short-lived, primarily because of his ego, though it would be lucrative enough to add at least $5 million dollars (in 1930's money. The equivalent would be close to $30 million today) to his fortune. He wanted to become a famous producer, and he wanted Gloria Swanson to be his leading lady. He commissioned a comedy for her, though from two less than brilliant writers. They were Josephine and John Robertson, with Vincent Youmans composing the songs. The screenplay that resulted was terrible, and Kennedy was convinced by others in the industry to change it. Ultimately a quality comedy was developed utilizing the talents of such people as Sidney Howard, a Pulitzer Prize–winning playwright. He was also the author of the new story's title—*What a Widow*—for which Joe Kennedy gave him a new Cadillac.

What a Widow was a success with *Daily Variety*, which delighted in Swanson's acting, the dialogue, and the direction. The more important New York critics were less enthusiastic, the *Times* viewing it as slapstick where most of the attempts to be funny were "rather pathetic." Even more embarrassing for Joe Kennedy, whose name had not been on the highly successful *Trespasser*, the movie utilized new special-effects techniques. The titles were animated at great cost, and the result was riveting. No one could miss the credit that read "Joseph P. Kennedy Presents," a credit he originally thought would assure that everyone knew the brilliant Swanson success was his doing. Unfortunately the public, like the critics, was not impressed.

Comedies such as *What a Widow* had lost their popular appeal in 1930. More and more Americans were out of work. Based on ticket sales, Americans wanted either the glamour of elaborate musicals or they wanted the drama, the violence, and the ultimate "good guy" triumph of gangster films. Comedies did not offer the type of pure escapism they were seeking. And while Gloria Swanson's popularity had not slipped, her name alone was not enough to sell a movie. With the special credits, the last film of Joe's Hollywood career would always be seen as *his* flop.

Joe Kennedy decided that it was time to get out. On December 6, 1930, the film industry and Gloria Swanson learned the truth about Joe Kennedy. Pathé, which he headed, was ending the year with a $2.6

million loss and was being sold to RKO for $5 million. The *Motion Picture News* for that day explained that "RKO is assuming the leases on the Pathé exchanges throughout the country, Pathé News, the laboratory at Jersey City, the building at 35 West 45th Street, the studio in Culver City, and all product, features, and short subjects, beginning with *Sin Takes a Holiday*." RKO also acquired many of the leading stars and directors from the other company, ironically including Constance Bennett, who had become Henri's lover following the separation from Gloria Swanson.

The deal was wonderful for RKO and Joe Kennedy, and the merged assets would result in substantial corporate profits for RKO. Joe personally made millions; the only people truly being hurt were the stockholders, who were convinced that they were victims of deceit, mismanagement, the illegal use of proxies, and other frauds.

By the summer of 1931, several facts were evident. The merger of Pathé, RKO, and indirectly RCA, which came to own 60 percent of the new company, paid excellent dividends for the leadership of those firms, including Kennedy. The new company eventually consolidated production at the Gower Street facility, closing the Culver City studio. David Selznick, the twenty-nine-year-old genius who would bring immense success to the business, took over, working closely with publicist Russell Birdwell. The latter helped make both *King Kong* and *Gone With the Wind* international favorites. Thus the company prospered, the executives who worked with Kennedy to change the business were successful, yet the early stockholders were left with unexpected losses.

There were other discoveries as well. The dressing room of the bungalow Kennedy had arranged for Gloria Swanson when she was on the lot had a listening device Kennedy had planted in case Gloria cheated on him with someone other than her husband. (Joe considered himself monogamous because he could brag to Gloria that, for the previous year, Rose had not gotten pregnant.) In addition, the Cadillac given Howard had been billed to Gloria's accounts instead of to the cost of the film as agreed. (Joe's accountant kept the books until their parting.) Joe gave Gloria a fur coat, then charged the present to her account. The cost of the bungalow he had bugged also came out of her income. In addition, she later learned from producers and other business executives that Joe had acted behind her back to prevent her from acting in films that could have brought her greater income and prestige. However, these would have required her working with others, not Kennedy, and he would hear nothing of such arrangements. In effect, Kennedy had wooed and won his mistress fair with her own money, not his.

For his part, Joe returned to Wall Street without saying goodbye to Gloria. He stayed with his family in Bronxville most nights and every weekend. He fathered Teddy, the ninth Kennedy child. Rose felt that both he and their seventeen-year-old marriage had been saved. In reality, the philandering was simply on holiday, though the children were happier than they had been for most of their lives. For the moment, their father was home.

BG: Teddy was both perhaps the loneliest of the Kennedy children and ultimately the most treasured. Mrs. Kennedy often talked about how people thought her foolish when they discovered that she was pregnant with Teddy. "They warned me I would lose my figure, I would be tied down for years to come, I would never escape the demands of such a large family."

She worked hard to regain her figure, and as for the demands of a large family, they were almost nonexistent for her. The staff was available to rear the children whenever she wanted to get away.

But once he was grown, Rose began to favor Teddy. He was the son most like her father. Tall and fat where John Fitzgerald was short and wiry, Ted nonetheless had the sense of humor her father enjoyed. He was like the stereotypical beloved, drunken Irish uncle who has ale in one hand and a tale of blarney coming from his lips.

After the deaths of Joe junior, Jack, and Bob, Ted's importance grew. As Mrs. Kennedy would often say, had she not gone against the "wisdom" of others and let herself get pregnant, she would have had no sons left at all.

The relationship between mother and son was flirtatious. She always wanted him to see her as being special. The daughters Pat, Jean, and Eunice would come to lunch and were likely to encounter their mother in a dressing gown and pink pajamas on her way to take a nap. A nap might have been planned for a time when Teddy would drop by, of course. She was habitual in her actions. But with Teddy she would not be dressed for the rest she would take after he left. Instead she would put on one of her colorful suits from Courreges, add a matching wide-brimmed hat, and modify her voice so it was girlish. They were more like close friends who knew how to make each other laugh than mother and son.

The relationship was a sharp contrast from the past with Teddy. It also contrasted with the way Mrs. Kennedy treated her far less favored daughters.

What spin did Rose want to put on Joe's affairs in Hollywood? As she later recalled in *Times to Remember:*

"During Joe's years in the movie industry he was surrounded daily by some of the most beautiful women in the world, dressed in beautiful clothes. Obviously, I couldn't compete in natural beauty, but I could make the most of what I had by keeping my figure trim, my complexion good, my grooming perfect, and by always wearing clothes that were interesting and becoming. And so, with Joe's endorsement, I began spending more time and more money on clothes. Eventually I began landing on some lists of 'Best Dressed Women.'"

6

The Years Before the War

Joe Kennedy was scared when he returned to the East. He had not been hurt by the stock market crash. He had always understood the economic crisis he and others like him had created with their stock manipulation. Thus he had anticipated an end to the twenties' speculative boom. That was why Joe Kennedy had shifted his money before the collapse, leaving his family with a minimum of $100 million in safe assets.

Joe Kennedy feared what the Depression could mean for the country. With families starving, radicals were calling for drastic changes in politics and society. A revolution might take place. Certainly it was to the federal government, not the business community, that the public would be looking. In the near future, if a man wanted ultimate power, as Joe Kennedy did, he had to look to government. Whoever was in the White House or held a meaningful position with the national government would have the power and respect that the CEO of a major corporation previously held. While Joe had not yet formulated thoughts of running for the presidency, he decided that he could at least buy government prestige.

Rose, by contrast, looked upon the family's fortunes as typical of what she had come to expect from Joe's business acumen. She may have come to hate him as a husband, but she knew she had been right in thinking that he was smart enough to be an excellent provider for her family. They were secure. The troubles affecting the rest of the country were not a concern. Instead, she could continue to focus on clothing buying sprees and international travel. As a result, she traveled alone to

Europe seventeen times during the first six years of what, for most people, was a period of extreme poverty.

Hyannis Port and all of Cape Cod were also seemingly oblivious to the economic disaster. The year-round residents had always had little money; frugality and self-sufficiency were long a part of their lives. The summer residents, like the Kennedys, had protected their money from the vagaries of the stock market.

Jack Kennedy attended the prestigious Canterbury Day School, where the parents of the pupils were likewise untouched by the Depression. In a note to his father, Jack asked that magazines and newspapers be sent to him "because I did not know about the Market Slump until a long time after."

Yet while the finances were in good shape, Rose was increasingly becoming an eccentric whose concerns were clothing, appearance, and control. She was undoubtedly reacting to the shock of her husband's flaunting his mistress in their home, yet her behavior did not help her marriage or her children.

Some of the oddities had been occurring for years. In addition to the file cards kept on each child, Rose liked to write notes to herself. Then, so she wouldn't forget to check them, she would pin them to whatever dress she was wearing. At any given moment one or a dozen notes might be adorning her clothing as she went about her day's activities.

She also began using what she called "frownies." These looked like pieces of cloth tape that she placed anywhere on her face that she felt she was developing frown lines. Often as the staff dealt with Rose, concerned with her next clothes buying trip to Paris, she would be walking about with hair curlers, taped lines, and pieces of notepaper adorning her body. She was determined to be beautiful for Joe no matter how unattractive her efforts might make her look when he was away from home.

BG: MRS. KENNEDY WENT SWIMMING every day as part of her exercise program, but she was concerned about the effects of the sun on her skin. Before going outside, she placed a bathing cap on the front part of her head, and a second one, slightly overlapping, for the back part of her head. Over that she would wear a straw hat tied on with a silk scarf. She wore dark sunglasses and a sun shield. Only then would she go into the water.

It must have taken Mrs. Kennedy ten minutes to get ready. Sometimes she would try to make things easier by stretching one of her bathing caps over a drawer from her bedroom night table.

I still remember one time when the water became a little rough and a wave swamped us. I had to retrieve her hat from where it was still bobbing in the ocean. But her sunglasses and sun shield sank to the ocean floor, and I had to scoop them up.

It was ridiculous, but she would protect her skin at any cost.

The relationships at this time between the Kennedy adults and their offspring are difficult to know. The boys were to be sent to boarding schools. Joe had already decided that Jack and Joe junior would eventually go to Harvard, and he wanted them able to stand on their own with Protestants, so he was focused on the Choate School in Wallingford, Connecticut. It was headed by an Episcopalian, though, which troubled Rose.

Rose tended to justify her travels by saying they gave Joe a chance to have a strong influence on the children. The family tried to convey the image of great parental involvement. Rose talked of her influence on the children's spiritual development, their regular attendance at church, and their learning to use their time wisely. She was constantly drilling them on names, dates, and facts of history. She treated life's lessons like a catechism for which there were questions and answers to be spouted at the dinner table. Many a Kennedy guest was astounded to have to endure what felt like a quiz-show atmosphere when having a meal with the family.

By contrast, Joe believed in spirited discussions about current affairs. He expected his children to be knowledgeable and to have developed their own opinions. He did not care how naive these might be, so long as they were reasoned.

Rose Kennedy believed that religion was the primary builder of character. Joe Kennedy believed that experience was the better teacher. However, the character he wanted from his children was at once obedient toward himself and aggressive toward others.

During the summers in Hyannis Port when Joe was at home, he oversaw the children in a variety of competitive events. Sailing was especially popular, and Joe Kennedy hired a series of "skippers" to lead the children. These were professional seamen who acted as instructors. Often their backgrounds put them in a different class from that to which the family aspired, but Joe felt their crudeness was important in exposing the children to people they would otherwise not meet.

Always the Kennedy children had to win. Joe Kennedy did not sail competitively. He did not play tennis. Just as he would later demand that his sons serve in the military he had deliberately avoided, so he wanted them to triumph in sports in which he did not participate.

At one time Joe kept a full-time physical education instructor in residence to teach calisthenics and otherwise supervise his children's bodily development. As a result, all of the children were pushed to their limits, including Rosemary, who sailed in races as part of a team with Joe junior and Jack.

All the girls became as competitive as the boys, especially Eunice and Kathleen, who regularly won their competitions. Their best year was the 1935 season of the Hyannis Port Yacht Club. With six of the children competing—Bob, Jean, and Ted being far too young—and seventy-six races that summer, the children took a total of forty prizes in first, second, and third place.

The size of the family and the odd mixture of strictness and laxity of the Kennedys made summer help difficult to obtain. At best, maids and kitchen help were reluctant to work for large families. The Kennedy children were undisciplined in many areas, expecting others to do things for them. Jack would drop wet towels on the floor, empty dresser drawers on his bed when looking for an item of clothing, then expect the maid to completely remake his room. In this he was little different from the others: even the neatest among them would leave their clothing wherever they removed it, inside or outside. And always they expected a staff person or even a lesser being among their neighbors would pick it up and place it wherever it belonged.

Before the Kennedys became too well-known with various Boston employment services, Rose would personally drive to an agency to hire full- or part-time help. She explained that she had five daughters, never mentioning the four sons until she and the new maid were in her car on their way to Hyannis Port. The story was told that one new hire was told only about the girls, then one son, presumably Joe junior, was brought to the table the first time a meal was served. At the next meal, a second boy was present. Bob was added to the third meal, and within two days, the staff person was serving all four boys and five girls.

Punctuality was the one discipline both Rose and Joe demanded. Hyannis Port lunches were served at one-fifteen, and dinners were at seven-thirty. A clock was placed in every room to assure that no one in the family could justify being even a minute or two late. Rose was also known to get in her car and drive all over the Cape in search of any child who dared stay out past curfew.

3G: THE ONE EXCEPTION was Jack. Both Mrs. Kennedy and Joe were sticklers for punctuality, but when Jack was late, he was so sickly and thin that Mrs. Kennedy would not let him go to bed hungry. She did not argue when Joe banished his son from the table. However, she would arrange with the cook to fix him something to eat in the kitchen.

Joe Kennedy carried punctuality to overnight guests. He announced that if they were not ready to eat breakfast at nine A.M., they would go hungry. Joe Gargan told me that the reason was that Joe did not want to upset the cook. He felt that not to be punctual for meals was too great a burden for the cook and that she might leave. Joe Kennedy wasn't like that. He used to announce, "If the cook leaves, I'm following right after her."

Rose never saw anything odd in the pressures placed on the children by Joe. "We don't want any losers around here. In this family we want winners," he would frequently state. "Don't come in second or third—that doesn't count—but win." This attitude seemed to glorify the individual, yet stories were told of how Eunice, who one summer raced in sailing events fourteen times in a single week, would start a competition by demanding that her entire crew say a Hail Mary.

Later Rose would temper the pressure by saying that the goal was not to win as such, but rather to do the best of which they were capable. However, the reaction of both parents when a child did poorly made clear that winning was what mattered in the family.

The home life during those years is usually described as a happy one. The children have admitted to periodic bouts of loneliness because of parental absences, and Jean Kennedy Smith did talk of feeling that her life had been made difficult by frequent changes in schools. Yet no one would detail how terrified of their parents the children seemed.

BG: I WAS IN THE swimming pool with Mrs. Kennedy and Jean Kennedy Smith when Jean commented, "You were the first promoter of women's lib, Mother. You stayed in one hotel and Daddy was in another.

"My friends at school were always amazed at how my parents didn't live in the same apartment in New York."

Rose Kennedy has spoken of instant discipline, using a coat hanger or other handy object for punishment. Yet such "whippings" have never been the subject of horror stories by the children and may have been no different from what other children experienced during this period. Yet one incident that occurred when Eunice was an adult hinted at much harsher discipline than anything to which the children have admitted. Eunice's reaction was automatic, a response, to a verbal scolding, that seemed out of line for a woman who had experienced only appropriate discipline while growing up.

BG: MRS. KENNEDY NEVER thought she would live to be 104. She was in her eighties when she decided that she should get her possessions in order, distributing to her children the family's acquisitions she had been storing in the attic in Hyannis Port. She was like the captain of a sinking ship, assigning priorities to everyone, and that day it was Eunice's turn to stop by to look over the silver pieces in the attic.

Eunice was late, never a wise situation with Mrs. Kennedy, so she and I went up the stairs to begin the work. I had my inventory book as we entered one of the smaller rooms of the attic. There were low exposed beams and one small window, our only source of light.

Suddenly we heard the door slam on the first floor. "Motha!" shouted Eunice, running noisily up the stairs despite being barefoot. She ran into the room, grinned briefly in greeting, but said nothing further.

Despite the public image of glamour, Eunice was dressed as I usually saw her. Her unkept hair had been permed, then pulled back on the side with a comb. She wore no makeup, which seemed to make her leathery skin look harsher in the limited light. She did have on some simple, though expensive, jewelry—a large sapphire ring encircled by diamonds and her wedding ring.

Mrs. Kennedy was never known for her generosity. She gave a dollar a day to the church when she went to mass. She gave me her cleaned but well-worn bras when she decided she was done with them. And when she passed family possessions on to her children, she often wanted them to pay for them. That day was no exception. Mrs. Kennedy had told Eunice that she wanted her to have an English silver sauce set and two other pieces of silver as part of her inheritance. It was part of a collection and quite valuable, so she intended to charge Eunice $4,000 for it, the fair market price.

Eunice was used to her mother's actions and was willing to buy the items. However, she would not pay until they could be authenticated. She had no idea if her father had been taken when he bought the silver while in England during World War II.

My inventory book had a complete description of the valuable sauce boat, and as we went through the holdings, we found a second silver sauce boat of slightly different design. The three of us bent over them to see which matched the description of the expensive one. Mrs. Kennedy and Eunice disagreed as to which was which.

Outraged over being contradicted, Mrs. Kennedy rose to her full height of barely five feet tall and, eyes blazing, coldly said, "Eunice, be still!" Then she calmly returned to work.

To my amazement, Eunice Shriver, a grown woman in her fifties, seemed to return to what must have been a harshly disciplined childhood. She had been reprimanded like a little girl, and she immediately knew what to do. She closed her mouth, all life seeming to drain from her eyes. Then she walked over to the corner of that small room and stood with her arms folded in front of her, her head slightly bowed. She was taking the required "time-out," standing in the corner as penance so she would learn to behave better next time.

I knew then that there must have been great pain in their childhoods. Eunice Shriver was an internationally respected adult, the founder of Special Olympics. Yet her mother's wrath turned her into a small child, fearfully taking the punishment she knew would be demanded of her if she did not comply voluntarily.

———————————

While Rose Kennedy was spending an increasing amount of time anywhere in the world except with her family, Joe had decided to get involved with national politics. Joe Kennedy was certain that if he gave a few thousand dollars to both Roosevelt and the Democratic National Committee, he could have his choice of government positions. But after he gave $25,000 to Roosevelt and loaned $50,000 to the Committee in 1932, he discovered this was a fantasy. Although he was given a position on the campaign finance committee and allowed to travel in a private railroad car with close advisers, no one felt obligated to Kennedy because of his contributions.

Part of the problem was that Joe Kennedy was a cynical pragmatist, convinced that everyone and everything had a price. Joe was convinced that he should be able to buy the loyalty or at least the support of men who had previously been his antagonists. He underestimated Roosevelt.

Franklin Roosevelt had a skill rarely encountered in politics at the level of the presidency, though ironically John Kennedy would come close. Without saying anything misleading or deliberately trying to alter the facts, he could convince almost anyone that they were more important to him than they really were.

Years later, entertainers such as actress Angie Dickinson and comedian Joey Bishop would tell of dinners at the White House and elsewhere with John Kennedy where he would ask them questions that indicated he was truly interested in their work. He would listen to the answers and then ask more pointed questions. He seemed to genuinely want to know, to put their interests over concerns of the nation. He made them feel important, and they repaid him with intense loyalty on the campaign trail. It was a trait he had learned, in part, from watching Franklin Roosevelt, his father's nemesis.

In the 1930s, Joe Kennedy was taken in by Roosevelt's style, even though some of the closest campaign personnel deliberately showed their disdain for the businessman. However, he never realized that the staff was reflecting their employer's true feelings.

Kennedy decided to make himself invaluable to Roosevelt. He raised money throughout Massachusetts and personally supplied most of the cost of the Massachusetts primary in April 1932. Roosevelt lost Massachusetts to Al Smith, one of the three contenders for the Democratic nomination for president, but no one questioned that Kennedy had done his best. In addition, he tried to assure Roosevelt's nomination at the Democratic National Convention, and after the nomination, Kennedy cast himself in the role of adviser to Roosevelt.

Rose understood the world Joe had entered and was far more comfortable with what he was doing than she had ever been with Hollywood. The glamour that had once excited her had long since turned too painful to discuss. But trying to buy a position in government was little different from working with the ward heelers to buy votes for local office. Joe was at last working toward an end that would possibly bring the family the respect they had long desired. Joe's being an intimate with the president was certain to bring her prestige, and for once she was supportive of Joe's behind-the-scenes manipulations even if she was not included in them.

Kennedy's greatest benefit to Roosevelt seemed to be his ability to place him in contact with other important business leaders. Personally he delighted in working with the press, being the center of attention even as he spoke about Roosevelt. He was neither the future president's best supporter nor were his actions hindering the campaign. Ignored at the time, his efforts were not forgotten by the loyalists.

The election of Roosevelt delighted Kennedy, who planned to take advantage of it in several ways. He fully expected to be named secretary of the treasury, so he could control the nation's money supply.

The work with Franklin Roosevelt had led Joe to a friendship with the new president's oldest son, Jimmy, and his wife, Betsy. Jimmy frequently represented his father at various events, and many people had the impression that whatever he did in business had his father's approval. As a result, with the amendment to repeal Prohibition about to pass, Joe used his friendship to arrange for a joint business trip to England. Supposedly the business was a minor part of a European trip, the majority of the time to be a vacation. However, Joe had no intention of staying with his wife and friends when he had finished getting what he was after. They could sightsee. He would go back to the States to make more money.

The year was 1933, and Joe knew from his bootleg days the quality of Britain's alcoholic beverages. Since liquor would soon be legal to import and sell, the trip was meant to acquire U.S. distribution franchises for some of the more respected products. Joe obtained the Scotch whiskey accounts of Haig and Haig, Ltd., and John Dewar and Sons, Ltd. He also gained the rights to the American distribution of Gordon's Dry Gin Company, Ltd.

Exactly why the president's son went along to the business meetings will probably never be known. Jimmy Roosevelt said that his presence was innocent, that the couple traveled as friends. Others, allegedly "in the know," claim that Joe traveled with Jimmy to make the deals since Roosevelt's name was a selling point. Jimmy was believed to have received a piece of the action (25 percent is the most frequently mentioned amount), which Joe Kennedy later talked him out of. Joe allegedly convinced Roosevelt that word of the arrangement could embarrass the president.

Joe probably used Jimmy's presence for his own benefit. It was the only major business deal he conducted in such a manner, returning to New York immediately afterward while Rose and the others traveled to Rome and the Vatican.

The import business was profitable. Joe made a million dollars a year from the time Prohibition was repealed until 1946, when he sold his franchises for another $8-million profit. He would probably have continued in the business, but Jack was making a run for Congress, and being the son of a liquor magnate would not make for good press.

Kennedy's involvement with Roosevelt was always troubling to the summer residents of Cape Cod, all of whom were either Republicans or claimed to be. Roosevelt could validly lay claim to having had ancestors in the area, including some who had come over on the *Mayflower*. Some of his staff tried to imply that he had support on the Cape because of that fact, but actually he was universally hated.

Franklin Roosevelt understood men like Kennedy, understood that their ambitions for power grew with their rewards. In politics, as in business, the more he achieved, the more he would want. Kennedy could become a political opponent if the president-elect was not careful.

The first thought Roosevelt had was to make Kennedy treasurer of the United States. Unlike the secretary's position, the nation's treasurer was a high-profile position without authority. Joe's name would appear on the nation's currency, he would be feted and photographed, but he would be dead-ended without being a danger or help to anyone.

Kennedy was irate as he realized that he was being shunted aside after his work. Confronting the issue directly, he was so outraged that he used no tact whatever. He informed men close to the president that he might sue the Democratic Party for immediate repayment of the $50,000 loan. Then he turned to bribery, offering to establish a fund to support Raymond Moley, one of Roosevelt's closest advisers, much better than his government salary would allow. Kennedy cited ample precedents for such subsidies, including that provided for John W. Davis when he was ambassador to the Court of St. James. But Moley had too much integrity. Rather than hurt Kennedy, he said that his tastes were simple, the salary adequate under the circumstances. He knew he had to work with Kennedy to some degree in the future, but he did not share Kennedy's moral and ethical reasoning.

Kennedy visited Roosevelt in the Oval Office in May 1933, but he found himself at that moment too in awe of the power and majesty of that location to keep fighting. Eventually all he could do, according to a letter he later wrote Joe junior, was to explain that the only government position he desired was one that would bring prestige to the family. What he did not realize was that his tirades against Roosevelt, his bribery attempts, and his other actions had made both the president and his close advisers wary. Kennedy had been an irresponsible speculator, one of the people who had helped destroy the nation's economy by draining businesses instead of helping them to grow.

The most logical post for Joe Kennedy was ambassador to Ireland, a position his daughter Jean Kennedy Smith would eventually hold under the Clinton administration. But Kennedy wanted nothing to do with a position that would play up his ethnic background. Finally he was given what seemed the least sensible appointment—chairmanship of the newly created Securities and Exchange Commission (SEC). The SEC was to be the watchdog for the public as it dealt with the stock market and Wall Street.

Roosevelt had no illusions about what he was doing. He knew that Joe Kennedy had been thoroughly disreputable. He had proven himself unethical at best, potentially an uncaught violator of numerous laws at worst. However, Roosevelt understood two things that ultimately revealed the wisdom of so seemingly dubious an appointment. The first was that no one had more knowledge of how to improperly manipulate the stock market than Joe Kennedy. If he could devise ways to prevent people such as himself from taking advantage of Wall Street, then everyone would be safe.

The second fact was that Kennedy had an ego. The SEC appointment would bring him massive public attention. He would do everything in his power to prove his value because, by doing so, he would get public acclaim.

Raymond Moley did the final interview with Kennedy concerning the chairman's position. Moley asked him if anything in his career could lead to embarrassment, could hurt the president. In his book *After Seven Years*, Moley wrote: "Kennedy reacted precisely as I thought he would. With a burst of profanity he defied anyone to question his devotion to the public interest or to point to a single shady act in his whole life. The president did not need to worry about that, he said. What was more, he would give his critics—and here again the profanity flowed freely—an administration of the SEC that would be a credit to the country, the president, himself, and his family—clear down to the ninth child."

The announcement of Kennedy's appointment came on July 1, 1934, the same day Hitler crushed a revolt by rival Nazi Party members, many of whom were murdered and many others sent to the Dachau concentration camp. The Kennedy announcement, not the story of Hitler, caused editorial writers, financial experts, and others to react with shock. Most understood the reasoning, that a fox knows more about henhouse security than the chickens or even the farmer, but the fear was that Kennedy could perform crooked deals on a larger scale.

However, Joseph Kennedy performed as Roosevelt had been led to think he would. Kennedy used his knowledge to help clean up Wall Street, to improve disclosures of stock offerings, and to publicly reveal the inner workings of corporations. For the first time, even small investors had the opportunity to understand the potential for success of the companies whose stocks were for sale. And speculators were denied many of the vehicles for making money they had previously enjoyed. Within months Kennedy emerged a hero, unrepentant in his personal ways, yet having performed a truly valid public service for the nation.

What mattered to Rose was his success in government. She always respected his abilities as a businessman and thought it perfectly natural for the president of the United States to utilize him. She had no sense of Joe's behind the scenes maneuvering to get the appointment.

Joe may have acted honorably toward Wall Street for the first time in his career, but he decided to distance himself from Rose and the children. He rented an estate called Marwood with thirty-three rooms on 125 acres in Maryland. The public impression was that during his year of service to the SEC, his wife, children, and servants would regularly be joining him. They would share the beautiful escape from the pressures of his job. However, Joe had no intention of bringing Rose or the children to Marwood. Eddie Moore joined him, of course, but family would cramp his style. The estate became the scene for lavish parties, some raucous enough to reveal a side of Joe to guests that went unreported in the newspapers. Franklin Roosevelt could play there without bringing his wife, Eleanor, and journalists knew they were invited precisely because they could keep quiet. Silence was the price of access, and access was such a privilege, everyone played the game.

The wild living would increase in later years. In 1946, for example, Joe became a regular at the Colony and Colonial Clubs in Florida. He always had a woman with him, frequently introducing her as his "wife." But the women never included Rose, and the "wives" changed from visit to visit.

Joe Kennedy resigned from the SEC in the fall of 1935, the departure planned from the start and thus not a surprise to anyone. His tenure had been successful, and he had shown his critics that he could have integrity. He also claimed to have no political ambition, though he continued to advise Roosevelt from time to time, especially after taking a European vacation where he visited nations of concern to the United States.

After spending most of 1936 making money and working to ensure FDR's reelection, Kennedy was offered a chance to return to government service, something he did in the spring of 1937. This time he took the chairmanship of yet another new agency, the Maritime Commission, established under the Merchant Marine Act of the previous year. But 1937 would reveal an even greater opportunity. Robert Bingham, America's ambassador to the Court of St. James's (England), was terminally ill, and when he returned to the United States, Joe Kennedy wanted to take his place.

Becoming ambassador to England promised Kennedy everything he had dreamed about since he first understood the disdain the Brahmins held for Irish Catholics. He had received a Harvard education without being accepted by the Protestant elite. He had become a self-made multimillionaire and not been accepted by them. He had become a movie mogul, a government leader, a man written about in the major newspapers and magazines of the day. And still the family was not accepted. To be the first Irish Catholic ambassador to the Court of St. James's would give him a chance to thumb his nose at the people he had hated all his adult life.

Rose, in her memoirs, talked of asking Joe the president's reaction to his desires. Joe had not passed them on, explaining to Rose that he did not feel he could just walk into the Oval Office and announce them. She said that he was eventually told that if he did an excellent job at the Maritime Commission, he could have an ambassadorship. The specific one was not mentioned, though Joe and Rose assumed it would be the Court of St. James. However, real life was slightly different.

The British post was an important one, England being America's most important European ally at a time when Hitler was amassing a vast military machine. Joe Kennedy was not considered the best man for the job.

Using his connections with Arthur Krock, the *New York Times* reporter whose friendship Joe had cultivated, and other reporters who looked favorably upon him, Kennedy received press attention that made him seem a national figure. He had wealth and knew how to influence others. Kennedy obviously had political ambitions, with hints that he might become a candidate for president. This was still an era when a man did not have to have a major national constituency to become the party standard bearer. For example, Wendell Wilkie, a completely unknown and politically untried figure from Wall Street, became the Republican candidate in 1940. Kennedy had the money and the reputation to challenge Roosevelt in 1940 if he so chose, perhaps successfully. Influential newsmagazines such as the weekly *Life* would eventually be on Joe's side as a candidate, another warning to Roosevelt, who saw that Kennedy could undermine his administration through criticism in the press or displace him on the party ticket. For FDR, getting Joe out of town was a good idea.

Roosevelt also had a sense of humor about Joe's appointment as ambassador to England. He knew that Kennedy would both shock and impress the British. As James Roosevelt said of his father's reaction to the discovery that Joe Kennedy wanted the position, "He laughed so hard he almost toppled from his wheelchair."

Roosevelt later thought further about the appointment. He realized that while he was having fun imagining how Kennedy would get on in Britain, the reality was that Kennedy was crude, insulting, and insensitive to established protocol. There could be serious problems and it would be better to pay him off with a different position. He sent his son James to see if Kennedy would, instead, accept an appointment as secretary of commerce.

According to Arthur Krock, who was present at the time and recorded the incident in his memoirs, Kennedy was outraged. The London job was the only appointment he would accept. One week later the appointment was approved. Krock broke the story on December 9, 1937, even before Roosevelt could make the official announcement.

Roosevelt secretary of the treasury and longtime friend of the president, Henry Morgenthau, wrote in his diary following the appointment that Roosevelt "considered Kennedy a very dangerous man and that he was going to send him to England as Ambassador with the distinct understanding that the appointment was only good for six months and that, furthermore, by giving him this appointment, any obligation that he had to Kennedy was paid for."

Morgenthau also noted that Roosevelt had said to him: "I have made arrangements to have Joe Kennedy watched hourly—and the first time he opens his mouth and criticizes me, I will fire him."

7

The Kennedys vs. England

Rose Kennedy's arrival in England was the high point of her life. It is doubtful that any other experience, including seeing her oldest surviving son inaugurated as president of the United States, would ever be as meaningful. As wife of the ambassador to the Court of St. James's, she would know the ultimate triumph over the Brahmin elite who had shunned her throughout her life.

At 7 P.M. on April 9, 1938, Rose Fitzgerald Kennedy arrived with her husband, The Ambassador, at the gates of Windsor Castle. A maid and valet had been sent ahead with their luggage because Joe and Rose were to be the weekend guests of the King and Queen of England. Their suite of rooms—two bedrooms, two bathrooms, and a sitting room—had formerly been the private chambers of Queen Victoria, England's longest-ruling monarch.

The sitting room was upholstered in red damask, Rose's weekend bedroom covered with white wallpaper, the furniture in gold and white damask, the same colors as the washstand. The canopied bed on which Rose would sleep that night was so high off the ground that a step stool was needed to get on top.

Brig. Gen. Sir Hill Child escorted the Kennedys to their rooms shortly after their arrival. They were to prepare for dinner, and as a courtesy, a liveried servant brought them each a glass of sherry.

The couple had slightly over an hour to prepare for the evening. The women would all be dressed in expensive gowns, most of them custom tailored and trimmed with silver and gold. Diamond-studded tiaras were worn by most of them, and the jewelry was often museum-quality heir-looms. The men wore standard Windsor dress—black suits with red collars.

It is hard to know what Rose and Joe were thinking as they sat before the fireplace, finishing dressing before their escort arrived to take them to meet the other guests waiting for the King and Queen. Years later, in 1948, when Joe Kennedy wrote his memoirs with the aid of ghostwriter James Landis (the book was later discarded to avoid hurting Jack's fledgling political career), he tried to downplay how much the appointment meant to him:

"The President's suggestion was a complete surprise. Diplomatic service had not suggested itself to me. To this day I do not know whether the offer initiated with the President himself or with one of his advisers. I asked for time to consider it."

Friends sent Kennedy letters of warning prior to his going to England. They pointed out the difference between success in business and being a diplomat. They reminded him that he had no background for the responsibilities of a world on the brink of war. They felt that this would be his first disaster, and their concerns were well-founded.

Even Joe understood that the appointment would probably not last. He was quoted by Harvey Klemmer, who had been his aide at the Maritime Commission and planned to go to London with Joe as both speechwriter and publicist: "Don't go buying a lot of luggage. We're only going to get the family in the *Social Register*. When that's done, we come back and go out to Hollywood to make some movies and some money."

When they were summoned to the castle, Joe had only been in England two months, and Rose even less. He had been presented at the court according to protocol, but this night was different.

Joe looked at Rose and said, "Rose, this is a hell of a long way from East Boston."

And then, at eight-twenty, they entered the ballroom to await the royal couple—King George VI and Queen Elizabeth—who would arrive exactly ten minutes later.

Rose was fascinated by the Queen, who wore a Winterhalter-style, rose-pink gown with opalescent trim. The blue ribbon of the Order of the Garter was across her body, and she wore both a diamond-studded tiara and double necklace.

The Kennedys, along with the other guests, shook hands with the royal couple. Both Joe and Rose also showed the additional respect due the King and Queen by bowing and curtsying respectively.

Rose sat to the right of the King, Prime Minister Neville Chamberlain's wife on the left. Joe and Chamberlain were seated in a similar manner next to the Queen. Lord Elphinstone was on Rose's right, but she later claimed to have spent most of the time talking about children with the King. Two of the royal couple's children, Princess Elizabeth, who would become queen, and Princess Margaret Rose, were the same ages as Bobby and Jean. Like most parents of children the same age, the frustrations and joys were shared interests, even in the royal gathering.

BG: THE QUEEN WAS both a political figure and concerned with social image. She took the time to give Mrs. Kennedy advice on her appearance, advice Mrs. Kennedy regularly passed on to her daughters and daughters-in-law, much to their amusement. For example, Rose told them that whenever their photographs were taken, they should be certain to bend their arms, holding them away from their bodies. This, she was informed, would give them an image of greater slimness.

Jean Smith delighted in the photographs of her mother standing or sitting with her arms bent away from the body. She used to laugh that the pose always made Mrs. Kennedy appear to have a broken arm.

Other tips included always wearing a hat that would not conceal the face, and to always wear bright colors, which would call attention to you when in a crowd.

The only flaw in the evening delighted Rose. The King controlled the dinner table, signaling his wife when it was time to leave so that she would rise. But the flowers had been cut longer stemmed than normal and he was unable to be discreet.

Following the dinner, the Queen went to a drawing room, stood before the fireplace, and acknowledged the bows of the departing men. They went to an adjoining room while the women stayed with the Queen, Lord Halifax remaining in the room to handle protocol. As wife of the ambassador, Rose was given the first exclusive audience, fifteen

OLD-WORLD NOTABLES HAVE WRITTEN TO HER

Miss Rose Fitzgerald, Daughter of Mayor, Has Interesting Album—Roosevelt Among First to Contribute

MISS ROSE FITZGERALD,

Who, in Writing to Eminent Personages for Their Autographs, Was Assisted by Her Father, Mayor of Boston.

About five years ago, when a student in the Dorchester high school, Miss Rose Fitzgerald, the eldest daughter of Mayor and Mrs. Fitzgerald, conceived the idea of an autograph album containing signa-

From the same source also came an autograph of Dr. Solf, who divides the honor of ruling Samoa with Gov. Uoore.

Probably the most elaborate reply to the many requests made was received from John Prince of Fichen-

Miss Rose Fitzgerald featured in an article in the *Boston Herald* about her correspondence with the world's rich and famous, November 12, 1907

ROSE FITZGERALD TO BE BRIDE OF J. P. KENNEDY

Betrothal Announced by Former Mayor and Mrs. Fitzgerald—Bridegroom Youngest Bank President in the State.

(Photograph by Conlin.)
Miss Rose Elizabeth Fitzgerald.

Miss Rose Elizabeth Fitzgerald, daughter of former Mayor Fitzgerald and president of the Ace of Clubs, is to be married soon to Joseph P. Kennedy of Winthrop, the youngest bank president in the state. Her betrothal was announced yesterday by her mother and father. Although the date of the wedding has not been announced, it is believed that it will be this month.

Miss Fitzgerald is a graduate of Sacred Heart Academy, Manhattanville, N. Y. She completed her education at Blumenthal Academy of the Sacred Heart at Vaals, Holland. In Dorchester society she was the leader among the young people. The last important social event of which she was the leader was the dancing party of the Ace of Clubs at the Hotel Somerset.

Announcement of Rose's pending wedding to Joseph P. Kennedy, the "youngest bank president in the state" June 21, 1914

Rose with her father, "Honey Fitz," embarking on a South American tour (*UPI/Bettmann*)

Rose, *far right,* with her mother and father at Palm Beach

Mr. and Mrs. Joseph P. Kennedy on their return from Europe aboard the S.S. *Aquitania* in 1928, when Joseph Kennedy was president of First National Pictures (*UPI/Bettmann*)

Rosemary, *far right*, enjoys a hot dog picnic with friends.

Rosemary, *right*, and a friend in London, c.1936

Ambassador Kennedy and family aboard the S.S. *Manhattan* on February 28, 1938, on their way to Great Britain. *From left to right:* Patricia, Eunice, Kathleen, Ambassador Kennedy holding Edward, Rosemary, and Joseph Jr. Robert and Jean are in front. John F. Kennedy is not in the photograph. (*UPI/Bettmann*)

Mrs. Rose Kennedy and Jacqueline Kennedy beam as President-elect John F. Kennedy rises to deliver his victory speech at Hyannis National Guard Armory Press Headquarters on November 9, 1960. (*UPI/Bettmann*)

An unidentified man helps Joseph P. Kennedy take off his topcoat at an inaugural ball in 1961, as Rose and a crowd of thousands look on in delight. Anne Gargan, pictured in the foreground, became Joseph Kennedy's closest aide and companion and was with him when he suffered his stroke. (*UPI/Bettmann*)

Barbara Gibson in her office at Hyannis Port, 1977

minutes in length. Then each of the other women was escorted in for a similar conversation. Similar protocol was followed for the men meeting with the King.

While Rose talked children with the King, Joe talked of war with the Queen. He was later quoted as having stated, "What the American people fear more than anything else is being involved in a war. They say to themselves, 'Never again!' And I can't say I blame them. I feel the same way."

The Queen commented, "I feel that way, too, Mr. Kennedy. But if we had the United States actively on our side, working with us, think how that would strengthen our position with the dictators."

Rose was so relaxed that her knowledge as a politician's daughter was put to use when the couple had lunch the next day with Chamberlain, among others. She knew that Joe's work with the prime minister was critical for American relations. She also knew that Chamberlain was an odd man, a loner who was uncomfortable with casual conversation. He was also darkly pessimistic about the future of England at the hands of the growing German militancy. Both he and Joe Kennedy could see the Germans dominating or destroying England, and though Joe felt that such domination was not a bad situation, it was Chamberlain's worst nightmare.

Rose explained to Chamberlain how much he and Joe were alike. She mentioned their shared love for classical music, for walking long distances to think more clearly, and their backgrounds as successful businessmen. She was trying to make clear that the prime minister and the ambassador had common grounds from which to work, something Joe had also noted, though not directly to Chamberlain.

On Sunday morning, the King, the Queen, and all their guests except the Kennedys attended Anglican services. The Kennedys attended a small Catholic church in the area. This statement of their independence and the seriousness of their beliefs did not strain the relationships developed that weekend. The only affront to the royal couple would have come if the guests had not attended any church. They understood the Kennedys' desires concerning where to attend mass, even though Joe and Rose did not mention their plans in advance.

Later, the couple would review their weekend and see it as a personal, social, and political triumph, all of which were accurate readings. This was the high point of their lives, Rose reliving the weekend in conversations with others for many years to come.

BG: Mrs. Kennedy told me that when they were visiting the King and Queen at Windsor, the royal children were outside playing. The telephone started ringing, the women understanding that they were expected to leave so the men could conduct business. Mrs. Kennedy and the Queen stepped onto the veranda, looking down at Margaret and Elizabeth. Rose said that the Queen explained that Elizabeth was easily controllable, while Margaret was always going off—a foreshadowing of the future.

Elizabeth remembered Mrs. Kennedy, though. Years later, when she had married Philip and become queen in her own right, the royal couple were dining in New York at a gathering where Joan Kennedy was present. Queen Elizabeth turned to Joan and asked, "And how is your charming mother-in-law?" When told of the question, Mrs. Kennedy was delighted that she had made such an impression on the Queen.

If there was any stress between them, it was Joe's anger with Rose's comments to Chamberlain concerning the similarities of the two men. Oddly, this action may have benefited Joe in his work with Chamberlain. What the Kennedys could not comprehend was how ill equipped Joe was for world diplomacy. The couple were out of their element, yet neither realized how naive and lost they actually were.

Rose Kennedy had traveled, but her world was one of either isolation or conspicuous consumption, of convent schools and Paris couturiers. She knew cutthroat politics at the level of city and state campaigns. She had no sense of nations at war with other nations, of power alliances that could lead to world war.

Joe Kennedy had a view of the world totally incompatible with real life. First, he looked upon governments as having lifetimes much like those of people. What was important to the world was not who was in power, or how they maintained it. International trade was paramount. International trade assured the success of nations. International trade assured jobs in every country of the world. International trade assured that the wealthy could continue their rightful quest of greater wealth, and the average person could pursue a modest, though comfortable life, fully employed from adulthood to death.

Joe also believed that turmoil in Europe was of no concern to Americans. He was outraged that the American stock market could be impacted by Chamberlain's obvious desire to appease Hitler no matter what happened to Czechoslovakia and other countries whose independence the British prime minister was willing to cede. Joe was quoted as complaining, "I wish our fellows at home would attend to the worries they have on their own doorsteps and keep Europe out of their minds until they made some headway in their own country." He was convinced that should war break out in Europe, it would not have any serious impact on the United States.

When analyzing Hitler's reported anti-Semitism and his hatred for the British, Joe saw the speeches and the posturing as a business gambit. Germany had been a bankrupt country after the First World War. There were endless stories of German inflation. The Germans were further humiliated because, though a people proud of their tradition of a strong military, they were stripped of their weapons and their right to form even a self-defense force.

Adolf Hitler had ended those problems. He had drastically strengthened the German currency, both within the country and in the eyes of the international community. He had gained the permission of the allied governments to rebuild his military, thus restoring German pride in its government. But Germany needed to increase its production of quality products for international trade.

Joe understood motivation. To Joe, Hitler was using the Jews and the British as scapegoats, the "enemy" to be beaten through increased productivity. The German worker thought of Jews and the British and was motivated to work harder.

Rose Kennedy tried to understand international matters, perhaps more than her husband. Certainly she was aware that he had to look at his public pronouncements in light of the impact they could have back in the United States. But she mistook the views of the wealthy social elite whom she encountered on her travels for the thoughts of the masses. Her support of her husband, her belief in his diplomatic skills, were based on false assumptions and limited knowledge. As the world teetered on the brink of chaos, Rose spent most of her time shopping.

In addition to his remarks sympathetic to Hitler, Joe outraged the British by flonting traditions. Joe's relatively casual attire, his refusal to engage in all the rituals of the court, were held in disdain. The British people looked upon tradition with the same reverence that Catholics held for Church ritual. Joe would never have tolerated a visitor to his church limiting his observance of ritual to those parts of the service he enjoyed. Yet this was exactly what he did as ambassador, and the majority of accounts indicate he was seen as rude, insensitive, and a man to be privately scorned.

Oddly, the size of the Kennedy family delighted the British. Men in government service were known to be sexually active with women other than their spouses. Even the royal family had their periodic sex scandals and well-publicized "secret" dalliances. But the idea of so obviously having had frequent sex with one's wife, and bringing the nine children as proof, had not occurred with past diplomats. The British press jokingly called him "the Father of His Country" and often repeated his remark when he had made a hole in one on the Stokes Poges course in Buckinghamshire: "I am much happier being the father of nine children and making a hole in one than I would be as the father of one child making a hole in nine."

Joe began his work in England with a degree of amusement. He wrote to James Roosevelt on March 8, 1938, giving his first impression of his new office in the American embassy, saying: "I have a beautiful blue silk room and all I need to make it perfect is a Mother Hubbard dress and a wreath to make me Queen of the May. If a fairy didn't design this room I never saw one in my life." The offices were actually newly remodeled, three adjoining town houses having been purchased, then renovated to consolidate embassy staff offices that were previously scattered throughout London. The town houses had more space than the government needed, so the extra was divided off and provided with a separate entrance so it could be leased as housing. Joe Kennedy was obviously not impressed.

Kennedy used his regular, close business associates for staff members, avoiding experts in government, international relations, or any other area that seemed appropriate for the job. Chief secretary was his longtime aide Eddie Moore, who came in May when Rosemary and Eunice could leave school. James Roosevelt suggested Page Huidekoper be hired as a personal assistant, and the young woman became close to Kathleen.

On the advice of Arthur Krock, Kennedy hired *New York Times* reporter Harold Hinton to be his press secretary and speechwriter. The British believed he was also present on behalf of his paper, his position allowing him to scoop the competition with insider information. However, the British government raised no objections because the *New York Times* was objective in its reporting.

The Kennedys vs. England

Arthur Houghton was brought along from the Hays Office in Hollywood, Joe apparently having hired him because he enjoyed Houghton's company. Joe apparently wanted only trusted friends and business associates, except for those with writing and publicity skills.

The casualness of Joe Kennedy's day-to-day attitude succeeded in simultaneously alienating the British elite and delighting the British commoners. Average Britishers had a bawdy sense of humor and a tendency to thumb their noses at the wealthy, the pompous, and the highborn despite cherishing a monarchy that cost them millions of dollars for ceremonial purposes.

Joe Kennedy fit their sense of humor. He refused to adopt the formal clothing, stilted speech, and stiffness of carriage that were expected of diplomats. One critic claimed that Joe dressed like the waiters at official functions. Kennedy liked to chew gum, a vulgarity among the highborn, put his feet on a highly polished antique desk in his office, and regularly referred to the Queen as "a cute trick." All classes of society declared him to be "representative of modern America," and most of the British meant it as an insult.

Because Roosevelt did not expect to keep Kennedy in the London post for long, he was expected to handle minimal concerns. The first was the hostility between Britain and Ireland. The president felt that Joe was the ideal person to act as mediator, perhaps settling the conflict. Certainly he would be acceptable to both sides.

A U.S./Britain trade agreement was to be negotiated—a task where Kennedy truly had some experience—and also a trustee dispute concerning several Pacific islands.

Rose Kennedy saw her husband's concerns as her own. She did not want to get involved with the negotiations, but she did feel that she was as much a representative of the government as he was. For the first time in several years she was concerned with the impression she made on others. She evaluated her strengths and weaknesses, then tried to change those areas she found lacking.

Voice lessons were of primary importance. She had the accent of her origins, a voice that did not sound particularly pleasing on radio, in the newsreels, or when talking with royalty.

Air attaché Michael Scanlon, the protocol expert for the American embassy, began working with Rose to eliminate the Boston speech pattern that used the sound of *ah* instead of *r*, as in "He pahked the cah in Hahvahd Yahd."

Gladys Scanlon, Michael's wife, took Rose to Paris so that she, Rosemary, and Kathleen would have the proper gowns for meeting the Queen. Style was important in England for an ambassador's wife. It was not enough to have the right dress. You also needed to have the right dressmaker. The nation was steeped in pomp, proper protocol, and tradition. Any deviation left the wrong impression.

Rose, who thought her husband was doing a masterful job on behalf of President Roosevelt, was convinced that the president thought so, too. She had even sent him a thank-you note from the Waldorf to let him know how pleased the entire family was for the opportunity.

In truth, Joe was summoned back to the White House in June of 1938, Kennedy's cover being that he wanted to see his oldest son graduate from Harvard.

The president was irate over Joe's isolationist statements. He was also wary of a casual meeting with the press in which Joe had explained that he would not be a candidate for president in 1940. The denial was actually a trial balloon, as Roosevelt well knew. The Boston papers picked up the idea, as did the *New York Daily News*. The latter coverage was coordinated by friends who had earlier stressed that the ambassador's position was given to Kennedy because the president looked upon him as the finest member of the administration. He was called the "Crown Prince," implying that he was next in line to the "throne."

The one negative reaction to Kennedy came from writer C. L. Sulzberger, who was on assignment for the *Ladies' Home Journal*. The magazine's publisher was a friend of Kennedy's, so Joe felt comfortable encouraging his staff to be completely open with the writer. Unfortunately Sulzberger realized that everything Kennedy was doing was meant as a prelude for a run for the presidency. When Kennedy saw the draft submitted to Sulzberger's editor, he insisted upon changes. The writer refused, though the changes were made in-house before the article appeared.

The president wanted to keep Joe Kennedy on a short leash. Roosevelt understood Rose's delight in the family's new position. He understood how important being The Ambassador was to Joe. And he also knew that if he could maintain Kennedy's support, Joe would not make a bid to unseat him as Presidential candidate at the 1940 Democratic convention.

Despite Roosevelt's unhappiness with Kennedy's performance, he had no choice but to return him to England. It was too soon to replace him without serious international repercussions. But Roosevelt related to Secretary of the Interior Harold Ickes, a longtime friend, his belief that Kennedy would not last more than a couple of years. Roosevelt believed that Kennedy followed a definite pattern in the jobs he took on. He would throw himself into the work until a crisis arose, then bail out. Certainly that had been his pattern in Hollywood, and the international arena would probably be no different. And the world was quickly becoming one big crisis.

Rose Kennedy was unaware of Joe's problems. She had arrived in London in March 1938, a month after Joe. She traveled with Kathleen, Pat, Bobby, Jean, and Teddy. Kathleen was eighteen, a convent-school graduate who had been attending Parsons School of Design in New York. She dropped out for the London adventure, happily traveling to Europe with her family. Joe junior and Jack were both attending Harvard, planning to travel to England when possible. Since Joe junior was graduating that year, it was thought that he could gain valuable life experience by finishing school, then becoming his father's most junior secretary.

Rosemary would be attending the Montessori school, and Eunice, Pat, and Jean would go to the Sacred Heart boarding school just outside London. Only Bobby and Teddy, thirteen and six respectively, would stay at home, getting their educations in a day school.

Rose was scared as she traveled to England. She seemed to think she was equal to the ambassador in importance. Since she received the pampering of someone held in great esteem, a part of the British desire to keep the Americans on their side, her attitude seemed to be rewarded. Thus despite her great joy in the warmth in which the family was received by the press and the public, she always had an underlying concern that she not do anything wrong.

Her daughter Kathleen, by contrast, felt a freedom she had never previously experienced. The restrictive life of the convent school was over. She was interested in boys, and they seemed to flock around her. She was fascinated by society, as intrigued by the royal lineage as she had previously been intrigued by movie stars.

BG: MRS. KENNEDY DEVELOPED a sense of propriety while in England, and she judged everyone by those standards. She thought President

Gerald Ford should not have tried to feed Queen Elizabeth and Prince Philip elaborate continental cuisine when the royal couple visited the White House. She felt that the president should have entertained them as she had entertained the Queen's parents. "When I gave a dinner for the King and Queen at the embassy, I thought it should be a regular American dinner with corn on the cob, turkey, sweet potatoes, ice cream, and strawberry shortcake."

She also felt that children should know their place. She read in the newspaper that Amy Carter had played the piano during a dinner President Carter and his wife had given at the White House. "How absurd!" she said, horrified. "To get all dressed up and attend a dinner party and afterwards have to sit and listen to some nine-year-old play the piano."

The children had no interest in their parents' world. Rose Kennedy was delighting in her new social status. Joe Kennedy, mistrusted by the British, was being spied upon, wiretapped, and having his memos intercepted by British intelligence. Even Roosevelt arranged for additional dispatches from embassy personnel he considered more accurate and reliable. However, Rose and the children thrived in England. The oldest four—Joe, Jack, Rosemary, and Kathleen—seemed to come into their own for the first time. This was especially true for Rosemary, who tragically experienced her last taste of freedom.

Rosemary had suffered in the United States. By contrast, the Montessori school the family found in England had teachers who adapted to each student's needs. Students who grew tired at a certain time of the day were encouraged to nap, regardless of age, so that they would be fresher. Studies were planned around a student's best time for learning, whatever that might mean. Rosemary not only began learning more and faster than she had in the United States, she was also able to share in the instruction of the younger children. Her skills improved as she helped the others with their reading and writing.

Rosemary and Kathleen would make their debut together. They were close in age, and their temperaments complemented each other. Rosemary, whose classes were in the countryside, was the better dancer of the two yet shy and retiring. She had spent a lifetime being made to feel inferior because she did not learn in the way of the other Kennedy girls, nor was she aggressively competitive.

Kathleen, by contrast, exuberantly embraced every experience and delighted in including everyone around her in whatever she found amusing. Rose impressed upon her girls the solemnity of the occasion since the coming out would include a presentation before the Queen. Yet Kathleen, by then almost universally called Kick, a nickname that reflected her flamboyance, delighted in referring to the royal couple as "George and Lizzie." She knew to be polite in person, yet her sense of irreverence made her comfortable in the more pompous settings.

The presentation of the season's seventeen- and eighteen-year-old debutantes took place at Buckingham Palace. Each girl was trained in the proper curtsy for royalty, the teachers coming from special schools that held classes to meet this need. (Most, such as the Vacani School of Dancing, considered curtsy training a minor part of their business but a major way to get their names before the prominent and wealthy.) Rosemary and Kathleen were no different, each practicing extensively.

The debut raised more questions about Rosemary. The royal family, along with upper-crust British society as a whole, were allegedly hostile to mental retardation. There were stories of royal children being hidden away, the dirty little genetic secrets that were never discussed. Yet Rosemary was going to be presented, and toward that end both she and Kathleen were trained to curtsy, provided with white gowns, and otherwise prepared.

The three Kennedy women were beautiful. Rose, though in her late forties, was an extremely handsome woman. Photographs from this time show a woman who appeared much younger than her years. She could easily have been the older sister of Rosemary and Kathleen when viewed dressed for the most sophisticated evening of the girls' young lives.

Rose and her oldest daughter had white gowns made by Molyneux, the most respected British designer of the day. Rose's was white lace with silver and gold beads for embroidery. (She later wore the same gown, without alteration, for Jack's inauguration. Eventually it was given to the Smithsonian.) Rosemary's was a white net with silver trim. And Kathleen's dress, purchased from Lelong's of Paris, was white net with silver croquettes. Rose was delighted with the snobbery of the British press since the reporters mentioned the Molyneux design but did not mention Lelong. The implication was that Kathleen had gone to the Paris branch of Molyneux rather than a rival with no connection to the crown. The purchase did not represent a breach of etiquette but did show Rose the snobbism of the day, Lelong's being at least as expensive and respected a design house as Molyneux.

White was not required by protocol. The women knew that debutantes had white plumes adorning their hair.

Rose also had a borrowed diamond tiara, shoulder-length, skintight gloves, and Prince of Wales plumes. The hairstylist who prepared her for the evening was skilled in helping women for such formal occasions and planned her hair to hold the tiara. But Rosemary was easily the most beautiful of the three.

The only flaw in the evening was Joe Kennedy's attire. He wore a black tailcoat, long trousers, and white tie—formal attire for the United States, an insult to the royal family at the debut. All the other men of any importance who were present, including the male members of the embassy staff, wore formal black coats, silk stockings, and knee breeches. Kennedy thought he would look foolish in the knee breeches, but without them he looked like an out-of-place, improperly dressed waiter. The Queen was displeased, but nothing was said because he represented an ally of great importance to the British.

The ceremony itself was simple. The King and Queen entered the ballroom at nine-thirty. Then, for what could be a couple of hours, the debutantes to be presented would first be checked by the court usher, then announced by the lord chamberlain, who stood at the entrance to the Throne Room. The debutantes walked with their trains draped over their left arms so they would ultimately trail eighteen inches.

The Throne Room had place markers much as are used for theatrical productions. In this case, a small gold crown was placed on the red carpet. The girls were to stop at the mark, smile, give a quick back kick to free their gowns, curtsy, take three steps to the right in a gliding movement, and curtsy again. Then they would continue the rightward movement to the door, never turning their backs to the royal couple.

Rosemary reportedly tripped slightly on the way out, recovering without falling. If the report was accurate—Rose never mentioned it—Rosemary was not the first nor would she be the last young lady to have such an experience.

The entire presentation was like living theater, whose participants would pay any price to be there. The fully costumed beefeaters, each holding a mace, formed a line from the Grand Stairway, through the anterooms, on to the ballroom. Liveried footmen were everywhere in attendance. And the diplomats and their wives were positioned according to the length of time they had been serving their countries in England.

The coming out meant more for Rose than it did for Kathleen and

Rosemary. Debutantes invited Kathleen and Rosemary to all their parties, but according to British protocol, a young woman could not accept without parental approval. It was the custom for the mother of the debutante to first pay a visit to the mother of the invited guest. This meant that some of the most prominent people in England were coming to see Rose, hoping to gain *her* acceptance. This role reversal added to her joy in being the wife of the ambassador.

The more Rose found acceptance through her position as the ambassador's wife and the mother of debutantes, the less she concerned herself with her younger children. They were left almost totally in the care of the staff. Rose was up late at night, then slept until late in the morning. By the time the children were home from school, she was getting ready for the evening. The smaller children were simply in the way.

Ironically, Rose was gently rebuked by the Queen during an embassy dinner on May 4, 1939. The subject got around to children. Rose recalled that the Queen "asked me if I got up in the morning to see the children off, and I said I used to in what I called the good old days, but that now I was usually up late at nights and rested in the mornings. To my astonishment and humiliation, she said she usually got up, half-dressed, to see her children and then went back to bed again." Despite the gentle royal rebuke, Rose did not change her ways.

Kathleen fell in love with England and was delighted to find that her mother's snobbery assured that she could stop going to school. An education was of critical importance in the United States, but at that time, the more educated a British woman, the lower her place in society. It was a mark of honor never to have to earn a living. Working-class girls might attend a university or otherwise engage in intellectual pursuits. The upper class had no need. Kathleen had an easy time convincing her mother to let her stop her education or at least postpone it.

Kathleen became the darling of Britain's Protestant elite. She was frequently the weekend guest of Lady Astor, the Duke of Marlborough, or some similarly titled person. Sometimes she went alone. At other times, Joe junior or Jack accompanied her.

Nearing the end of her teenaged years, Kathleen was sensitive, sensual, outgoing, lively, and crazy about boys. She easily made friends of both sexes, was interested in British society, British culture, British history. It was as though she saw herself as having been permanently transported to a strange country where she wanted to be assimilated as thoroughly and rapidly as possible. She was like a sponge for everything British, a refreshing contrast to her father, who was often hated by the same families that genuinely welcomed Kathleen into their homes.

That Kathleen impressed Lady Astor was probably not surprising. Nancy Langhorne had been born in Virginia before marrying Waldorf Astor and making England her home. She had the reputation of being a British society leader, her home filled with the political and intellectual notables of the day. Yet though Kathleen wrote to friends back in the States about the games she played at Lady Astor's parties, such as musical chairs and charades, the woman had an intensely serious side. She eventually succeeded her husband in Parliament, becoming Britain's first woman MP.

Joe Kennedy fit nicely into the world of Lady Astor. The majority of her friends were against any war with Hitler. A few felt that appeasement was best. Others were outright pro-Nazi. They were nicknamed "the Cliveden set," and some American writers felt that Joe had been seduced by their ideas. The association with Lady Astor's social circle seemed to many to be further proof of Kennedy's anti-Semitism and insensitivity.

Kathleen came of age in England, both physically and emotionally. Because of her father's prominence, she met the social elite, ranging from the Earl of Rossly to Prince Ahmed Hussain to Peter Grace, heir to the W. R. Grace shipping-lines fortune. Among the Americans at Oxford, she found one to be a small-town boy out of his element. That was the brilliant scholar and athlete named Byron "Whizzer" White. Eventually he would be involved with her brother Jack's fitness efforts during the early days of the Kennedy administration. He would also be named an associate justice of the Supreme Court of the United States by President John F. Kennedy.

While Kathleen was the favored daughter, in 1938 Rosemary was also attending society functions. It has been suggested that Kathleen was gracious and loving enough to look out for her "retarded" sister during these events. Certainly that is a possibility. But that there was a stigma to mental retardation, and that no one could hide Rosemary's actions when she was out enjoying herself with her peers, further indicate that a learning disability was her problem.

The Kennedys did cover for Rosemary the night they gave a dinner party for the debutantes. The party, at the American embassy, was held in the ballroom. The Ambrose band played, Harry Richman sang, and dozens of guests moved gracefully about the dance floor. A young man named Jack Kennedy (no relation to the family) was assigned to be Rosemary's constant escort. Everyone, including Rosemary, referred to him as London Jack to keep him from being confused with the ambassador's son. Kathleen had dozens of men trying to dance with her throughout the night, and it was only the night of her own party that she stayed for the evening.

Kathleen was finding London nightspots exciting to visit. During the parties given by other debutantes, she and a few of the relatively "wilder" young men and women attended the more reputable nightspots in London, though the evenings were always chaste. She was not ready to become serious about anyone, in part because she was convinced that all men had affairs. She knew of her father's infidelities and the increasingly bad reputation of her brothers, so marriage did not appeal to her at the time.

On July 18, 1938, Kathleen began on a course that her mother was convinced led to her death, a punishment from God. Kathleen was one of twelve thousand guests at a party given by the King and Queen at Buckingham Palace. All the debutantes of the year were invited, the ambassador and his family being part of a limited number of special guests also invited to a private tea. At the party within the party, Kathleen met Billy Cavendish (officially, William Cavendish, the Marquess of Hartington, eventual heir to the title of Duke of Devonshire). A tall, lean youth, he was considered a proper suitor for Princess Elizabeth when she grew a little older than her twelve years. Billy was as quiet as Kathleen was outgoing, and they talked for two hours. A week later she visited his family home, meeting his parents in Compton Place, Eastbourne, where they attended the horse races.

Billy's parents delighted in Kathleen. They understood their son's friendship and seemed to enjoy the novelty of it. Kathleen was Irish Catholic. Billy's father was as hostile to the Catholic Church as old Joe was to the Brahmins of Boston. Any sort of intimacy between the couple would have been a scandal. Kathleen, though smitten enough to begin a scrapbook containing every article she could find related to Billy, was considered nothing more than a friend.

Kathleen Kennedy had a very different reaction to the impending war from her father's. She and her British friends discussed what was happening without illusions, yet they saw no alternative. Hitler was on the march, they were threatened, and they had to stand together to stop him. They were all surprised about the doom and gloom the relatively isolated, probably quite safe Americans were expressing. The boys Kathleen knew understood as best as their parents could tell them what hardships were coming, and while they did not wish to fight, if that was what it took for the survival of England, they were not afraid to do their part.

England had a tradition of the upper classes going to war, whereas the American rich frequently found a way to avoid military service. The higher a man's position in English society, the more he was expected to return to his country through service in battle. Kathleen's friends all had fathers, uncles, and other relatives who had been killed or wounded in battle. They had no illusions about war. Yet with Hitler's challenge, the men who had endured war a generation earlier were about to commit their sons, their nephews, and the sons of their friends to the same uncertain nightmare they had experienced.

Kathleen's friends joked about her being at odds with her father. They said that during the first German air raid, they'd shoot a member of her family, claim it was the Germans, and force America into war to avenge the honor of the ambassador.

Ironically, it was Joe Kennedy's daughter who best understood what might happen. She, Joe junior, and Hugh Fraser, a mutual British friend, went to Spain in July 1939, four months after the end of the Civil War. Young Joe fancied himself an aide to his father and had been to Madrid in February against his father's wishes. He had long wanted to see the triumph of Francisco Franco, who emerged victorious over a coalition of liberals and Communists. And like his father with Hitler, Young Joe saw only what he wished to see during the earlier visit.

Young Joe talked of the remarkable spirit of the people who had undergone terrible suffering. He talked of murdered priests and little food. He was thrilled that Franco was emerging triumphant so that the people could at last get on with their lives in a positive way.

Kathleen understood that the Franco dictatorship was not good, that peace had come through a vicious suppression. The quality of life may have been relatively better, but it was far from good.

As for Rose, her diaries were filled with notes reflecting a constant misunderstanding of the troubles in Europe. Her thinking was Joe's thinking, and Joe was strongly for appeasing Hitler.

After Chamberlain agreed to Hitler's infamous annexation of Czechoslovakia, Rose made her September 30, 1938, diary entry: "We all feel that a new psychology for settling issues between countries has been inaugurated and that henceforth war may be out of the question.

The Kennedys vs. England

"Chamberlain's words, from Shakespeare's *Henry IV*: 'Out of this nettle, danger, we pluck this flower, safety.' The result of the Munich settlement, he said, would be 'Peace in our time.'"

Joe Kennedy's words and actions ultimately gave the impression that America had a new foreign policy. War was not a viable option for handling international conflict. The boundaries of countries might change, but so long as there were no wars, international business could continue and the American economy would thrive.

Such thinking eventually led to the end of his diplomatic career.

Roosevelt had additional reason to dump his ambassador. According to reports passed on to the White House by British intelligence officers who routinely wiretapped the entire embassy staff, Joe was using inside information for financial speculation. By knowing when announcements would be made in Europe that would affect certain types of American stock, he could position himself for a quick killing.

Investigations over the years failed to turn up records of transactions Kennedy made. However, a number of career diplomats from various countries who worked with Kennedy in England, such as Sweden's ambassador to London, Baron Erik Palmstierna, all made the same allegations.

During his years in exile in London, according to Czech leader Jan Masaryk, Joe manipulated Czech investments based on Chamberlain's planned actions. Masaryk alleged that Kennedy's profits were twenty thousand British pounds.

Joe was also helping friends in the film industry. Britain had some serious needs as the war with Germany was developing, and only finite funds. To maintain morale, Britain imported American movies, and Kennedy worried that money for movies would be cut back. Joe negotiated to help the American film industry—and to increase Britain's costs —while work on agreements in other areas languished. Britain had to cut back imports of apples and pears and raisins. It had to delay shipping the rubber it owed for cotton that had been shipped in a barter deal. Food and other necessities for fighting a war and assuring the survival of the people of an island nation were all that were important. Kennedy would not make the deals for the necessities without first protecting American film interests, and Britain went along because it was assumed he spoke for Roosevelt.

The beginning of the end of the family's tenure in England came with the torpedoing of the British ship *Athenia* on September 4, 1939. Britain had declared war on Germany four days earlier after Hitler's troops invaded Poland. Joe was supposed to handle the logistics of helping the nine thousand Americans who remained in England, all of whom were asked to return to the United States. Joe junior was contacting the various tramp steamers that were sailing, arranging for them to take as many people as possible. James Seymour and Eddie Moore were also helping.

The *Athenia* was a British liner heading for Canada, with 311 Americans among the 1,400 passengers. At 3 A.M. Seymour, who had been napping on a cot near the telephone, relayed the news that the unarmed ship was sinking in the Atlantic. However, other ships had successfully rescued all of the passengers with the exception of 112 men, women, and children, including a dozen Americans, killed in the initial explosion. The survivors were being taken to Scotland, from where the Americans would be desperate to get to safety.

Joe was terrified of German air raids, even when he was in no danger. His favorite golf course was being used for antiaircraft guns, and he would be extremely nervous his remaining time in England. However, the crisis he faced was far more serious.

This was the first act of war that affected Americans. German propaganda minister Joseph Goebbels was claiming that his country's U-boats were not responsible. Rather, it was a deliberate act of violence by the British government to build sentiment against the Nazis.

The passengers were terrified. They wanted assurances that they would be safe. The United States Navy had ships in the area and the people wanted to be escorted back by a convoy.

Joe should have and could have gone to Scotland, but he chose not to. He may have felt his duties in London were too important to leave or perhaps he was terrified of being caught in more violence, but whatever his reasoning, he had to act, and the most expendable person was twenty-two-year-old Jack.

Jack was a college student who looked even younger than he was. One paper reported his age as eighteen, another as nineteen. Reporters hailed him as a "schoolboy diplomat." The passengers thought the U.S. government did not care about their safety.

Jack, acting for his father, explained that the American liner *Orizaba* would take them to New York. A convoy wasn't needed. Germany was at war with Britain and had attacked a British ship. Germany was not at war with the United States, the liner would be clearly marked as an American vessel, and they would be completely safe.

In the end, the surviving passengers reached New York safely, and Jack received excellent press for his actions. But Joe Kennedy was about to compound his insensitivity.

On September 11, convinced that the British government could not survive war with Hitler and knowing that England would soon be bankrupt, Joe asked Roosevelt to mediate an armistice: "It seems to me that this situation may crystallize to a point where the President can be the savior of the world. The British government as such certainly cannot accept any agreement with Hitler, but there may be a point when the President himself may work out plans for world peace."

Roosevelt understood what Joe meant. Once more Joe was trying to get peace at any price. Secretary of State Cordell Hull, as outraged as Roosevelt over Kennedy's comments, wrote:

"The President desires me to inform you, for your strictly confidential information and so that you may be guided thereby without divulging this message to anyone, that this Government, so long as present European conditions continue, sees no opportunity nor occasion for any peace move to be initiated by the President of the United States. The people of the United States would not support any move for peace initiated by this Government that would consolidate or make possible a survival of a regime of force and aggression."

G: WHEN I FIRST WENT to see Mrs. Kennedy in Hyannis Port, she had me sit on a couch that I quickly learned was special to her. Eugenio Cardinal Pacelli had sat on this couch when he visited the Kennedys many years earlier. The cardinal had become Pope Pius XII on March 12, 1939, and they had attended his coronation.

What Mrs. Kennedy did not mention was how boorishly the family had behaved. Pope Pius XI had died unexpectedly while Joe was ambassador to the Court of St. James. Since Joe was a Catholic in an important diplomatic post, he was asked to attend the coronation in Rome as the representative of the United States.

Joe was supposed to attend the ceremony alone, though I assume he could have arranged for Mrs. Kennedy to officially accompany him. Instead, they decided to make the event a family affair. They figured that it might be their only chance to take at least some of the children to see a pope's coronation, an event none of them would ever forget. However, it violated protocol and disrupted the seating arrangements for the event.

I was later in the John F. Kennedy Library where Cardinal Giovanni Battista Montini, later to become Pope Paul VI, had provided a taped remembrance of the day for the oral history collection. A transcript of that interview noted:

"It happened that the ambassador of the United States to London, Mr. Kennedy, father of the dead president, was charged by his government to represent the United States at the ceremony; and indeed he arrived punctually but bringing with him five children, who proceeded to occupy places that were reserved for the members of the official missions, with the result that the arrangement of places was altered; and when there arrived the Italian minister of foreign affairs, Count Ciano, the son-in-law of Mussolini, he found his seat in the gallery of the official missions was occupied and he began to protest, threatening to leave the Basilica and to desert the ceremony. The situation was immediately resolved; but there remained in our memory the procession of the children of Ambassador Kennedy."

Boston's Cardinal O'Connell was also present and apparently was also outraged. He had married the Kennedys and might have said something. However, periodically Joe Kennedy would need a favor, and each time that occurred, he would give the cardinal a large donation for a favorite project. The two men fed off each other, and the cardinal was not about to offend the ambassador by pointing out the latter's rudeness.

Mrs. Kennedy said that the new pope gave seven-year-old Teddy a rosary. She would later joke, "I thought that with such a start he would become a priest or maybe a bishop, but then one night he met a beautiful blonde and that was the end of that."

The entire Kennedy family was back in the United States by the end of 1939. Joe would stay three months, not returning to England until February 23, 1940, when neither he nor the British wanted him there.

Roosevelt wanted to further reduce Joe's political threat, and Rose was so proud that Joe was still The Ambassador that she also supported his return. However, the children were readjusting to the United States, and the lives of the three oldest were rapidly changing.

8

From Ambassador to the War Years

In stark contrast to her father, Kathleen Kennedy had become the darling of the British press. When society columns mentioned her, she was considered British society, not American, and she was placed on a number of committees, including that of the 1939 Derby Ball. She had also become even closer to William "Billy" Cavendish, the Marquess of Hartington.

Ironically, Hartington's ancestors had, for generations, represented the British government in Ireland. A bachelor in his early thirties, he was tall—six feet two and a half—and stood with a slight stoop, always embarrassed by his towering presence. He had graduated from Eton and was attending Trinity College in Cambridge where he was majoring in history. By inheritance, he would eventually be known as the Duke of Devonshire, a title that assured him great wealth and a position as part of Britain's powerful elite.

For generations the Cavendish family had worked against the Roman Catholics. In the seventeenth century, for example, William, the first Duke of Devonshire, had rebelled against James II, a Catholic, to topple him from the British throne.

The Cavendish men were notorious for increasing their wealth and power through carefully selected wives. Billy no longer had to consider such matters, though, being one of the first Cavendish men to be able to follow his heart. This was because he would inherit a castle in Ireland, a mansion in London, a massive estate in Derbyshire, and numerous other holdings. The only family of greater prominence was that of the King and Queen of England. And the royal family was nowhere near so bigoted as the manner in which Billy was reared. For him to fall in love with an Irish Catholic girl was as much a surprise to them as Kathleen's growing romance was to Rose.

During the same year, 1939, Eunice had her coming-out party. It was quite a different affair, the impending war turning English society somewhat less formal. At the party on June 22, Eunice wore a peach-colored dress from Paquin. The King, Queen, and their daughters dressed for the photographers, wearing light-colored clothing so they could instantly be identified at a distance.

The orchestra played a new line dance that night, called the Big Apple. The young women and their escorts treated the event more like a prom held during the week following final exams. Even some of the fathers, usually absent from such events, came to enjoy the party. Although shocked by the way the event had "deteriorated" in just over a year, Eunice accepted the appropriateness of what took place because the Duke of Marlborough led the Big Apple when it was danced. (To give a sense of Kathleen's ability to tweak the noses of the upper crust without sounding offensive, she called him Dukie-Wukie.)

Eunice had begun dating, but young men took little interest in her. She was considered awkward, unable to wear her clothing well, and rather shy at social events. Dance sets averaged twenty minutes each, and anytime no one had signed her card, she would retreat to whatever area had been set aside for the young women. She was always most comfortable with women, though she enjoyed men perhaps as much as Kathleen. But while Kathleen was aggressive, Eunice waited for the men to come to her. She was not comfortable in the world of social events in which Kathleen moved with such ease. In fact, even Rosemary handled her year of debutante parties with more grace, beauty, and happiness.

The impending war changed everything. Joe ordered the family, except for Rosemary, to return to the United States in September. So long as the danger did not extend to the countryside, he would not ask his oldest daughter to leave the one school where she was physically and mentally thriving as never before. Unfortunately for her, Joe brought her with him when he returned a few weeks after the others.

Kathleen and Jack adjusted to being stateside, but Joe junior changed inexplicably when he returned home. He was angry in a way that had not been so obvious in the past.

Joe junior had always been somewhat arrogant, even vicious. The physical violence against his brother Jack was family legend. Yet the constant battles between the two brothers were offset by Joe's treatment of Teddy. The greatest family nurturing Teddy received came from two sources—Joe junior and Rosemary. They were surrogate parents, loving and supportive. Many of Ted's later problems, such as with alcohol and his inability to sustain a relationship, may have stemmed from the anger he felt after Joe died in World War II and Rosemary's life was destroyed by the prefrontal lobotomy. It was as though the parents who should have loved him allowed the "parents" who did love him to disappear.

But those losses were in the future. As Joe junior returned to the United States, his problems began to multiply. He was in danger of flunking his first year at Harvard Law School. At times he was also sullen and given to rages when he could not be the center of attention. He frequently talked about his trip to Spain, though he became outraged when a listener either disagreed with his conclusions or showed little interest in what he had to say.

Joe senior tried to ease his son's scholastic problems by hiring a tutor. The father was even more arrogant than the son in this regard and hired Superior Court judge John H. Burns. It can be presumed that the judge was handsomely rewarded in either money or influence for trying to teach a first-year law student of limited promise.

Just as Kathleen's friends had shunned Joe junior in England, American girls his age were little interested in dating him. He began seeking out older women, many of them somewhat hardened by life, at nightclubs, including the Stork Club, Roseland, the Plaza, and numerous other popular nightspots.

Once back in America, Kathleen could not attend her college of choice, Sarah Lawrence, unlike her mother, who was easily accepted by Wellesley. Kathleen had never been interested in academics, and her convent-school training had been of limited value. Sarah Lawrence, the experimental women's college, was perfect for her flamboyant personality, but her educational background was so limited, she was certain to fail. The school refused to admit her. Instead she enrolled in Finch, a cross between a finishing school and a junior college. The school seemed to specialize in the daughters of the rich who either had more money than intellect or who had never applied themselves to their studies. Years later, Tricia, the less bright of Richard Nixon's two daughters, would also attend Finch.

Kathleen, the most outgoing Kennedy, dated frequently. Her name was always linked to whichever wealthy young man whose family was most in the news, such as Winthrop Rockefeller. Many times she invited Jack and Joe along when they had no dates of their own, but such evenings invariably had problems. Joe would become sullen and withdrawn, and Kathleen would ignore him. Yet it seemed as though Joe junior could not handle the idea that anyone could come in the way of the family.

Jack, by contrast, tried to act like Kathleen's big brother. He was being as sexually active as he could, at least if his letters to his friend Lem Billings are to be believed. He was discreet, though Kathleen was well aware of his activities. However, he was invariably upset with her when she showed what, for a woman of her upbringing, was a wild streak. Kathleen liked to have as many men pursuing her as possible, and she would often go to a dance with one man, then leave with another. Jack was outraged by her behavior, but she felt she did nothing wrong.

Rose was still basking in the afterglow of the British experience. She was invited to women's clubs and other groups fascinated to hear of her adventures. The organization's members wanted to know about the King and Queen, about the debutantes and the inside of a real castle. They were interested in the society that was quickly coming to an end.

Joe, however, was in trouble on both sides of the Atlantic. He had returned to England in 1940, a time when his political prospects were, of course, ended.

The British openly criticized his politics and associates. Perhaps the sharpest blast came from journalist Harold Nicolson. On March 8, 1940, he wrote in *The Spectator*:

"He will be welcomed, as is fitting, by the large and influential Anglo-American colony in London. He will also be welcomed by the native or unhyphenated rich, who hope that he may bring with him a little raft of appeasement on which they can float for a year or so longer before they are finally submerged. He will be welcomed, of course, by the bankers and the isolationists, by the knights and the baronets. He will be welcomed by the shiver-sisters of Mayfair and by the wobble-boys of Whitehall. He will be welcomed by the Peace Pledge Union, the Christian Pacifists, the followers of Dr. Buchman, the friends of Herr von Ribbentrop, the Nuerembergers, the Munichois, Lord Tavistock and the disjecta membra of former pro-Nazi organizations. A solemn gladness will even crown the brows of M. Maisky, ambassador of the USSR. Few envoys, on returning to their post, can have received a welcome of such embarrassing variety."

Joe returned to the United States in October, reluctantly giving a speech in favor of President Roosevelt's reelection to an unprecedented third term. Political promises made to Kennedy were now seen as either meaningless or unlikely to be fulfilled, no matter what the original intention of those concerned. The two men were barely civil to each other, and to add to Kennedy's perceived insults, Roosevelt remained close to Joe's father-in-law.

John Fitzgerald was 77, the avid reader of nine newspapers a day, and still involved in backroom politics. When the president's campaign train stopped in Boston during his whistle-stop tour of the country, Roosevelt inadvertently further upset Joe by meeting with Honey Fitz.

According to Jack Kennedy, who related the story thirteen years later when he was a senator, Jack, Joe junior, and Honey Fitz met the train, where Roosevelt embraced the ex-mayor warmly, saying, "Welcome, Dulce Adelina." Roosevelt claimed that he had visited South America in the 1930s, traveling to locations Honey Fitz had also visited. FDR said that he had encountered a band that tried to honor him by playing the American national anthem. However, the music was actually "Sweet Adeline," the song Honey Fitz sang everywhere, anywhere, and at any time.

Roosevelt said that the South American leaders explained that a distinguished Bostonian had visited them, always singing "Dulce Adelina," the Spanish name for "Sweet Adeline." They assumed it was the national anthem.

Jack did not know if the story was true or if Roosevelt was having fun teasing an old friend. However, for the rest of his life, whenever FDR had to talk with Honey Fitz, he called him by the nickname Dulce Adelina.

It was in the midst of Honey Fitz territory that Joe Kennedy was asked to speak with newsmen from the local papers immediately following Roosevelt's reelection to a third term in office. The press conference was arranged by John Fitzgerald and was held in the Ritz-Carlton. What occurred is in question because the interview is available only in the newspapers, and Joe Kennedy later claimed that he was misquoted by Louis Lyons of the *Boston Globe*. Joe said that Lyons, a distinguished newsman, took no notes.

Oddly, some of the reporting that upset Kennedy actually resulted in greater support for England from the Boston Irish. His reported cattiness, such as explaining that Queen Elizabeth seemed more like a housewife than someone of regal appearance in the clothes she wore, seemed to delight the locals. They had been anti-British during World War I. They were strongly pro-England during World War II, supposedly because one of their own had been appointed ambassador.

Lyons quoted Kennedy's pessimism. He said that democracy was finished in England and that the only reason to supply aid was to borrow time for the United States. England was fighting for self-preservation, whatever that might mean, not one government form over another. "It's all an economic question. I told the President in the White House last Sunday, 'Don't send me fifty admirals and generals, send me a dozen real economists.'"

There was also a backhanded compliment of Eleanor Roosevelt. He told of her sympathy for everyone and said that she was constantly bothering them to "take care of the poor little nobodies." He said, "She's always sending me a note to have some little Susie Glotz to tea at the Embassy."

Accurate or not, the reported comments sealed Kennedy's fate. He resigned his post the same month, much to everyone's relief including Rose. She worried about his safety and his health, severe ulcers having periodically sent him to the hospital in the previous years. But others came to see that he had been a much stronger isolationist than is normally reported. The British understood that Joe felt that the war was Britain's, not that of the United States. And by 1941, Joe was stating publicly that his country would be better off to develop a barter system with the Nazis after they had captured all of Europe rather than to wage total war on behalf of Great Britain.

The coming of the war caused several changes for the Kennedys. They moved to Palm Beach, closing the Bronxville home in favor of a larger ocean-front property. With the children getting older, they only needed two permanent residences, and the Florida location was a perfect complement to Hyannis Port.

BG: JOE HAD ONE odd souvenir of the war. I used to see it all the time on a table in the sunroom of the Hyannis Port house. It was a large shell, like an oversize bullet perhaps two inches in diameter and cylindrical. It had the initials JPK carved in it. I never did learn if this was one of the shells that had fallen near his country estate in England from which he worked during the blitz or if this was from a British antiaircraft weapon. I'm not even certain it's still there, because when the grandchildren became old enough to have parties, souvenirs like that kept on display were frequently stolen by the guests.

While her sons were reconsidering their father's political views and Joe was pessimistically awaiting disaster in Europe, Rose realized that the war might limit some of her pleasures. She decided it was time to travel, letting Joe handle the children: "It was a system we had always followed: as long as one of us was there, the other was free to go."

Rose traveled with Eunice, visiting Barbados, Rio de Janeiro, Argentina, Chile, Peru, Ecuador, Panama, and Cuba. They were gone for more than a month, the smaller children at home, the older ones scattered to various schools. The travel made Rose feel in control of a life that was gradually unraveling for many reasons.

The war was a factor, of course. No mother wants to see her children in uniform. That Joe would go to war was bad enough. That Jack also wanted to put on a uniform was devastating.

Jack Kennedy was an extremely sickly young man. The problems with his adrenal cortex would not be diagnosed until 1947, at which time the relatively new drug cortisone could be used for treatment. But he had been born with a bad back, a condition so serious that he was frequently in crippling pain. He could never be counted upon to carry his weight in the military.

As he suspected, Jack was unable to pass any of the military physicals, but was determined to join anyway, and for some reason his father was determined to help him. Jack began exercising, attempting to gain muscle strength, weight, and stamina, though it was all in vain. He was still 4-F—physically unfit for service—by any objective standard. However, Joe contacted Adm. Alan Kirk, formerly the naval attaché at the London embassy. The admiral was both head of the Office of Naval Intelligence and high enough in the military to be able to enlist whomever he chose.

The admiral had Jack get a physical from the family physician. Naturally it "proved" that Jack was in excellent condition for the military, though the truth was that the genetic back condition could be seriously aggravated in basic training. If Jack proved the slightest unlucky, he would become crippled for life.

Jack was given a desk job, perhaps part of the arrangement with the admiral. He gained an ensign's commission before his older, physically fit brother. But Jack's work kept him in the middle of obtaining, then passing on, appropriate intelligence concerning the buildup of Japanese forces. Such work should have been vital to the United States' strategic planning for the Pacific, but in September of 1941, no one took it seriously. Not until Pearl Harbor did anyone realize how poorly they had analyzed what was happening.

Kathleen also had a new job, though her plans were quite different from anything Rose understood. Kick had fallen in love with Billy Hartington.

Billy was with the British Expeditionary Force defending the Maginot Line in 1940. After Dunkirk and his evacuation, she understood that their relationship might not survive the war. Billy might die without their being together again. The idea horrified her and she insisted upon going back to England.

Rose misunderstood Kathleen's concerns. She thought that her daughter, like herself, simply missed the glamour and excitement of prewar Britain.

If Kathleen had to do something for the British war effort, she wanted to do it where it was needed most, in the nation under attack. Not only would she feel closer to Billy, but anytime he got leave, they could be together for at least a few hours or a few days.

With her parents opposed to a trip to England, Kathleen wanted something she could respect to occupy her time. She had mentioned that she might like to learn journalism, so Joe turned to his friend Arthur Krock for help. Krock suggested the *Washington Times-Herald*.

In 1941, the *Times-Herald* was the type of newspaper on which many journalists get their start. The founder, Eleanor "Cissy" Patterson—the sister of the founder of the *New York Daily News* and the granddaughter of Joseph Medill, the owner of the *Chicago Tribune*—was fifty-nine in 1940, the first female editor/publisher of a major American newspaper. But though it was profitable, it had no influence on anyone who mattered in Washington. The paper seemed a combination of gossip, news with a right-wing, isolationist slant, and features of one sort or another. The staff was generally dedicated, hardworking, with dreams of moving up in the field.

Kathleen did not want to receive special favors from the newspaper.

She did not want to be known as the daughter of Ambassador Joe Kennedy, the multimillionaire. She just wanted to be Kick, living in an apartment that matched her salary, leading the same life as the others on the staff. If she could not be in England waiting for chances to see Billy, then she would go as far as she could as a reporter.

There were few expectations of Kick when she arrived at the newspaper. Everyone knew she was another of Krock's debutantes, but she refused to stress who she was. She dressed inexpensively, worked hard, and used her political and diplomatic connections to get stories others couldn't. She did accept dates to parties, but she noted all that was said, using whatever was appropriate for her work.

Kick's only problem was her winter coat. Joe had purchased his daughters expensive fur coats of their choosing, and Kathleen's was a long mutation mink that cost almost as much as she earned in a year. She bought herself a cheap coat to wear to the office, but she used the mink for evening wear.

Kick was so successful at hiding her identity that no one realized who she was. If she had to go to an event right after work, then she stuffed the mink in a shopping bag, changing after she left the office. However, one night, as Kathleen later told her mother, she was on her way to a diplomatic reception when she realized she had forgotten something she needed at the office. When she returned to the office wearing an expensive dinner dress and her mink, she mistakenly thought it was late enough that no one would see her.

The next day some of Kathleen's friends tried to talk with her about self-respect, men, and success. They assumed from her expensive clothes that she had become a part-time, high-priced call girl or rich man's mistress, not knowing of her family's wealth.

Kathleen progressed rapidly at the newspaper. After being an assistant to Executive Editor Frank Waldrop, learning the business, she worked with John White, who was in charge of the "Did You Happen to See?" feature. This was a short-profile/gossip item that was quite popular.

By 1942, Rose Kennedy was feeling jealous of her children. Both Joe junior and Jack had written books, and Kick was increasingly skilled as a journalist. Yet though Rose was better educated than most of her family, no one consulted her. In a February 16, 1942 letter to her children, she seems almost petulant about it:

"Kathleen has been transferred to the Play Department; that is, she has a column and is giving her opinion of plays and pictures. I am a little confused as to whether it is both or one, but anyway, that is the general idea. My suggestion would be that she have a nom de plume. My second suggestion would be that she have a decent picture taken, but she and her father seem to think both of these matters are okay. She is quite thrilled at the idea of people watching for her column and I am quite crushed to think that my three or four children got into print with works of their brains and I was never allowed to edit one little word. I believe it is the Bible which says—'The twig cannot be greater than the root from which it has sprung.'"

Kathleen ignored her mother's letters, more concerned with a new woman who had come to work at the newspaper, Inga Arvad. Her presence would lead to a scandal that would change Jack Kennedy's life.

Inga Arvad, at twenty-eight, had one of the longer careers in journalism among the men and women who began work at the *Times-Herald*. A tall, blond beauty, she had won a French beauty contest, and an early marriage to an Egyptian diplomat had ended in divorce before she was twenty.

Born in Copenhagen, Denmark, Arvad was educated in Brussels, London, and Paris. As the Nazis came to power in Germany, she took a freelance job for a Copenhagen newspaper and went to interview Hitler. She was officially listed as the paper's Berlin correspondent, and she was fortunate, for that year was one of the last times when the Nazi high command willingly made themselves accessible to journalists. Because her beauty seemed to fit the Aryan ideal, she quickly obtained interviews with many in the Nazi high command. Ultimately she attended the 1936 Olympics with Hitler. By the time Arvad came to the United States, she was under investigation by the FBI.

Inga Arvad was the major love of Jack Kennedy's life. She was like no one he had ever met. As cultured and worldly as Rose wanted to be, though with a better understanding of international affairs, she was also uninhibited in her lovemaking.

Kathleen and Inga became friends, and since Jack and Kathleen shared a Washington apartment, inevitably he met Inga. They were immediately taken with each other, she by his naive intensity and sense of humor, he by her sophistication and uninhibited sharing of herself. Their relationship became so important to him that he saved at least some of their love letters. These were the only love letters he ever saved, even though her comments were about wanting to have his baby, their lovemaking, and other intimate details of the relationship.

Joe was extremely worried about Jack's relationship with Arvad. A woman of such intensity was likely to marry his son, and Joe was already grooming his sons for the presidency. He wanted nothing in their pasts that would hinder them.

Kennedy legend has Joe senior preparing Young Joe for office. The youth's selection as a delegate to the 1940 Democratic National Convention was an obvious introduction to the world of politics. And the myth says that Joe would be president, followed by Jack and then each brother in turn. According to both myth and the beliefs of friends he made immediately after the war, Jack had no serious interest in politics until his parents helped move him into Congress.

However, the Arvad letters show that Jack was already planning on the White House, and the amused Inga (called Inga-Binga by Jack) was talking of visiting him there. With Joe having such concerns so early, Inga must have seemed his worst nightmare. No Catholic could marry a twice-divorced woman and be elected president. Joe wanted to assure that the two lovers were not in the same city. Just as he had arranged for Jack to enter the Navy, so he now saw to it that his son was assigned to active duty in the Pacific.

Joe knew that Jack was physically unfit. Yet just as Joe had destroyed Rosemary the previous year by ordering her unneeded, improper prefrontal lobotomy, so he now put his second-oldest son at deadly risk. Angered over the Arvad relationship, Joe contacted a former Wall Street associate who had been appointed undersecretary of the navy. James Forrestal never questioned the request. He just made certain that Jack's time in Naval Intelligence was ended and that he was transferred to Midshipmen's School at Northwestern University. Jack was going into combat despite the fact that if the enemy did not kill him, his own sickly body might handle the job.

Rose Kennedy simply accepted the family activities by then, no longer personally involved with her children. They were all able to read, including the youngest, so she simply typed up greetings, made nine copies, and mailed them to each child. Sometimes she praised one child or another. Sometimes she was petulant, as in her comments about Kathleen previously quoted. Sometimes she gossiped. And sometimes she inadvertently caused pain.

Ted Kennedy was an afterthought, the post–Gloria Swanson child Rose never truly wanted. He was moved from place to place, from school to school, and bedroom to bedroom. He was closest in age to Jean, his best friend within the family. He was most nurtured by Rosemary and Joe junior, though the former was now mentally destroyed and the latter was overseas with the military.

Ted was not particularly bright, not particularly coordinated, and ate with the same obsession he would later devote to alcohol and women. Instead of being lovingly supportive, Rose damned him with faint praise, essentially ridiculing him within the family. Her letters frequently held such comments as:

"Teddy is the same and is very busy. He assists at Mass and the Priest invited him to breakfast last Sunday. Teddy said he informed him that he had already had his breakfast but the Priest misunderstood, and anyway he ate his breakfast with the Priest. *I think he has put on the ten pounds which he lost at Riverdale.* He dances very well, has remarkable rhythm, and shakes his head like a veteran when he does the conga. *He only fell down once last week, so he is improving.* He has a little dancing partner, just the proper height, and as they are the two youngest in the class, it is just as well that they prefer each other." (Emphasis added.)

"To Bobby's amazement when he saw him at dancing school, Teddy knows all the steps from the zomba [sic] to the old-fashioned waltz. He also scans the movie columns, makes his dates, and goes confidently off without bothering anyone. *I am afraid he is getting too fat as he now weighs about 105.*" (Emphasis added.)

"We expected darling Teddy home over this weekend, but it seems the little angel got into a water fight in the lavoratory [sic] and 'after he knew his way around he got full of biscuits' and got himself into a little trouble, so he was put on bounds for two weeks. It seems quite unfair because I am sure the boys who were there before provoked him to mischief. Also, these are our last two weekends when he might come home as we now expect to close the house about the 19th. I suppose he has learned his lesson, but a little too late."

Rose's letters also indicated that she was intellectually aware that Jack was at risk in battle, though the seriousness of his situation never seemed to touch her. As she wrote to the children:

"Jack, you know, is a Lieutenant, J.G. and of course he is delighted. His whole attitude about the war has changed and he is quite ready to die for the U.S.A. in order to keep the Japanese and the Germans from becoming the dominant people on their respective continents, believing that sooner or later they would encroach upon ours. He also thinks it would be good for Joe's political career if he died for the grand old flag, although I don't believe he feels that is absolutely necessary."

By the end of the war, Jack would barely survive the destruction of his PT boat and Joe junior would be dead.

At first Joe saw Jack's near-tragedy in the Pacific as a way to repair the family's reputation. Joe senior knew that Jack's "heroic" actions in the Pacific aboard PT 109 made great copy, and he played up the story of his son as hero for all it was worth. He held a dinner for Jack when Joe junior was in town. Both brothers knew the truth. In fact, years later all Jack would say was that he wasn't a hero. All that happened was that the Japanese sank his PT boat. But no one would contradict old Joe, and the speeches were so pompous and self-serving that one witness, Joe Timilty, a friend of the elder Kennedy's, would later be quoted as saying that Young Joe wept in his bedroom from the frustration of failing to please his father with real acts of courage. It's even possible that his desire to show his toughness for his father drove him to the mission that would take his life.

Joe junior had wanted greater action and volunteered for the Aphrodite Project, a desperate attempt to halt the new, highly devastating German V-1 missiles.

The V-1s were being launched from sites in France that had been identified by intelligence gathering, surveillance, and reports by the military personnel who had survived the attacks. But the Americans lacked missiles of their own and nothing less than a missile could be safely used. Finally, a Liberator bomber was modified for remote-control operation. A television camera was fitted in the nose to guide the plane from a manned mother ship. The rest of the robot plane was to be filled with explosives, the actual arming for electronic control to be done in the air just before the plane was released. Practice was conducted with the PBY-4 planes, on which Joe was an expert, and he was fascinated with the project.

On August 11, 1944, Joe was preparing for the flight. The weather was excellent and would hold for the next two or three days. The attack of the robot plane was scheduled for the twelfth, but there would be no problem delaying it until the thirteenth or fourteenth.

Joe's job, along with a second pilot of less seniority, would be to fly the Liberator filled with 21,170 pounds of high explosives, then maneuver until two mother planes could position themselves for total radio control. Once the electronics were set and the plane had become a drone missile, the two pilots were to bail out over England and the Liberator would attack a V-1 rocket launch site in Normandy.

After a preflight check, electronics officer Earl Olsen went to Joe and informed him of problems with the circuits on the plane. The remote control might possibly cause premature detonation. Olsen needed twenty-four hours to be certain everything would work flawlessly, but he felt there was little risk. Since the mission would not be hurt by a day's delay, the commanding officer had said that it would be Joe's judgment call whether to postpone the flight.

After his conversation with Olsen, Young Joe wrote out a will, divided his possessions among his friends, and mentioned that his only regret was that he couldn't call his girlfriend, Pat Wilson, to say goodbye.

This might be considered routine for a man going on what amounted to an experimental mission. However, Joe was an experienced pilot who had frequently faced danger before without going to such lengths. More important, he knew that a day's delay was not critical. So, disregarding Olsen's request for delay, Young Joe took off at 6 P.M. on Saturday, August 12, 1944. Twenty-eight minutes into the flight, the feared accidental detonation occurred.

On Sunday, August 13, 1944, most of the Kennedys were in Hyannis Port. According to Rose Kennedy, the family had enjoyed a front-porch picnic lunch, after which Joe went inside to take a nap. The younger children were sitting in the living room, talking quietly among themselves. Rose was reading the Sunday newspaper.

At approximately 2 P.M. two priests arrived at the door and requested to speak with Joe. This was not unusual because, though Rose refused to support the church financially, Joe was regularly contacted concerning one or another charity. He was frequently more generous than his wife, which kept the cardinal beholden to him. His generosity was often timed around a problem, such as his entanglement with Gloria Swanson.

Assuming the call related to a contribution, Rose refused to awaken Joe. She knew he would not be resting much longer, so she invited the priests to sit with the family. They declined, explaining that their mission was urgent.

Instinctively Rose knew something was terribly wrong. She raced to get Joe, then the two of them sat with the priests, who informed them that Young Joe was dead. There was no hope. He had died in the explosion of the Liberator bomber.

According to Rose, Joe went to the porch and told the children. He said that they should be brave as their brother would want them to be. He told them to race their sailboats as planned, which they did.

Jack was the only one not to listen to his father. He began walking the beach, lost in thought.

After that, according to Rose, she and Joe sat holding each other, weeping "inwardly." Then Joe supposedly stated, "We've got to carry on. We must take care of the living. There is a lot of work to do."

Other versions of what happened are harsher and probably more accurate: After telling the children, Joe retired to his room to grieve. He again shut Rose out of a moment they should have shared.

Even Doris Kearns Goodwin, both a respected biographer and a woman close to the Kennedys, tells a different version: "When the priests left, Joe held on to Rose for a moment and then went into the living room to break the news to the others. 'Children,' he said, 'your brother Joe has been lost. He died flying a volunteer mission.' Then, with tears in his eyes and his voice cracking, he said, 'I want you all to be particularly good to your mother.' And with that he retreated into his bedroom and locked the door."

Unlike Jack, Joe junior had been a true hero. He was posthumously awarded the Air Medal and the Navy Cross. In addition, Destroyer #850, launched from the Fore River Shipyards in 1946, was named the USS *Joseph P. Kennedy, Jr.*

Kathleen was not in the United States when Joe junior was killed. She had gained the courage to follow her heart, returning to England in 1943, where it became clear that she was in love with Billy Hartington.

Rose was outraged and frustrated. Kathleen could not abandon her Catholic faith. In Rose's eyes, Catholicism was as much a part of what defined her Irish heritage as the language and customs. Catholicism had kept the people united while under British domination. As Rose saw it, to become a Protestant was to deny the history of her existence.

Rose also felt that Billy Hartington's family would be equally hostile to his leaving his Anglican roots. (In the United States, the Episcopal Church is rooted in the Anglican tradition, though deviating slightly from the rituals.) This proved correct, though both families realized that, with or without approval, a marriage was possible. And when Jack was almost killed, Kathleen realized that she could lose Billy at any moment. She did not want to lose him before they were married.

Rose and Joe used every connection they had. They contacted Francis Spellman, whom they had known both as bishop in Boston and as cardinal based in New York. They were also friends with the former Cardinal Pacelli, the man who had become Pope Pius XII. Direct contact had become difficult, so Cardinal Spellman acted as go-between.

The Kennedys did not want anyone to know what they were doing. However, Kick was with the Red Cross, an American in a nation at war, and that meant that everything was being read and censored. Refusing to risk embarrassment, the Kennedys used codes when writing across the Atlantic. As Rose later explained, instead of referring to Francis Cardinal Spellman, they chatted breezily about "Archie Spell."

Finally Kathleen talked with both Billy and Joe junior. Young Joe understood war and had stayed more closely in contact with her because of his work in the Atlantic theater. Kathleen could not bring herself to hurt her family by marrying in the Anglican Church. Billy would not hurt his parents by agreeing to rear any children in the Catholic Church, a requirement for either a Catholic ceremony or a Catholic Church–sanctioned civil ceremony.

Rose was outraged and sickened by what was happening. She felt that the marriage would be a rejection of her, of her values. She believed that her daughter was making a choice between Billy and her mother, something Kathleen never considered.

Eventually Rose entered New England Baptist Hospital as a way to escape the press. When, two days before the marriage, Kathleen made clear that her choice was irreversible, Rose cabled her daughter with the message: "Heartbroken. Feel you have been wrongly influenced—sending Arch Spellman's friend to talk to you. Anything done for our Lord will be rewarded hundredfold."

Rose refused to think that Kathleen could love a man more than the Church. She was fairly certain that her daughter's soul would go to purgatory for such a marriage. Even worse, since the Kennedy family was seen as the most important Irish Catholic family in America, or so Rose believed, news of Kathleen's marriage could influence other Catholic girls. It horrified Rose, as a Child of Mary, to think that her daughter could become the example cited by other Catholics in love with other Protestant boys. Nothing could be worse than Kathleen's marriage to a man of the wrong faith causing other girls to marry men who were not Catholic.

Despite their mother's concerns, Joe junior and Kathleen decided that she and Billy had only one option. They would marry in a manner that would cause the least difficulty for everyone. On May 6, 1944, they had a civil ceremony, unsanctioned by either church, in the Chelsea Registry Office. The ceremony would not meet the standards of either set of parents, but those problems they would work out later. Family friends in England helped Kathleen dress and acted as witnesses. Young Joe also attended. Then, after the brief ceremony, the couple honeymooned at Compton Place in Eastbourne.

Kathleen and Billy had a little more than a month together. Then Billy was ordered to be a part of the invasion of Normandy, France, and Kathleen visited in Hyannis Port. When word of his death in Belgium on September 10 was relayed to his widow, Lady Hartington, she immediately returned home to England.

Rose made no record of her feelings, but Billy's sister was extremely close to Kathleen and spent extensive time with the grieving widow. She later claimed that Kathleen said her mother had tried to convince her that Billy's death was God's way of handling the improper mixed marriage. She said that Kathleen worried about losing her soul for what must have been a sin or Billy would not have died. Although perhaps not all that rational a thought, Kathleen was grieving, she had violated the principles on which she was raised, and Rose undoubtedly felt that a sin had been committed.

Gradually Kathleen was effectively excluded from the Kennedy family to a great degree. She was British, not American, if only through the adoption of the country as her home. She had married outside the Church, and Rose did not want her to be seen publicly near Jack after he began running for political office.

Having lost everything, Kathleen returned to England at the end of 1944, determined to find happiness. This she did after the war ended, in the arms of the very married Peter Milton, Lord Fitzwilliam. The lovers made no effort to hide their affection, and Milton left his wife, filing for divorce.

Joe senior had come to recognize his own wild streak in Kathleen and accepted her actions. Milton may have cheated on his wife, but not until they were emotionally estranged. He was being honorable by leaving her and filing for divorce. And if he and Kathleen were having what could be considered illicit sex while waiting for the day they could marry, who was Joe to say anything? At least they were faithful to each other, something he had never been to Rose.

But again there was tragedy. Joe was in Paris in May of 1948, while

Peter and Kathleen were vacationing in Cannes. They had hired a private plane to have lunch with Joe in Paris on the thirteenth.

The day of the lunch a storm was moving toward Cannes. The lovers were anxious to be on time since the date with Joe was a welcoming into the family they had received from no one else. The pilot felt he could outrace the storm. However, he was wrong, and the plane crashed, killing all three.

BG: I HAD BEEN WORKING as Mrs. Kennedy's assistant for seven or eight years when the subject of Kathleen's death came up. Rose had been dictating a letter to her friend Moucher, a woman I learned was Billy Hartington's mother. Although the two corresponded regularly, this was the first time Rose had brought up the funeral when talking to me.

Mrs. Kennedy mentioned that she did not attend, and when I asked her why, she said, "I was in the hospital having a hysterectomy so I didn't go."

Mrs. Kennedy never said if the surgery was an emergency or if it was elective and could have been delayed. I later learned that her version of what Kathleen was doing when she was killed was not accurate, though. She told me rather disdainfully that Kathleen was killed when going to a party in Switzerland. She never mentioned that Kathleen was going to meet Joe or that she was traveling with her married lover.

Again Rose saw God's work. Kathleen's soul was not in a state of grace. It would be in purgatory and Rose refused to grieve. She did not acknowledge the truth of the plane crash, saying only that Kathleen was with "a few friends." She also refused to attend the funeral.

Kathleen was buried in the William Cavendish Family's Devonshire ancestral estate of Chatsworth. At her former mother-in-law, the duchess's suggestion, the gravestone read: "Joy She Gave, and Joy She Has." But Rose saw only a fallen daughter, more lost in life than Rosemary had become. And Rosemary had been a victim of others. Kathleen had died because of her own choices. Or so Rose believed.

BG: ODDLY, THOUGH THERE was great pain for the way Kathleen had lived at the end of her life, Mrs. Kennedy could not avoid her awe at the title her daughter had achieved. Whenever she learned someone was traveling to England, she suggested they go see Kathleen's grave at Chatsworth. And then, as though they would need the ultimate incentive, she would add, "She was a duchess, you know."

9

Politics

Joe Kennedy had denied his wife a chance to be his partner, and she had lived for years in his shadow. She had become a self-centered eccentric. She had seen one son die and one daughter destroyed by the man she once thought she would do anything to marry. Jack had almost lost his life in combat because Joe's anger toward his son's lover had led him to use influence to send a chronically physically unfit man into a war zone. But Jack had managed to survive the war, and though he was increasingly in ill health, he was following in the family tradition by running for public office.

In 1946, with Rosemary in Wisconsin, Kathleen in England, and the other children either in school or exploring the working world, Rose was able to do for her son what Honey Fitz had trained her to do from the time she was a small child. Rose Kennedy determined to get Jack into his first political office.

* * *

In politics you have no friends, only coconspirators.
— Joe Kane, campaign strategist for James Curley in
his successful 1913 campaign to unseat John
Fitzgerald, and campaign strategist for Jack
Kennedy in 1946 in his bid for Congress

* * *

Rose may have felt God's blessing in 1946 when Honey Fitz's old nemesis, James Curley, left Congress to run for mayor of Boston. Curley had no successor in mind, nor did any of the ward bosses. The seat was up for grabs, and the Eleventh Congressional District, though redrawn slightly over the years, was almost identical to the one Honey Fitz had held when Rose was always at his side. She knew the district, knew the people, and while her life had taken her far from Boston, little had changed in the "dear old North End."

Joe Kane was officially the coordinator of the John Kennedy for Congress campaign, but Jack's first important election was a Fitzgerald affair from the start. Kane was hated by Jack's grandfather, of course. Kane had helped James Curley with the smear strategy that had led to Honey Fitz's downfall over the Elizabeth Ryan affair. Yet because of Kane's very success in the rough-and-tumble world of corrupt Boston politics, Honey Fitz was pleased to have him on board. What mattered most was electing his grandson to Congress, and Joe Kane was the best available "pol" for the job.

John Fitzgerald was an elfin man of eighty-three, still singing "Sweet Adeline" and still willing to dance an Irish jig on a barroom tabletop. That he was intimately involved with the campaign was obvious from the location of Jack's headquarters, specifically selected so he could use his grandfather for advice. The entire Fitzgerald clan was relocated to the Bellevue Hotel in Boston, a residential and transient facility. Honey Fitz and Josie had an apartment in the Bellevue. The Democratic Party's headquarters was in the Bellevue. Jack's campaign office was in the Bellevue. And when Rose and Joe wanted a place to live while helping their son with his first campaign, Rose saw to it that they also took an apartment in the Bellevue.

Joe Kennedy knew how to buy a vote, a favor, or a political appointment. He knew where and when to use his vast fortune. But he didn't know the streets, had never understood them in the way of his father, P. J., of the seemingly innocuous yet brilliantly cunning Honey Fitz, of his own wife, Rose Fitzgerald Kennedy.

Jack was not a politician. He was a kid with an infectious grin, a friendly personality, a broken body, and so little guile that he was dismissed as a man naive enough only to attend a wake if he actually knew the family.

In fairness it must be said that Joe Kennedy had one idea—that of the new generation of leaders—that set the tone for every Jack Kennedy election campaign.

Ostensibly to honor his oldest son, but actually to give Jack a base, Joe had funded a new Veterans of Foreign Wars post named for Joseph

P. Kennedy Jr. Jack was one of the founding members, of course, and though he was well liked by the other young men, he was never a leader.

Edgar Grossman, long active in Democratic politics, was one of the first members of the Joseph P. Kennedy, Jr. VFW Post. The organizational meeting was held at the Puritan Hotel on Beacon Street near the Harvard Club. Approximately a dozen men were present, none of whom knew each other well. Jack Kennedy became the first commander of the post, a low-key position. "It was social, patriotic, and fraternal," according to Grossman. And when the first meeting was over, they had food and beer brought in, then played cards.

Jack Kennedy and the others never talked about the war, according to Grossman. Jack's only interest was domestic travel.

"Jack never had, in my opinion, the temperament, the desire, the ambition, the intestinal fortitude, the stomach, for a political campaign. He was a quiet, laid-back, somewhat introverted person, seemingly kind, gentle, and hardly one that you'd expect to get into the dirt which politics in general, and Massachusetts politics in particular, are duly noted," said Edgar Grossman.

June 17 is a regional holiday in Charlestown, the part of Boston where the Bunker Hill Monument is located. A large parade was held there annually commemorating one of the earliest conflicts of the Revolutionary War. Naturally all the veterans' organizations were invited to march in the parade, including, in 1946, the by then approximately twenty members of the Joseph P. Kennedy, Jr. VFW Post.

Jack Kennedy, the post commander, had announced his candidacy to be the Democratic Party's nominee for the open congressional seat. The primary had intense competition from professionals, including the mayor of Cambridge and a member of the city council. Jack had no experience, no constituency, and no history in politics. However, he did have Joe Kane guiding him, and Kane, though sixty-six at the time, knew how to analyze a community. He sensed the earliest change coming to an area and knew how to take advantage of it. He coined the campaign slogan "The New Generation Offers a Leader" and showed Jack how to use the June 17 parade to reflect this idea. As Edgar Grossman later commented:

"Every other veterans' organization came in full regalia with hats, uniforms, color guard, flags, sometimes a band. This group appeared without trappings, without anything fancy. In fact, they were told what to wear and everybody was asked to wear dark trousers, black shoes, white shirts, a simple tie, and no conventional military hats. No military at all. You'd never know what they were except that there was a little banner identifying them.

"And we marched the full route—I think it was two or three miles— Jack was up at the head of the line, and it was not in a military formation. It was a loosely jointed military formation. We were in rows, but not keeping step. But we made a nice appearance.

"It was the new look. A fresh wind was blowing. And this fresh wind was led by John F. Kennedy.

"It was refreshing.

"We had a good time. It was enjoyable. I liked the experience." It also reinforced the image of a new generation, born in the twentieth century, tempered by war, and ready to take command.

Not that Jack Kennedy was unique in this manner. Richard Nixon was from this era, as was the disreputable senator and Kennedy family friend Joe McCarthy. George Bush was also of this generation, but because he worked behind the scenes, including a stint as CIA director, by the time he became president he was associated with Ronald Reagan. And though Reagan was also from the same generation (his wartime service only in southern California), by the time of his election he seemed to be as much an old man as the nineteenth-century general Dwight Eisenhower seemed when Kennedy ran.

Jack Kennedy had two options that fateful year of 1946. One was to place himself on the ballot for lieutenant governor. Incumbent governor Maurice Tobin was running for reelection and needed a lieutenant governor on the party ticket. He was a friend of Joe Kennedy's, liked the idea of an innocuous twenty-eight-year-old who would not get in the way, and thought he could use Jack's image as a war hero to help his own campaign.

In Massachusetts, races for governor and lieutenant governor were conducted separately, so it was possible for a Democrat to be governor, a Republican lieutenant governor, or the reverse. Joe's idea was that both Tobin and Jack would win, then, because one of the Massachusetts U.S. senators was dying and would probably not complete his term, Tobin would move into the Senate and Jack would be governor.

The two problems with this reasoning, however, were that either Tobin or Jack could lose. The Republicans would be delighted to take on a twenty-eight-year-old running for lieutenant governor with pretensions to the higher office. Jack had no political experience. He had no meaningful work experience. He had no leadership experience except in saving lives after his bad judgment resulted in his PT-boat's being sunk.

Joe reluctantly supported the idea of the congressional race. He had been humiliated by Roosevelt. He had seen his father-in-law humiliated by Curley. The lieutenant governor would be supported by businessmen seeking favors, something Joe well understood. And to be one of the youngest governors in the nation would be an excellent stepping-stone. However, as Joe Kane pointed out, in the previous thirty-two years in Massachusetts, only one lieutenant governor had managed to make the switch.

Rose and Honey Fitz were naturally enthusiastic about the Eleventh District race, even though the primary had ten candidates. They understood that it would take far fewer votes to become the best of ten than if it were a two-person race. They also knew that if Jack lost, there would be no disgrace given the size of the field and the experience of some of the candidates. These included former Speaker of the Massachusetts House of Representatives Mike Neville, the popular mayor of Cambridge.

What was not said was that some of the ten might be called "non-candidates." Joe Kane knew that one of these men preferred money to power and made a deal with the man for $7,500. If the race was close and only the large field made a win possible for Jack, the man would stay in until the end. However, if it looked like a smaller field would help Jack, the man would drop out when told to do so.

In addition to Mike Neville, City Councilman Joseph Russo was on the ballot and extremely popular with the voters. Joe Kane located another Democrat in the district whose name was also Joseph Russo, then arranged for this second man to have his name on the ballot, too. The second Russo probably didn't campaign. What mattered was that the Russo supporters would have to guess which man was the one they wanted, and Kane hoped the vote for the popular Russo would be drastically diminished.

The politicians looked upon Jack Kennedy as a joke, and in a conventional campaign, he was. He was a spoiled rich kid who had played in California, played in Florida, played in England. He was a veteran, but so was candidate Major Catherine Falvey, a Somerville woman who had served with the Women's Army Corps. What mattered was that the district was a tough working-class area, and Jack had never been in a poor person's home in his young life.

There were other problems as well. Jack had not lived in the district since he was eleven years old. He had never voted there, and he knew no one who lived there. He was not even a member of the Democratic Party.

The charge of carpetbagger was made early on in the primary, then quickly dropped when it was learned that Massachusetts law did not require a congressional representative to live in his or her district. Jack's summer home in Hyannis Port made him seem a resident of the state, and that was all that mattered.

As for party affiliation, Jack had to be a member of a political party at least twenty full days before becoming a primary candidate. That was state law, and Jack complied with only a few days to spare.

Joe Kennedy's focus was on the best campaign money could buy. He hired an advertising agency. He arranged for press releases to stress Jack's war record, his heroism, and the massive support he was receiving from veterans. But while that had an appeal, it was not what mattered. As Rose would later write:

"Joe was wise in the fields of national and international political affairs, but his interest dwindled as the political unit grew smaller. Events at the level of district, city, town, and ward left him progressively bored. Particularly in Boston. It was a life he had left long ago without regret."

But not Rose. Not a Boston where she could use the political skills she had learned at her father's knee. This was her world and she would show her husband how much she understood power.

While many of Jack's classmates had entered the military, often compiling distinguished records, they were also likely to be officers. Well educated, they were trained for leadership. By contrast, the sons of the families in the Eleventh Congressional District were often of limited education and likely to have served in the front line. The district contained a large number of Gold Star Mothers, women who had lost one or more sons to the war. They needed to grieve, to know that there was compassion for what they had experienced. And Rose Kennedy was a Gold Star Mother.

Joe Kane hated Honey Fitz, and Jack was supposedly uncomfortable with his grandfather's guidance. Yet as much a character as Honey Fitz seemed to be, he understood the people who had voted for him. He went campaigning with Jack whenever his grandson was knocking on doors in areas where the people were primarily elderly. He had never lost contact with hundreds of constituents, and he never forgot their names. They had loved him in office, loved him as a fellow parishioner. When he introduced his grandson to them, telling Jack each person's name, he was essentially anointing his successor. He was symbolically passing the mantle, a gesture they understood and trusted.

But the campaign that mattered, the campaign that brought in the most unpaid-for votes, was the one conducted by Rose.

It was called "Coffee With the Kennedys." A friend of Jack's was part of a family that owned a printing company and were active in the Democratic Party. The company prepared paper coffee cups with the slogan printed on them for use in home gatherings. The gatherings were like Tupperware parties, only instead of being sold plastic storage ware, the participants were sold a congressional candidate.

To this end, Eunice and Pat began coordinating the "Kennedy-ware" parties, the gatherings in living rooms throughout the district where women, and occasionally men, would gather to hear the candidate. Eunice had been working for the State Department in Washington, working with former German prisoners of war who had been liberated and returned to the United States. Pat had graduated from Rosemont, then gone immediately to Boston for the campaign. And Jean, the youngest, took a break from her studies following her first year in Manhattanville. Only Kathleen was not present. As a darling of British society, she was told she was not welcome. She offered the wrong image to the voters.

The women of the Eleventh District voted more frequently than the men, and some of the older women remembered that Honey Fitz had given them patronage jobs before they got the right to vote. Some had told this story to their daughters, and Jack gained extra credibility among women for his family history.

But the Kennedys were concerned about Catherine Falvey's appeal to women. Probably the most competent among the candidates, she was attractive, intelligent, and had gained more publicity than Jack by having served at the Nuremberg war-crime trials. At thirty-five, she had proven herself as an attorney as well as a successful vote getter since she had served two terms representing Somerville in the Massachusetts legislature. She had a track record, a war record, and offered a maturity that Eunice and Pat lacked as they organized and coordinated the in-house gatherings of neighbors where Jack was to speak.

Rose understood all of this. She also understood that it would be her job to convert the crowd to her son.

One of Rose's strongest selling points was also one she chose not to stress: she was a Gold Star Mother herself.

Dave Powers, who accompanied Jack on some of his campaigns, then built a life and career around his friend, eventually heading the Kennedy Library, felt that Jack had won over the Gold Star Mothers. Jack would always mention that his mother knew the grief of the women with whom he was speaking. But Rose, not Jack, made the difference.

As Rose well knew from her own grief, Gold Star Mothers did not want anyone's sympathy. The pain was too great. The nation saw honor in sacrifice. The mothers saw a loss that would forever leave a hollowness in their lives.

BG: MORE THAN THIRTY YEARS later, when Rose was having people in for dinner, Rose asked Jean who was coming. Jean said, "Pat and Ethel and me. What more could you want, Mother?"

There was a pause, then Mrs. Kennedy said, "I want my sons."

Joe junior had been more than another boy killed in war. He was the firstborn child, the firstborn male. On Joe had rested all hopes for the family. He would guide the others. He would be the leader long after his parents were dead from old age. And suddenly he lived no more. In that Irish Catholic world that made up large portions of the Eleventh District, all the women shared the same hopes and beliefs concerning their firstborn. Both personally and culturally there was no greater loss to be endured. Others could have sympathy. Rose had empathy in the truest sense of the word. And if she asked them to vote for Jack, they would cast the vote to help one of their own.

The idea behind Coffee With the Kennedys was misunderstood by some of the newer politicians and even many of the older ones. They saw it as a way to introduce the candidate to small groups of voters, to get them acquainted with the young man. He was rail thin, his skin slightly discolored, and obviously not well. But his attitude and style were such that no one noticed. And as Joe senior would comment, it was the perception of the voters, not the reality of the candidate, that ultimately mattered.

Rose understood that people wanted something more, wanted to know that their own striving could amount to something. If they were going to vote for little more than a boy the same age as the women's own sons, brothers, or husbands, then he needed to be a symbol of success. They wanted to think that the men in their lives might one day be able to achieve what Jack was doing, and that was where Rose dominated the gatherings.

Rose did not try to dress to look like the women, especially not in the poorer tenement communities, which she understood far better than her children. (Jack was horrified at one point to discover how many people had to live in such cramped quarters that the toilet and the stove shared the same small room.) Instead she dressed as someone who had known success, who had been to dinner with the King and Queen of England. And when she spoke, she often talked of her weekend with royalty.

Rose knew that glamour sold. Jack Kennedy made certain he was never photographed with a cigar sticking out of his mouth, yet he enjoyed smoking cigars. He learned from Rose about image, and her son's first lessons came as she arrived at each gathering slightly behind her daughters. She usually made her entrance alone, letting them see this small, glamorous woman about whom they had been reading in the newspapers. They knew her father, of course. And she was one of their own, her heritage being their heritage, and she had made it in a world that sometimes seemed eternally hostile. She had almost a movie star's charisma, yet she knew what it was to raise a large family, to lose her firstborn to a war. She was both one of them and the culmination of their secret fantasies.

At times, the speeches Rose made seemed far removed from politics. Yet they had greater impact than the ones the men had written for Jack.

Coffee With the Kennedys was a masterful political stroke. Rose's life may have been self-centered, yet she had never forgotten the psychology of the women of the communities that comprised the Eleventh District.

The family tried to keep the meetings to a minimum of twenty-five participants, a maximum of seventy-five. Often several events were scheduled in an evening, and they had to be slightly more casual, with coffee and flowers, but little else that was fancy. However, when the gathering was manageable, they would also bring good china and silverware, increasing the glamour.

The men working on the campaign focused on Joe Kane's slogan, "The New Generation Offers a Leader." Shortly before the primary, Joe Kennedy paid to have ten thousand reprints of an article on Jack's heroism sent to homes in the district, each mailing accompanied by an endorsement from one of the crew members.

Joe also arranged to have an article printed in *Look* magazine the week of the primary. The numerous photographs included one with

Jack, Joe, and Honey Fitz. Quotes were also created for the publication, some stressing that Jack was only doing what Joe junior would have done, and others stressing the obligations of a rich man's son to those who still struggled. This skillful public relations seemed to give a national magazine's support to one of the least capable candidates in what was really a local election. Most of the country probably did not care, but Joe felt that the price, whatever it might have been, was worth it to reach the voters in a way the other candidates could not match.

But Rose knew best what the people wanted.

On June 15, 1946, Rose gave the women of Cambridge, the most hotly contested area in the Eleventh District, a taste of royalty. Using what she had learned in England, she rented the grand ballroom of the Commander Hotel in Cambridge. Then she insisted that Joe appear in formal clothes—white tie and tails—acting as the former ambassador to the Court of St. James. (It was his only public appearance during the campaign.) Rose and Eunice were there in their finery, though without the jewels that were expected in England. And of course there was Jack, transformed into the rather scrawny Prince Charming, the heir apparent to the congressional seat, eligible bachelor, hurting son needing to be fattened by loving mothers, and whatever else their fantasies might project onto him.

There was no charge, no dress code. Every registered voter was invited, Eunice coordinating the addressing and mailing of thousands of invitations. Charwomen, housewives, secretaries, and numerous others could, for one evening, be part of a fairy tale that came alive in their community. And it all happened three days before ballots had to be cast.

The response was overwhelming, though not unexpected. Harvard Square traffic came to a standstill. The ballroom could only accommodate 1,500 people, but hundreds more lined the sidewalk and streets outside. Stores that rented formal wear for women rented every garment they had. Some shopkeepers, perhaps exaggerating, said that they rented more for the one event than their combined rentals to women for the rest of the year.

The royal family was in residence, and even the lowliest of women could become ladies of the court. This ingenious combination of politics with theater was 100 percent Rose.

Mike Neville, Cambridge's mayor, was amazed at the tactic. He knew how to compete with the men. This was his town and he was expected to take the city by a landslide. Instead, he won by a squeaker, most of his lost support going to Jack.

The exact *honest* vote count was never known for certain in the Boston area. Even today Catholic priests in this area whose churches include a cemetery joke that when they tend to the graves, they are tending to a flock of voters. Corruption remains ongoing, and in 1946, certain men thought that not to vote more than once was unpatriotic.

Did Jack Kennedy's victory include vote buying and other forms of vote fraud? It would not have been Boston if it didn't. However, among the other nine candidates in that all-important primary, some, perhaps the majority, probably also had followers returning frequently to the polls throughout the day. Thus what matters is not the number of votes cast but the relative positions of the candidates. Jack Kennedy won by 40 percent in a field of ten. Even if a large percentage of his support was improper, he obviously was the favorite of the voters.

Rose was proud in the fall election when Jack beat the Republican candidate by a margin of three to one. However, that race was a foregone conclusion. The district was solidly Democratic, and as James Curley had shown when he was elected mayor of Boston a year earlier, even a known crook could get elected if he was a Democrat.

The public was well aware that Curley was going to be convicted of mail fraud, which he was in February 1946, not long after he took office. But so long as he was out of jail, they wanted him. And when he was sentenced to six to eighteen months in the federal penitentiary in Danbury, Connecticut, a sentence from which he was pardoned by President Truman after five months, he turned his time into a badge of honor. After that he said that he was an alumnus of "the University of Danbury."

One more lesson was to be learned, though. Following the primary, John Fitzgerald sat by a telephone and spent the next several days calling every party worker who had helped Jack. There were hundreds of them, and he did not stop until he was done. He thanked them for their efforts, telling them how much he appreciated what they had done.

It was the sign of the consummate career politician. Not only would they remain loyal to Jack, he would have an easier time during his next campaign.

When Jack arrived in Washington in January 1947, the elevators had operators, mostly young white men. Jack was twenty-nine but looked ten years younger because of weight loss from his illnesses and the back surgery he had had to undergo in 1944. Several people got onto an elevator with Jack, looked at him, and asked him to take them to their floor. He was stunned.

Rose Kennedy did not realize that the congressional campaign would be the last time she would have major influence in the family. Joe was switching his methods for making money, and while he still occasionally liked to make a deal with members of the mob, such as becoming a partner with Frank Costello in the Hialeah Race Track, he moved heavily into real estate. The liquor business was sold, and everything he did was meant to gain money to buy power for his sons. He could not orchestrate Jack's congressional campaign, but he could see to it that when the time was right, Jack could afford to run for president.

Rose Kennedy would never again have the chance to use her skills as a strategist and campaigner to the degree she had done in Jack's first congressional election. However, some of her ideas, raised to more sophisticated levels, were used when, after three congressional terms, Jack made a move for the Senate in the 1952 election.

The Senate race had been planned by Joe and his father-in-law, who both thought that Henry Cabot Lodge Jr., the incumbent senator, could be beaten. Lodge had served two terms in 1952, but support within the state was wavering as early as 1950, when Honey Fitz died.

Lodge was that rarest of all Massachusetts Republicans—a liberal whose history was that of the Back Bay. His sister-in-law spoke fluent Italian and translated when he campaigned in the growing Italian sections of the state. He spoke fluent French, using it with the French-Canadian community. He was popular throughout the state, yet the late Fitzgerald's judgment seemed right.

The vulnerability was nothing anyone could identify. Certainly no other Democrat wanted to make the challenge. The closest anyone came to pinpointing it was during the debates the senator and the congressman held.

The League of Women Voters arranged for a debate between Kennedy and Lodge in Waltham, Massachusetts. There, Kennedy learned the advantage of image versus substance when debating. He also triumphed brilliantly, though two stories emerged as to why.

The first, more heroic story is frequently repeated by even the more objective biographers. Kennedy was relaxed, handsome, and youthful. Lodge was older, more distinguished looking, and seemed senatorial.

Kennedy established the image of being young, brash, and in a hurry to change the nation after having been tempered by war. (Everyone ignored Lodge's greater bravery and more competent time in service.) When Jack pounded his fist or aggressively gestured at his opponent, the image was powerful. Lodge could not mimic the gestures because he would look like a teacher scolding an adorable, bright, overly energetic pupil for a youthful, rather meaningless indiscretion. While the conflict in images was both real and effective, there was more to Kennedy's success in the debate.

Joe was seated in the balcony of the school auditorium where the debate was held, positioned near an exit and alert to all that was taking place. Two Kennedy retainers acted as runners, sending notes down to Jack to alert him concerning what to say and do.

Joe Kennedy was playing off his knowledge of the Lodges gained over the years, as well as the "black book," a thick reference book created by Kennedy aide Ted Reardon. Although Jack had a terrible voting record, frequently absent from Congress, and never consistent on any issue, no one on the Lodge side had bothered to document him. The black book documented Lodge's failings. He was the better representative of the people of Massachusetts at the time, yet his attendance had also been poor, his voting sometimes inconsistent. Contrasting both records would have destroyed Kennedy. But Lodge was not prepared to go on the attack, so Kennedy's challenges over what Lodge had not done for the state could not be countered. Lodge was thrown on the defensive by what should have been a lesser opponent.

Lodge was also a good Kennedy target because he had been an isolationist before World War II and an internationalist afterward. Kennedy could attack Lodge for either stance, depending upon how he felt the audience would respond. But he had to avoid mentioning that Lodge had left government service to enlist in the military when he could have used his age and position to stay out of the war.

Jack Kennedy also exploited the issue of anticommunism and what the United States should be doing about such countries as China. The implication was that Lodge was not a strong anticommunist, though Kennedy was probably the weaker of the two in that field as well. With Joe's constant stream of suggestions, and Lodge's relative unpreparedness, Jack emerged triumphant.

For those voters concerned with emotions rather than issues, Bob Kennedy had married Ethel Skakel two years earlier, and she unexpectedly supplied another reason to vote for Jack. On September 23, a very pregnant Ethel made a speech in Fall River, Massachusetts, then went into labor, giving birth to her second child, Joseph Patrick Kennedy II. (Technically the youth should have been Joseph P. Kennedy III, and he is sometimes referred to in that manner. However, with his uncle dead, the family named him "II," and he uses that designation as a congress-man.) Archbishop Cushing performed the baptism, a well-publicized event that seemed to imply the Catholic Church's approval of Jack as senator. There was no such Church endorsement, real or implied, but when a campaign is built more on image and emotions than substance, the birth of a nephew helps to win votes.

Several campaign ideas—some new, some proven—were tried during the Senate campaign. Joe and Rose rented an apartment at 81 Beacon Street in Boston to help coordinate the campaign. This time money was at least as important as strategy, so Joe planned to play a bigger part. But still the "old ways" were critical.

Embellishing on Honey Fitz's strategy of personally thanking and in-volving every volunteer, the Kennedys renamed their area chairmen "Kennedy secretaries." This separated them from the other volunteers and made them feel closer to Jack. This also assured that they were working for John Kennedy, not a ward boss or party leader. Their work was the same, but the subtle psychological difference paid off. For ex-ample, nominating petitions were required to have a total of 2,500 valid signatures to get a candidate on the ballot. The Kennedy secretaries obtained 262,324 signatures. As a result, just the filing of the petitions became a major statewide news story. Jack was perceived as a possible winner right from the start.

The Kennedy siblings, especially the women, were devoted to the move for power among the men. They analyzed their strengths and weaknesses, then acted accordingly. Rose had visited Portugal and could talk knowledgeably about the country, so she took the largely Portu-guese New Bedford area. Eunice handled the Lebanese. Rose went after the French Canadians.

Rose Kennedy was also always the family representative at Jewish gatherings that Jack could not attend. Joe senior's anti-Semitism was still fresh in everyone's mind, but Rose was not suspect despite sharing similar views.

Polly Fitzgerald, Rose's aunt by marriage to Edward Fitzgerald, coor-dinated a statewide and high-tech version of Coffee With the Ken-nedys. Usually the volunteer hostesses were apolitical, wealthy, and celebrity conscious. They did not care about Jack. They wanted to help the wife of the former ambassador to the Court of St. James, and toward this end they utilized their personal silver services, expensive table-cloths, and time.

Voters saw Jack as single, handsome, rich, and having great appeal to women, another reason why Rose's efforts were so important. It was obvious that some women wanted to mother him, some wanted to bed him, and many wanted either to marry him or to have their daughters marry him. This sex appeal was utilized by having handwritten invitations prepared by the statewide organizations. These went to women inviting them to a "reception in honor of Mrs. Joseph P. Kennedy and her son, Congressman John F. Kennedy." Thirty-three such events were held in addition to the traditional Coffee With the Kennedys. Jack Kennedy would always be present at these, along with one or more family members. Dave Powers would unobtrusively stand with a counter, taking down the numbers. Approximately seventy thousand women passed through the receiving lines of these events according to his totals.

Bob Kennedy was in charge of registering voters. Some of those registered were women who came to the various social events. Others were from parts of the state where many of the residents had previously felt disenfranchised.

The importance of the receptions and the effort to register more voters cannot be underestimated. Jack won by 70,737 votes, indicating that without Rose's and Bob's efforts, the Senate race would have been won by Lodge.

Rose also put together a television show called *Coffee With the Kennedys*, which was run during the mornings when housewives might be taking a break from their chores. A toll-free telephone line took calls from viewers, and Rose chatted about rearing a large family. She showed the file cards she had maintained on each child, talked of family outings, and the like. She instinctively understood what the listeners wanted to hear, and she was more than willing to provide such information.

Lodge never knew what hit him. Nothing in his blue-blood background prepared him for Coffee With the Kennedys, Rose's three-by-five cards helping her keep track of the children, her homely stories of a little boy growing into manhood, picking blueberries, teasing little girls, going off to war, coming home a hero—all of which created a sense of neighbors gossiping happily over the back fence. The sisters, vivacious, wearing flared skirts embroidered with "John F. Kennedy," loving their brother so much that they would go anywhere, anytime, to help him. The willingness to be Catholic one minute, nondenominational the next, and seemingly a closet Baptist, Lutheran, Jew, or anything else the audience might be.

A vote for Jack Kennedy was a vote for family, for the boy next door your daughter was crazy over, for a war hero. And if anyone wasn't impressed with the heavily edited exploits of the commander of the ill-fated PT-109, nine hundred thousand copies of an eight-page tabloid were headlined "John Fulfills Dream of Brother Joe Who Met Death in the Sky Over the English Channel." The publication showed pictures of the brothers, and the tabloid, coupled with the birth of Joseph P. Kennedy II, added incredible impact to the campaign.

The vote was close, far closer than anyone had anticipated. By midnight the press was projecting a victory for Lodge. But Jack was optimistic. Everything possible had been done to win, and Lodge's support was so obviously eroding that Jack was confident he would triumph. Within hours he was proven right.

With Jack's move into the Senate, Rose would begin playing a secondary role in the family business of power politics. Her children were marrying, and her world was radically changing.

10

The Children Come of Age

In the 1950s, Rose's sons began taking wives, and their choices reflected a variety of women. Yet all of them shared an inherent insecurity coupled with enough flamboyance to gain the fascination of the American public.

Ethel Skakel was the first outsider to join the Kennedy family in a meaningful way. She was also the only one to become a Kennedy, thriving in the rough-and-tumble atmosphere of siblings reared to be so insular that Joe once joked that his children would only find happiness if they married each other. Kathleen dramatically proved him wrong, of course, but his sons-in-law would prove far more adept within the family than the Kennedy women.

The Skakel family was as rich and troubled as the Kennedys, though without the Kennedy success in society. They were also totally undisciplined alcoholics, their children eventually leading far more troubled lives than those of the Kennedys.

Ultimately Joe Kennedy would narrow control of his money so that neither his wife nor his children had access to it. A small office in New York—the Park Agency—became his primary management firm for all that he owned and did. He also had the equally small Ken Industries, though in later years it would be the Park Agency that the family knew about.

BG: BY THE TIME I went to work for the Kennedys, the New York office had about a half dozen employees. Most of them had been hired directly by Joe Kennedy so he could be certain they would follow his policies.

Joe Kennedy wanted his wife and children to lack any knowledge of the fortune he had built. Only the staff understood how this empire of entangling and disparate businesses all came together.

Taxes, mortgage payments, routine maintenance needs, insurance, and the like were all met by the New York office. However, the paternalism of the office was so extreme that family members had no understanding of real life. The bill for a prime rib of beef, a ring from Tiffany or Cartier, a rental car, or anything else was sent to the New York office. The situation was so bad that a Kennedy girl might walk up to an airport magazine stand, pick up a magazine or two, and walk off without paying. There was no sense of value to anything, and even Mrs. Kennedy had no sense of her worth.

For example, if Mrs. Kennedy decided to change her will to give her brother an additional $25,000, she had to call the New York office to see if there was enough money to do so. There were controls on the spending, and the children who overspent would be contacted by a staff member as forcefully as a father complaining when a child who get an allowance overspends midweek, then wants money for spending Saturday night. But the money available to the family was so vast that there were never problems. There was also never a sense on any of their parts as to how normal people have to live.

Sometimes Mrs. Kennedy would become frustrated and want to know how much money she had. She was always certain that she was rich, yet she seemed equally certain that the slightest extra expenditure would bankrupt her.

For example, I received a letter on stationery from the TWA Ambassador's Club at Logan International Airport.

"Dear Barbara," it read. "Be sure to phone Teddy's office and say I shall stay at Claridge's Hotel, London. Be sure my electric clock is off—I believe I told you both that. I was not certain.

"Thank you again for your generosity and your general efficiency, etc. etc.

"Sincerely Rose Kennedy."

The clock in question was a small white plastic electric alarm clock of the type that probably cost no more than $6.95 at K Mart. If it used more than a cent or two of electricity a day, I would be surprised. But such were her ideas of keeping track of the pennies, never realizing that the hundreds of millions of dollars that Joe had accumulated were more than taking care of everyone.

Knowing this, and convinced that Mrs. Kennedy could not handle all the details of her vast wealth, the New York office invariably promised to get right back to her with the exact figure. They never did tell her, and it would be months at least before she questioned again. Once more they would promise to get back to her. Once more they would not.

The family trust funds, expenses, allowances, and various needs were requested through the Park Agency and paid from the offices. None of the children were taught about their father's business holdings. None of the children were groomed to manage the family's vast wealth or even a portion of it. Yet ironically, when Jean Kennedy married Stephen Smith, Joe decided to let Smith run the Park Agency. Thus an outsider had far more knowledge of the family business than did the family.

BG: STEVE SMITH WAS always getting the children and grandchildren out of trouble. For example, Ethel was skiing in Aspen, partying all the time. She hired a caterer to handle the parties, ignoring his bills as though tradespeople should be honored to work for a Kennedy.

The caterer wasn't flattered. He was in business and Ethel had not paid. He sued her in court, and Steve Smith had to fly out there to appear in court on her behalf, ultimately paying the bill. Then, after telling Ethel, still in Aspen, that the problem had been handled, he asked if he could ride back home with her on her private plane. She indignantly told him there was no room, forcing him to buy a ticket and fly back on a commercial plane at his own expense.

Steve also had to assume responsibility for Bob's son David, a drug addict who later died of an overdose. David was constantly being arrested for buying drugs or driving under the influence, or otherwise getting into trouble. And Steve was the negotiator of a settlement when Joe Kennedy II, now in Congress, had a driving accident that left David's then girlfriend a paraplegic for life.

Joe Gargan told me that he laughed about all the work the family caused him through their unthinking attitudes and arrogance. Yet they never seemed to appreciate him. He also said that Steve Smith sarcastically commented, "I'm just waiting for the day when one of the grandchildren sues me for mismanaging their money."

Fortunately for Steve, he died before that could happen.

While the Skakel home did not encourage intellectual pursuits, Ethel's mother, called Big Ann, developed a hobby/business/philanthropy project involving rare books and book manuscripts. It somewhat mirrored Rose Kennedy's fascination with writers apart from Joe's belief that a book brought respect, even when solely or primarily the work of others. Rose preferred attending dinner parties with writers when possible. Her correspondence handled by Barbara Gibson was frequently with noted authors. But Big Ann took this a step further. She collected books on Catholicism, trying for rarity when possible, including original manuscripts from which the books had been produced.

Big Ann and George Skakel eventually financially supported the monks of Our Lady of Gethsemane Abbey in Kentucky, from which the Trappist monk Thomas Merton worked. Big Ann essentially created her own job as secretary to Merton when he was writing what became highly acclaimed books of religious philosophy and autobiography. She hired people to type for various authors so she could keep the original manuscripts with margin notes and corrections that would be the draft just prior to the final, corrected manuscript that was used by the publisher.

As a result Big Ann accumulated an immensely valuable collection, and she also opened the Guild Book Shop at 117 East Fifty-seventh Street in Manhattan, a location near Central Park and the apartments of the wealthy. Ironically, one of her partners in the venture was Hilda Shriver, whose son, Sargent, would also marry into the Kennedy family. The store ultimately failed, but it did help the Skakels add first editions and other valuable works to their home library.

Ethel had no interest in the intellectual side of the Church, though she was devout, faithful, and truly believed in the power of prayer. However, when it came to the rituals of her Catholic school, she was a rebel. She talked, used foul language, smoked, and was late for events she did not cut entirely. She had no respect for the property of others, destroying clothing, bedding, or anything else in the pursuit of a practical joke. At home, the Skakel boys were notorious for wrecking new cars the first time or two they tried them out. But beyond reckless driving, they would engage in such "humorous" incidents as driving a car into the swimming pool. So long as their fun never cost more than a few thousand dollars, George and Ann Skakel found it a small price to pay.

BG: ETHEL, LIKE THE OTHER Kennedys, frequently did not bother carrying money with her, and sometimes she would need a small sum, such as $5, for a purchase. Rose Kennedy's chauffeur had a wallet that was too large to place in the right front pocket of his slacks, and his uniform did not have a jacket to hold it. He would carry the wallet in his back pocket, then take it out and put it on the seat of the car while he drove. If he was driving Ethel somewhere and had to leave the car briefly, she would take $5 or $10 from his wallet and tell him about it later.

The money was *not* a small matter to the chauffeur. He would say nothing to Ethel, fearing the loss of his job. But he would come to me to see if he could get the money back from the petty cash I maintained for Mrs. Kennedy.

Mrs. Kennedy was also bothered by Ethel's ridiculous extravagance. Ethel loved tennis, but she used new balls every time she played. Even professionals would use balls far longer than Ethel. Mrs. Kennedy found this silly habit a complete waste of money.

Mrs. Kennedy was always cheap. One time she supposedly got caught by the cheapness of her children. During Jack's campaign for the Senate seat held by Senator Lodge, Mrs. Kennedy had been told by her friends that the best way to gauge the reaction of the little people, the voters who were outside her social circle, was to ask them which candidate they thought was doing best.

Mrs. Kennedy was in a taxi going to Jack's apartment when she asked the driver the question. The driver realized that he had taken the congressman to the same address a night or two before. He asked Mrs. Kennedy if she was related to Jack Kennedy, and of course she proudly said that she was his mother.

"Boy, am I glad to meet you!" the cabdriver supposedly told her. Then he explained that she owed him $1.65. Jack, as usual, carried no money and had stiffed the cabdriver. Rather than being embarrassed by her son's cheapness, Mrs. Kennedy just decided she would never admit to who she was when traveling.

———————

The Skakel home was beyond compare with most people's idea of the rich. The recklessness and wild living made the family home a nightmare; the family dogs ran loose inside and out, clothes were scattered about.

By contrast, Ethel found Rose Kennedy ran an ordered home, with fresh flowers all about, where fun was not stopped but where the house was never in a shambles. Ethel also saw her future mother-in-law as an intellectual helping to educate her children. Ethel had first met the family through Jean, the youngest sister and a classmate at Manhattanville, and her earliest memory of Rose was being lectured and quizzed on the history of Halloween.

———————

BG: ETHEL WAS LIKE a big tree with guests constantly around her. She loved to entertain and entertain lavishly, especially celebrities who were currently in the news. She thought nothing of having guests fill every bedroom in her house and the dollhouse (one morning I saw *Good Morning America* host David Hartmann bent over to descend from the dollhouse door.)

One weekend she informed her secretary she would have to return to Washington for a few days: Her room in the Secret Service house was needed. Oh yes, Ethel's staff and guests overflowed to the house once used by Jackie for her Secret Service agents. The secretary left, thinking she would return and spend the rest of the summer there in Hyannis Port, as she usually did. However, at the end of two weeks, Ethel had someone call her and tell her she would not be needed any further that summer and her clothes were being sent to her. The secretary told me that her clothes had arrived as promised. They had been casually stuffed in a plastic bag, sealed with a twist tie, and mailed to "The Secretary."

Eunice had habits similar to those of her sister-in-law. She would arrive in Palm Beach for the weekend, needing a new dress to wear to a cocktail party. She would then go to Martha's, an exclusive Worth Avenue dress shop, buy an expensive dress, and wear it to the party. Then, on Monday morning, on her way to the airport, Eunice would drop off the dress at my office, asking me to return it for full credit. In that way she would not have to pay for something she never expected to wear again. The fact that it may have been ruined for resale did not matter to her. She saw the dress shop as a lending library, having no sense of the expense she created for the hardworking owner.

Ethel was just as bad, and I still remember when Mary Kerry, one of her daughters, was sent to visit Mrs. Kennedy in Palm Beach. The girl carried a large pile of expensive clothes that I was asked to return.

Oddly, Ethel also became cheap after Bob's death. She always ordered several identical designer outfits in different colors. However, a staff person would usually remind her that such expenses were too great for her income. At some point even Ethel had to use some common sense, a fact she accepted—after the dresses were delivered. She was like a spoiled child who is told he can have one piece of candy, then grabs five.

I later learned that the problem had to do with the Skakel inheritance money. Her parents died in a plane crash in 1955, and not everything was fully sorted out for the various siblings. While she waited for her inheritance to be settled, she had to live on Bob's trust fund, which "only" gave her an income in the six figures. At least this is what a secretary at the Park Agency told me.

Ethel met the Kennedy brothers through Jean, and her first crush was on Jack. Bob was dating Pat Skakel, one of Ethel's older sisters, but she was wrong for him. Bob was not an intellectual, and he came to prefer the animal excitement of Ethel to the quieter sister, who liked school, liked order, liked a bit of privacy.

Jean had come to look upon Ethel as a sister, as would all the Kennedy women after they knew her. Jean wanted Ethel to marry into the family and thought that Ethel and Bob would be perfect for each other. However, at that time Bob seemed the shyer of the two, which did not excite her. What she quickly came to realize was that with her seriousness about the Catholic Church and a figure that came late (*skinny, boyish, flat chested,* and other terms were frequently used to describe her, despite the fact that she was prettier than most of the Kennedy girls and had the same vitality as their sister Kathleen, though channeled differently), Jack Kennedy had no interest in her. Fortunately Bobby proved her type, and when she came to know him, she adored him with an intensity that was similar to Rose's love for Joe.

Bob, like his brothers, had gone to Harvard, though his academic record was undistinguished, both there and at the private school, Milton, that he had attended. His interest, like Ethel's, was in sports, though while she excelled in the precision beauty of equestrian activities, he liked the rough and tumble of football. He was too short and too skinny for the game, yet he managed to play based on technical skill and pure aggressiveness.

Harvard let Bob play, but he was always on one of the squads that was little more than intramural. Although the varsity team, from which you could earn your letter *H*, took players from the lower squads, Bob was not someone of promise. When he eventually played with the varsity, there was some question about financial influence, a not unlikely possibility.

No influence was adequate to enroll Bob in Harvard Law School, though. He lacked the grades and, some hinted, the intellectual capacity. Harvard had long had a reputation greater than the education it provided. Many less well-known institutions were better preparing men for their careers in the first half of the twentieth century, and certainly in the years before that. But the school had been working to improve the quality of its graduate programs, especially law and medicine, the latter radically reformed beginning in the late 1940s. Meeting academic standards meant more than breeding for the Law School, and Bob was forced to attend the University of Virginia Law School.

Ethel's dating of Bob was a minor scandal in Manhattanville. Her classmates were romantic gossips, almost as naive about sex and life as Rose's generation had been. Few knew anything about male anatomy and little more about their own. Virginity was valued, and a "loose" girl would kiss her steady date. The students seemed a throwback to a time even before Kathleen's training. Thus the idea that Pat had "lost" Bob Kennedy to Ethel was the subject for gossip. No one realized that Bob had an apparently chaste (though not for his lack of trying) relationship with a British actress prior to his marriage, a more shocking relationship than the one with Pat Skakel.

Ethel graduated from Manhattanville in 1949, academically average and so fed up with that world that, though she, like Rose Kennedy, had earned the Child of Mary designation, she never returned. She attended her first reunion, then realized her place was not there. Her focus was Bob and what would prove to be a family of eleven children.

* * *

An excited hoarse voice, a shriek, a peal of screaming laughter, the flash of shirttails, a tousled brown head—Ethel! Her face is at one moment a picture of utter guilelessness and at the next alive with mischief.
　　—The Tower, Ethel's yearbook
　　at Manhattanville

* * *

The marriage took place on June 17, 1950, Bob surrounded by some of the Harvard football players, Ethel's friends having had last-minute retouches of hair and clothing after too wild a prenuptial party.

Ethel became Rose's newest daughter, which would not happen with the other daughters-in-law. Eventually Bob and Ethel bought a house next to Joe and Rose's place in Hyannis Port, assuring that their children would be constantly at play at both locations.

Ethel used her mother-in-law as a guide for child rearing. She knew her own family was undisciplined, but she did not see that her children needed far more attention than she was giving them. Only Bob seemed truly devoted to spending time with the children, to the point that, when he was attorney general, he had Ethel bring the brood to the Justice Department for dinners.

Ethel heard endless stories about the way he and his siblings were allowed to engage in all manner of physical activities, including sometimes violent fights, without parental interference. She encouraged the same uninhibited physical activity among her children, later commenting, "I try to do what Mr. and Mrs. Kennedy did." She added, "Sure there are risks . . . if they're going to develop independence, they have to do it while they're young. I want my children to grow up with as little fear as possible, because the less they fear, the more they can accomplish. This outweighs the risk."

Ethel followed other practices she had learned from Rose. Like her mother-in-law she clipped articles from the newspaper for them to read. Then these were discussed by the family at the dinner table and when traveling.

As more and more children arrived, Ethel again followed Rose's child-rearing practices by separating them by age groupings during dinner. There were actually two or three mealtimes, according to the ages. This made things easier for them, though the cooks hated the casualness and never being able to plan. (Ethel never learned to cook. The rare meal she prepared was invariably a disaster.)

Ethel turning to Rose for domestic advice showed her estrangement from the Skakel family, showed how much Ethel longed for greater discipline and order. She never achieved it in her home; kids, pets, and chaos always reigned even before Bob's death. After his death, Ethel distanced herself from her children, and their activities became notorious (Bobby junior nearly dying from a drug overdose; David dying from drugs; Joe the second crippling David's girlfriend for life in a wild-driving accident; and numerous other problems). But in those early years, Ethel tried hard to learn from and please Rose.

There were problems between the two women, but they were minor. Ethel used large quantities of perfume, her scent seeming to arrive several minutes before she did and lingering long after she had left.

BG: "ETHEL'S EXTRAVAGANCE!" That's what Mrs. Kennedy called it. She and her "other daughters" bought expensive perfume by the ounce. She claimed that Ethel bought the same perfume by the quart. Ethel not only used far too much, she also paid a small fortune each time she bought it. Mrs. Kennedy felt that if you could pay $25 for a small amount, it was somehow better than paying $250 for a much larger amount.

Mrs. Kennedy also wanted to be unique in her scent. Certainly she didn't want to be upstaged by her daughters and daughters-in-law. She had long used a fragrance by Guerlain. Then one day she realized that Ethel had begun wearing the same scent. Mrs. Kennedy felt that the overuse by Ethel spoiled the aroma, and she stopped using it entirely.

There were other signs of competitiveness. Mrs. Kennedy was a grandmother who always wanted to look youthful. She delighted in someone noticing that she genuinely seemed much younger than her years. However, despite the frownies—the white adhesive patches that looked like wing-shaped Band-Aids—she used to smooth out her wrinkles when she was at home, and her other "beauty secrets," she sensed that she couldn't handle close scrutiny. She never wanted to be photographed next to a younger woman, even Ethel or her daughters.

A famous photograph of the entire Kennedy family was taken in the living room of the Hyannis Port house just after Jack became president. Everyone is standing except for Mrs. Kennedy, sitting on the left, and Jackie, sitting on the right. Mrs. Kennedy told me that she never liked that picture: "I don't like to have my picture taken next to a younger woman because it makes me look older."

Another time, famous photographer Richard Avedon arrived at the Cape with his assistants to take her picture for the magazine *Rolling Stone*. I was standing at the back of the sunroom, talking with one of the assistants. Mrs. Kennedy said, "Would you please leave the room, Barbara. You're distracting everyone." What she meant was that I provided an unpleasant contrast since I was more than two generations younger.

Mrs. Kennedy did not believe in drinking, and Ethel loved vintage wine, especially Pouilly-Fuissé, which she purchased by the case. Mrs. Kennedy did not drink and did not want her family to drink, though of course they did, especially the senator. Ethel's secretary told me that Ethel regularly went to bed with her Pouilly-Fuissé and a sleeping pill. I always thought it was a dangerous combination, and she knew enough to keep it secret from Mrs. Kennedy. Her staff knew, though.

Pat and Jean were more blatant. They knew Mrs. Kennedy would have nothing in the house, so they would call me before they arrived at the Cape, asking me to buy them some of their favorite wines. Each of them would take a bottle to bed as well.

Ethel enjoyed her money, something Mrs. Kennedy also did, though in different ways. Mrs. Kennedy bought expensive clothes, as did Ethel, while Ethel also liked to eat well and had the cooks spare no expense. This made no sense to Mrs. Kennedy, who had no interest in food other than as nourishment.

I remember one night when Mrs. Kennedy was asked to Ethel's for dinner. She wanted to know what the meal would be, and I told her that it would be Alaskan king crab, rice pilaf, and spinach soufflé, a normal meal for the family despite their large size, yet the type of food Mrs. Kennedy might choose only on special occasions. She looked at me and said rather sarcastically, "Oh, my, what it is to be rich!"

Of course, Ethel and Bobby were rich. The Skakel and Kennedy fortunes were enormous, and they were each heirs. But Mrs. Kennedy did not respect anyone whose extravagances differed from her own.

Despite their differences, Ethel was the most considerate of the family members when she visited the Palm Beach estate. Mrs. Kennedy never hired adequate staff, and the situation was worse after Mr. Kennedy died. Ethel would often request the supplies needed to clean the bathroom she would be using and would clean it herself.

There would also be little gifts that showed she cared, such as replacing some strands of quality costume jewelry Mrs. Kennedy liked to wear to church. They had become dirty, losing their attractiveness, so Ethel gave her a new set.

In the years after Bob's death, the two women had an unusual empathy. It was as though Mrs. Kennedy thought her son acted irresponsibly by running for the presidency instead of staying in the Senate. She seemed to feel that he "allowed" himself to be murdered.

Ethel was unable or unwilling to cope with her children. They were allowed to be wild, undisciplined. Drugs and alcohol were the bane of their existence, and everyone was in denial. But what bothered Mrs. Kennedy was the mess—bicycles, clothing, and all manner of possessions strewn everywhere, the lack of an adult presence while the children created havoc throughout Hyannis Port. I still remember the time I saw her staring out the window at Bob and Ethel's home, the yard littered by the children as usual. She turned away, her face angry, and snapped, "I don't know what Bobby meant by going away and leaving Ethel with all those children to raise alone." He hadn't "gone away" voluntarily, of course. He had been assassinated in Los Angeles. She had as much resentment toward her son as she had shown toward her husband when she realized that his long absences were for the pursuit of women.

With her anger, there was an odd defense of Bobby. He was known to have had affairs over the years, though in a far more discreet manner than his brothers. He was also the one Kennedy male who seemed to genuinely enjoy his wife, and not just because he kept her constantly pregnant. He was also deeply religious. Both Bobby and Ethel had considered making the Catholic Church their vocation before they married. Ethel seriously thought of becoming a nun, and Bobby attended mass regularly throughout his life.

After Bobby's death, when it was known that Jack had had an affair with Marilyn Monroe just as Joe had had sex with Gloria Swanson, Mrs. Kennedy commented to me with a laugh about the rumors that Bobby, not just Jack, had had an affair with Monroe: "I don't believe it could have happened . . . Bobby was always so *sanctimonious.*"

Despite everything, Ethel came as close to having a mother-daughter relationship with Rose as would any of the girls. Joan was too weak, and Jacqueline was too sophisticated.

Jacqueline Bouvier had known little happiness in her life. Her father, John Vernon Bouvier III, was a cross among Errol Flynn, Joe Kennedy, and Jack Kennedy. He was known as Black Jack, both because of an illness that discolored his skin to a bluish black tone, and because he was as much a conqueror of women as the handsome pirates who grace the fantasy fiction of writers such as Rosemary Rodgers. He was handsome, lean, muscular, and sexually aggressive (allegedly with both men and women, one rumored affair having been with Cole Porter), a self-made millionaire in the stock market, who squandered his fortune and destroyed his health with alcohol. When Jacqueline was born on July 28, 1929, her twenty-two-year-old mother was sixteen years younger than Black Jack.

Bouvier was an ardent Republican who hated Joe Kennedy and Franklin Roosevelt. He and Kennedy had been fellow stock market manipulators, and Black Jack, like Joe Kennedy, had been consistently successful. When Joe took control of Roosevelt's Securities and Exchange Commission, he limited the ways in which Black Jack and others could do business. As a result, Black Jack Bouvier lost $43,000 in the stock market in 1935, and the story was told that, as a child, Jacqueline Bouvier thought that the name Franklin Roosevelt was another way of saying Satan.

Although Jacqueline came from a moneyed background, she had no wealth of her own. Black Jack spent his money, and father-in-law James Lee seemed to find his granddaughters a constant reminder of the despised son-in-law. He cut them off without any of his money.

To add to her insecurities, Jacqueline was a little like Eunice Kennedy. Attractiveness came long after puberty. She aged well, gaining beauty with the years. But while young she was always a poor second to her sister, and intelligence, personality, and the other important qualities of life seem unimportant during youth.

Withdrawn, sensitive, and with a desire to communicate, Jacqueline entered journalism. She worked for *Vogue* magazine, then obtained a $42.50-a-week job with the *Washington Times-Herald*. Among other tasks, she would ask people on the street a question, write down their answers, and take their pictures. Then the question, along with pictures of the people interviewed and their responses, was published in one of the man-on-the-street columns popular at that time. Many papers had them, a way of broadening their readership base.

Jack Kennedy was much like Jacqueline's father. He was twelve years older than she was, and when they began dating, he frequently was late or stood her up. He always had a seemingly justifiable excuse, especially since he was a new junior senator. And when Jack did show, he could be extremely attentive. The appeal was probably the same one her father held, and because of that, she admitted to him that she was worried that he would have an affair on their honeymoon the way her father had hurt her mother.

BG: I UNDERSTAND JOE THOUGHT his son's being single was going to be a political liability at some point. A handsome young bachelor could get votes for the Senate. An older bachelor making a run for the White House would seem to have a character flaw. Americans wanted a family man as president. That was why Jack was told to get married in 1953. That was probably also why he was not particularly attentive to Jacqueline. He agreed to marry her, but there was no strong emotional commitment right from the start.

The wedding list was seemingly endless when Jacqueline Bouvier married Jack Kennedy on September 12, 1953. His father had been busy planting stories about "the nation's most eligible bachelor." The implication was that no woman had ever met his high standards until the young Jacqueline Bouvier, and the couple became an object of fascination. In addition, the wedding was meant to be a business affair. Every United States senator was invited, along with their spouses. There were numerous business contacts of Joseph Kennedy, including Hollywood stars, producers, directors, and others. There were acquaintances from when Joe was ambassador. There were twelve hundred guests for the reception alone, though Hammersmith Farm, the country estate of Hugh Auchincloss, could handle the crowd, the caterers, and the Meyer Davis society orchestra that supplied the entertainment. The wedding itself was held in Newport at St. Mary's Roman Catholic Church. Naturally a cardinal, in this case Richard Cardinal Cushing, presided.

Jacqueline invited her father to give her away, which outraged her mother. According to rumors, Janet Auchincloss paid the room-service waiters to bring large amounts of liquor to Black Jack's hotel room from the moment he arrived in town. Black Jack was by then a newly recovering alcoholic. He was working hard to avoid drinking, but Janet knew her ex-husband was weak. Coming to Newport was an emotional experience. The marriage of his daughter would be stressful. He would not voluntarily go out and get drunk. But if liquor kept arriving at his hotel room, in some moment of weakness he would take a sip. And he was too much of an alcoholic to have any control once he did. An hour before the wedding he was found unconscious, too drunk to be roused. Janet was pleased. Jacqueline was shattered.

Earlier the Kennedys had given Jacqueline a taste of the future. The engagement took place when Jack was about to be the subject of a *Saturday Evening Post* cover story about his life as a bachelor. Joe feared that the story would be killed when Jack became engaged, and Jack agreed. Although claiming to be thrilled and wanting to tell the world of his love, Jack did not release the information until after the story ran.

Then there were the rounds of parties that included popular games of the day, such as a treasure hunt. During one such engagement party, Pat Kennedy decided to win the category for finding the "longest object." She found a city bus momentarily abandoned by the driver while he stopped inside a station. She climbed on board, then drove it back to the home where the party was being held. One of the other participants stole a policeman's hat. Ultimately the youths were caught by the police, Joe Kennedy having to bail them out of what would otherwise have been a charge of grand theft against Pat.

Jacqueline was not pleased with the wildness, but she was amused by the meeting of Rose Kennedy and her mother. The two women were determined to impress each other. They each wore fine dresses, pearls, hats, and white gloves. Jack wore bathing trunks, an old undershirt, and bedroom slippers. Jacqueline watched while Rose treated her son, a thirty-six-year-old United States senator, as a small boy.

BG: ALTHOUGH NO ONE THOUGHT about it at the time, when I went to work for Mrs. Kennedy, the staff realized that she had not been accepting invitations to social gatherings unrelated to a wedding or one of her son's election campaigns. Looking back, we realized that this practice seemed to have begun after the family returned from England and were no longer a part of the Court of St. James's.

We first concluded, based on what Mrs. Kennedy told us, that she felt that her homes were too shabby to reciprocate. Certainly she was lax in the way she maintained the Palm Beach house (Hyannis Port was always beautiful), and she was even worse after Joe died. But she could well afford to replace peeling wallpaper, repaint, and do whatever else might be necessary. She had as much or more money than the people who invited her to their homes, and making things nicer would have been no hardship.

The more we got to know Mrs. Kennedy, the more we realized how insecure she was. She was intimidated by the rich and by the socialites of her day, even though she was one of them. She had been comfortable in England because of the strict social protocol to be followed. As the wife of The Ambassador, as the mother of debutantes, she was as one with the men and women who socialized with the King and Queen. The title, not the person, had brought the family into the Social Register, and I think that deep down she knew that.

Yet oddly, she had achieved the status of royalty just by being who she was. She seemed to fear that somehow if she pushed too hard, made too many appearances, she would be "unmasked." The Brahmins would take all the pleasure from the Irish Catholic daughter of Honey Fitz. It made no sense, yet her insecurity was evident. That was why you never saw photographs of Mrs. Kennedy and her husband in the social columns. That was why they never went to parties or held them for others. That was why Joe only went to places like the Everglades and Palm Beach country clubs to socialize. They did not accept him for full membership, but he was allowed to eat there. Someplace else might not. Yet the reasons they had accepted him were the same ones that made them a step below the elite WASP organizations that might finally have admitted the Kennedys had they tried to get in.

Mrs. Kennedy had an even better excuse for avoiding people when Joe had his stroke. She said that she had to stay home and take care of him. But she didn't. Their niece, Ann Gargan, did that, along with a full medical staff. Besides, Mrs. Kennedy no longer liked her husband by then. She didn't want to be with him, and he became agitated anytime that she was. He didn't want her there either.

It was sad. For all she accomplished in American society, she never had the courage to take advantage of the pleasure she might have gained from it.

Joe made certain that news of the wedding, and a photograph, made the front page of the Sunday *New York Times*. There were two truckloads of champagne, a five-tiered wedding cake, and an estimated three thousand spectators standing just off the grounds, straining to catch glimpses of those in attendance. It is presumed that the spectators were genuine, for such crowds would continue to appear at Kennedy events. But had Joe had any concerns whether the wedding would be properly covered, he would probably have hired them the way movie studios hire extras.

Joe was the one person delighted by the match. His daughters and Ethel hated Jacqueline. They ridiculed her shyness, her rather thin voice, her devotion to the arts, her intellect, her language skills, and her insistence on pronouncing her name in the French manner, even though that was the correct pronunciation. But Joe thought of Jacqueline as French Irish, a social class much higher than the Kennedys. Jack was marrying up in the same manner as Joe had done. Love did not matter. She was a good catch and would make the proper wife for a politician on the rise.

Joe was fascinated that his new daughter-in-law had the same inner strength he seemed to see in himself. They both saw Rose as rather self-centered and selfish, yet Jacqueline, like her mother-in-law, firmly believed in being a mother and creating a home environment for her husband. Her White House years were spent restoring the splendor of the president's residence, not just for reasons of history but also because this was where her husband and children lived. And unlike Rose, although there was always help, Jacqueline was devoted to her children, Caroline and John junior.

If there was any strain with Joe, it was Jacqueline's lack of interest in politics. The manipulation of power was not important to her, yet it was all-consuming to the family. She often ignored such talk, whether at home or at parties, and was considered a potential liability by the Kennedy sisters. Jack's wife seemed to be a snob, someone who spoke foreign languages fluently, loved the arts, and did not see the winning of an office worth the phoniness of being everyone's friend long enough to win a vote.

BG: JACK AND JACKIE BOUGHT a home next to Mrs. Kennedy and Joe to use each summer in Hyannis Port. They saw each other frequently, though Jackie tried to keep her children from being too involved with their cousins. She did not like the lack of discipline she saw with the other families, and she did her best to provide as normal a life for John and Caroline as she could.

Mrs. Kennedy was extremely sensitive to the troubles Jackie had seen. Mrs. Kennedy understood loss. She also knew that the horror of Jackie's being with her husband when he was shot was far greater than anything she had endured. She had great respect for Jackie's having endured the shooting and the pain of its aftermath.

Mrs. Kennedy greatly admired Jackie's sense of art and interior decoration. She also delighted in the glamour that Jackie brought her.

Many people think that Mrs. Kennedy was unhappy when Jackie eventually married Aristotle Onassis. I learned from Mrs. Kennedy that this was not true. He was an odd man, physically unattractive and so little concerned about personal appearance that his trousers were usually baggy. At the same time, Onassis was one of the richest men in the world, and Mrs. Kennedy was a practical woman who could see the appeal for a shy, private person of being able to escape to private islands and yachts. As rich as Onassis was, his wealth could shield Jackie and the children enough to give them more of a private life than they would have staying in New York or Hyannis Port.

Mrs. Kennedy was also impressed by the generosity of Onassis. He periodically brought his private yacht to Palm Beach, docking, then going to visit her. He invited Mrs. Kennedy and her entire staff of domestics to come on board and see the massive floating home, so large that helicopters could be used in place of life rafts. He also went alone to visit her New York apartment.

On one of the New York visits he brought a gift of a gold bracelet with a snake's head encrusted with red and white stones. Onassis had obviously spent much money on this magnificent piece of unusual jewelry. However, she was certain that the bracelet was merely an expensive piece of costume jewelry that he had picked up at Bonwit's on the way.

Years later Mrs. Kennedy decided to include the bracelet with some other pieces of jewelry she knew little about, having them all appraised. To her astonishment, the stones were genuine rubies and diamonds.

Onassis's thoughtfulness may have been extreme, but Jackie always took special care in the gifts she gave her mother-in-law. She genuinely thought about what would give Mrs. Kennedy pleasure, whether it was an ornate silver cross she found in Greece or hand-embroidered bedding carefully matched to Mrs. Kennedy's decor. Jackie obviously wanted the gift to be appropriate and appreciated, though she never tried to impress her. (Mrs. Kennedy was not so appreciative of the sheets as Jackie had hoped. She returned the gift to get the same sheets embroidered in pink, not the green of the original present. They had cost $500 because of the quality and the hand work, and the shop complied. However, once Mrs. Kennedy saw the pink ones, she returned them as well. She decided she did not want any hand-embroidered sheets.)

Mrs. Kennedy normally simplified her Christmas shopping by calling Elizabeth Arden's on Worth Avenue in Palm Beach to order sweaters for each daughter and daughter-in-law, considering that the extent of her shopping—with one exception. For Jackie she would spend more time. She would go from store to store, browsing. And if the gift also proved to be a sweater, it would be radically different from the others, a fancier design, a better material. There were limits, of course.

I remember one time she found what she thought was the perfect sweater in Courreges on Worth Avenue. Two sales clerks were standing there as Mrs. Kennedy asked the price. Told it was $80, she said, "I'm not spending that much money on Jackie!" Then she turned and we walked down the street to Cartier's, where Mrs. Kennedy bought Jackie a gold pillbox, not paying for it but using a credit from a picture frame given to her by journalist Barbara Walters. The clerk was asked to gift-wrap it, send it, and charge it to her credit.

As we were leaving the store, I thought, Jackie's really receiving a Christmas gift from Barbara Walters.

And always Jackie was prompt to thank Mrs. Kennedy, writing letters rich with details of what she was doing.

The notes actually were part of a tradition. Because Mrs. Kennedy saved many of the family's letters, I came across Jackie's writing from as far back as the couple's Acapulco honeymoon. Instead of seeming to perform a duty, she wrote to let Mrs. Kennedy share in the adventure and amusement of what they were doing, whether fishing or listening to Jack attempt to speak Spanish.

Finally there was Joan, the third "outsider" among the females who came to marry Kennedy men. Joan Bennett was that seeming rarity at Manhattanville, at least among the Kennedy women and their friends. She was a serious student, using her time to learn. She was also a beautiful blonde who, at five feet seven inches, was taller than many of the other girls. She worked during the summer as a model and actress, selling Coca-Cola on Eddie Fisher's television show, working for *The $64,000 Question*, and generally combining part-time glamour with her education.

Ted Kennedy, by contrast, was a less than brilliant student at the University of Virginia Law School. He was never particularly bright, though when he eventually became a senator, he had the sense to surround himself with one of the finest staffs on Capitol Hill. No matter what else might be said about him during his career, no one ever faulted any of the men and women who surrounded him, working on the legislative matters he presented.

Ted seemed like the stereotypical fraternity boy at law school. He studied hard and partied harder. He loved to drink, loved to drive too fast, and was always rather surprised when the police stopped him.

Joe Kennedy had long been orchestrating the family's limited philanthropy with events that would promote themselves. For example, when Joe decided to give money to help fund a Catholic hospital for handicapped children, he used the Joseph P. Kennedy Foundation, whose president was Jack. Jack was newly into politics when he handed over a check for $650,000 to Archbishop Cushing. The check had nothing to do with Jack, and some will argue, based on Joe's very limited philanthropy almost always being tied to the need to make headlines, that the gift might not have occurred without the congressional race then going on. Jack was the front man and the papers showed a congressional candidate giving money to help the disabled.

In October 1957, Manhattanville College dedicated a new physical education building named after Kathleen. This was of special interest to the Kennedy women, but Ted was twenty-five years old and being groomed for public office. He, not his mother, gave the high-profile speech at Manhattanville.

Ted was a skilled speaker in front of a crowd, though he was not particularly good one-to-one. It was as though he could lose himself in a mass of people because they did not get too close to him.

Joan avoided Ted's dedication speech. She had no interest in anything but her schoolwork. However, the nuns wanted to encourage more philanthropy, and they had insisted that all the students attend the dedication and reception. At least one nun was stationed at the reception to note the names of all the students attending. Whichever young women failed to show would be given a demerit, something Joan, a senior, wanted to avoid.

A friend convinced Joan to meet Ted at the reception. No one would know how much of the program she had missed. She could stay out of trouble and finish her term paper.

Joan knew some of the Skakel family and had been at their home at the same time as Jean. When Jean saw her at the reception, she introduced Joan to her "little brother." Ted had grown to six feet two inches tall and two hundred pounds. Joan was intrigued.

Ted and Joan began talking by telephone after he left the college. Within a matter of weeks they had their first date, a Sunday brunch over the Thanksgiving holiday.

Joan, in contrast to Ted, was an obedient young woman, rarely breaking the rules of the convent or those of her parents.

Dates were limited until June when Ted invited her to Hyannis Port to meet his mother. Joan brought along expensive clothes, then realized they would be inappropriate. She stayed casually dressed all weekend.

Rose was concerned with the spiritual side of Joan Bennett. She also wanted to know about Joan's experiences with her Catholic schools, many of which Rose had attended a generation earlier. In addition, she learned that Joan was a musician specializing in the piano. This connection delighted her.

Ethel had been the perfect Kennedy sister. Joan was the perfect outsider to join the family. She was what Rose wanted in a daughter-in-law —beautiful, stable, a child of the Sacred Heart, from an upper-class family, and trained as a musician.

Imitating Joe, who always checked on his children's dates, Rose called Manhattanville to learn more about Joan from the president of the college. The background proved as fine as she had hoped.

Harry Bennett had a successful career in advertising. He was not an entrepreneur like George Skakel and Joe Kennedy, but he had made money through hard work. And Virginia Bennett, Joan's mother, had been a harsh disciplinarian who pushed Joan in music. Both parents were heavy drinkers, though the risks for Joan in such an upbringing were not understood by anyone in her family. More important, the drinking did not result in public awareness as with the Skakels.

Ted Kennedy understood what his parents desired from him: he was twenty-five and should get married. Joan seemed perfect to them, though Ted had been interested in another blonde, a young woman who later became the secretary for Tom King, the husband of Mrs. Kennedy's niece Ann Gargan. I don't know why they did not marry, but Joe Gargan told me that the woman never married.

Ted proposed casually. There was no ring and he spent most of his time working on Jack's reelection campaign for the Senate. Eventually Joe Kennedy bought Joan a ring, handed the package to Ted, and he gave it to his bride-to-be, never looking to see what his father had selected.

A few years later, long married to Ted, Joan lost the ring, which was worth $25,000. She was apparently drunk at the time, but the insurance company replaced it. This happened again, the insurance company refusing to pay a second time. Ted, disgusted, told her to go down to the dime store and buy another ring.

BG: MRS. KENNEDY WAS NEVER certain just what to do with Joan. She was always so busy trying to please everyone that you wondered if Joan could ever please herself. I guess that's why she could not get control of her drinking until after she separated from the family.

I remember a time in the 1970s when Joan was obviously alcoholic. She had visited her mother, then taken a bus to Palm Beach to visit Mrs. Kennedy. She arrived unexpectedly, apparently drunk, and went to her bedroom, where Mrs. Kennedy went to greet her. She looked so terrible that Mrs. Kennedy came out, rolled her eyes, and said, "Oh, *baby!*" A telephone call to the senator's office led Ted to summon his wife back to Washington. Joan left the house within hours, both her arrival and departure unexpected.

Mrs. Kennedy did not understand drinking problems. She held anyone sick in disdain, even though Jack was sick his entire life, perhaps the most disabled of all our presidents when he first took office. (Mamselle, who worked as a combination cook and maid for

Mrs. Kennedy, told me never to get sick. ("Mrs. Kennedy does not like sick people around.") She was always studying Joan, whether drunk or sober, as though watching an animal that might be expected to turn at any moment. Ted did the same. Yet Joan was a quiet drunk. She tried to always be a lady, but lost control without realizing it. For example, once she was in the kitchen with me, Nellie the cook, and the security guard. We were standing around chatting when Joan decided to show the guard how successfully she was tanning herself. She pulled down her pants and showed him her tan line.

I think what confused Mrs. Kennedy was that Joan was unable to accept her life. She was beautiful, cultured, and married to a family of money and power. Her husband cheated on her, but everyone's husband cheated in Mrs. Kennedy's world. She seemed to think that Joan should bear her fate the way the Children of Mary had been taught to do. She liked to call her own marriage a happy one, though she and Joe seemed almost not to speak. If she could fool herself about that, it was not much of a stretch to feel that Joan should be happier.

As their November wedding approached, Joan realized she did not want to marry Ted Kennedy, at least not yet. He had been working on his brother's campaign. She had been planning the wedding with her family. And Joe Kennedy had been publicizing the match. What she and Ted had not been doing was getting to know each other. She really had little knowledge of what he was like or whether they could get along.

Joe Kennedy put a stop to Joan's talk, even though her father briefly sided with her. Joe was not going to let his son and his family be embarrassed by stopping a wedding everyone knew about. He had no reason to be concerned about Joan's feelings; he had ignored Rose for too many years. The two young people were married in November 1958, when Ted was twenty-six and Joan was twenty-two.

The marriage taught Joan more than she ever wanted to know about the Kennedy family. Joe made certain that the guest list was heavy with people he needed to impress or to whom he owed favors. It was a political and business gathering, not a family celebration.

In addition, one of Harry Bennett's friends gave a unique wedding gift. He had a film crew come with several movie cameras and sophisticated sound equipment. Everyone was given a microphone to hide in his or her clothing, as in a television production. Tape recordings were made of everything, then a sound track added to the edited film. This skillful production not only looked theatrical, it also caught all nuances of the wedding, from the vows to the private words of Jack to Ted as they waited for Joan to come down the aisle. Among other things, Jack told his kid brother how to cheat on his wife, the "Kennedy way" for handling a marriage. To Joan's horror in the years ahead, Ted took his brother's advice.

The men who came into the Kennedy family were of a different breed from the women. Sargent Shriver had the audacity to be poor, though a blue blood with pretensions.

BG: SARGE NEVER SAW the realities of the way Mrs. Kennedy lived. In 1975 and 1976, he ran for president. His shoes needed shining so he gave them to me to have them done, presumably by whichever servant Mrs. Kennedy used for the purpose. I took them to a shoe repair shop that charged $1.50, a bill Mrs. Kennedy found outrageous.

It was worse when he ordered food and drink for the Palm Beach house. He often charged hundreds of dollars to Mrs. Kennedy's account simply because it would be consumed in her house.

And he wasn't cheap. Money just meant nothing to him. If he had it, he spent it. If he didn't have it, he spent someone else's. Like Eunice, he didn't understand what it was like to be poor or even of normal income. Oddly he was not rich, for as Mrs. Kennedy said, "Blue blood but no money." Fortunately his extravagances only affected those who could afford them. Yet he really had no sense of normal life.

Sarge also had a slight arrogance that made me never really like him. The first day I met him I offered my hand, saying, "Hi. I'm Barbara Gibson, Mrs. Kennedy's new secretary."

Before walking on down the hall, Sarge smiled wryly, shaking my hand as he commented, "Well, la-dee-da."

Eunice was the most aggressive of the Kennedy sisters, and probably more aggressive than any of the brothers except Bob. If she had been born a generation later, she might have been the first member of the family to push for the presidency.

Eunice was the family activist, the one willing to go where events were taking place and be a part of them, not an observer squired by minions of a rich and powerful father. She was briefly a social worker in Harlem and also worked for the State Department. Later Joe helped her become an executive secretary for the Justice Department's commission on juvenile delinquency. Instead of staying in the office, though, she happily did some field visits in penitentiaries.

Oddly, Eunice dated Joe McCarthy. The two were serious enough about each other that some acquaintances thought they might marry. Their politics seemed at extreme odds, yet the areas of public service to which Eunice would later devote her life, such as Special Olympics, were neither in sympathy nor conflict with right-wing extremism. Her world would be the physically and mentally less fortunate, not those fighting poverty and racism. That Eunice seriously dated Joe McCarthy, the senator whose vicious lies and half-truths kept the nation in terror for years, hints at a harsher side to Eunice.

The connection of Joseph McCarthy with the Kennedy family has always been uncomfortable for them. The Wisconsin senator was a man on the move, and when he chose to make his focus the "Communist menace," he chose it strictly because he needed some issue as a political focal point.

Jack Kennedy and his sister Eunice were living together in Washington after Jack entered Congress, and Joe McCarthy was a frequent visitor. He was also frequently in the home of Joe and Rose, both of whom enjoyed his company. His earliest forays into anticommunist rhetoric were rehearsed with his friends, who listened to his ideas about gaining national attention for himself. Eunice dated McCarthy with some frequency, and when she realized that the friendship would not blossom into romance, she led Pat to date him. Only by chance and the aggressiveness of actor Peter Lawford did Joe McCarthy fail to become a Kennedy in-law.

Joseph Kennedy happily contributed to McCarthy's 1952 reelection campaign. Jack Kennedy referred to him as "a great American patriot" when his friend was attacked during a gathering of Harvard's Spee Club in 1952. Jack also seemed to see him as "shanty Irish," the only break

Rose Kennedy, 1972

President Kennedy's Summer Home on Cape Cod

The Kennedys as tourist attraction: postcards of the Kennedy homes at Hyannis Port.

Home Of The Late Ambassador Joseph P. Kenned

President
John F. Kennedy

Home Of Senator Robert F. Kennedy

Barbara Gibson and Rose Kennedy, 1974

Barbara Gibson, *left*, with a Palm Beach resident and Rose Kennedy leaving church, 1975

Rose Kennedy with
Jeannette, the maid, 1977

The Palm Beach Time

The Home Town Newspaper for All the Family

NO. 149   WEST PALM BEACH, FLORIDA, TUESDAY AFTERNOON, APRIL 6, 1976   ★ ★ ★   36 PAGES—

Times Photo by J.

Friends of Retarded hear advice

Rose Kennedy, matriarch of one of the nation's most prolific political families, offers a few words of advice as she prepares to leave a meeting of the newly formed Friends of Retarded Monday. Mrs. Kennedy recounted her own experiences as mother of a retarded child to 250 people Fountains of Palm Beach condominium complex Lake Worth. See story page B2.

Rose Kennedy featured on the front page of the *Palm Beach Times* for her work with the retarded. Barbara Gibson and Dennis, the chauffeur, are pictured to Mrs. Kennedy's left.

Mrs. Kennedy's bedroom. On her desk were mass cards for her dead children.

Barbara Gibson and Rose Kennedy during one of her daily swims

Rose Kennedy, 1976

from his father's opinion. However, he did not hold this opinion strongly enough to go along with the censure of the senator. Besides, Massachusetts voters were intensely anticommunist, so giving full public support to his friend seemed appropriate.

In 1953, Bob Kennedy joined Joe McCarthy's Subcommittee on Investigations. The elder Kennedy wanted his son named chief counsel, figuring that the exposure would be good for him. Instead, that position went to Roy Cohn, a young, arrogant, flamboyant attorney. However, Joe Kennedy's influence in Bob's selection was obvious. For example, when Peter Collier and David Horowitz interviewed Ted Reardon for their book *The Kennedys: An American Drama*, he told of a telephone call Francis D. "Frip" Flanagan, the general counsel for the McCarthy subcommittee, received a week after Bob was hired. According to the authors, Joe Kennedy said, "I understand Bobby's gonna work for you, and I just want you to know that by God you won't have any trouble with him. But if you do, I'll give you my private number, and just give me a call."

The story of the Army/McCarthy hearings is best told elsewhere. McCarthy's charges were ridiculous and overplayed, and then he came up against Joseph Welch, a Boston attorney who represented the Army. By the time Welch was finished with McCarthy, the senator was so damaged that those who had remained silent out of fear suddenly joined the attack. Television programs challenged the senator for the first time, and other senators realized that it was both time and safe to stop him.

He was condemned for behavior that violated the Senate's code of conduct in a 67–22 vote. The mood was clear. McCarthy, though still in office, had lost his forum, his power, and his reputation.

McCarthy did not lose the support of John Kennedy, though. During most of the hearings, the young Massachusetts senator was ill, suffering from a bad back and Addison's disease. He was usually on crutches, and when he went on the Senate floor, he usually spent long hours working, not out of dedication but because the pain of walking from the room was so great.

Kennedy did recover, of course, and was in good health, though not yet able to return to a normal work schedule, on December 2, 1954, when the Senate voted to censure McCarthy. In the oral history made by Kennedy's friend Charles Spalding for the JFK Library, Spalding told how Kennedy joked about what he would do when asked about McCarthy: "'You know, when I get downstairs, I know exactly what's going to happen.' He said, 'Those reporters are going to lean over my stretcher.

There's going to be about ninety-five faces bent over me with great concern, and every one of those guys is going to say, "Now, Senator, what about McCarthy?' " And he said, 'Do you know what I'm going to do? I'm going to reach back for my back and I'm just going to yell, "Ow," and then I'm going to pull the sheet over my head and hope we can get out of there.' "

Actually, that would have been more courageous than what he did. Kennedy did not and possibly could not have appeared on the Senate floor for the vote, but he could have alerted his office to pair him with an absentee Republican senator whose vote would be opposite his own. That way Kennedy could have gone on record for censure, and the Republican would have been recorded as opposed. Instead, Kennedy did nothing, so no one could prove that he was actually in favor of Joe McCarthy.

Kennedy eventually changed, becoming a McCarthy fighter in 1956, long after the senator had become so outrageous, almost no one supported him. As Kennedy later admitted, even his father no longer liked the Wisconsin senator by then. But never was Kennedy willing to face the moral issues of the era, though he would try to change history when he ran for president four years after that. But by then it was difficult to find anyone who admitted they had ever supported the man who had dominated Congress for so long.

BG: EUNICE WAS NOTORIOUS for doing good and being slightly reprehensible at the same time. Her special Olympics program has rightly been praised throughout the world. However, she used to have some of the retarded come to work in her home as domestics. She either did not pay them or else she paid them far less than she would have to pay for someone else to do the identical work. She justified it as some sort of on-the-job training. Everyone else just saw her as using cheap labor.

Shriver was one of the more interesting figures in all this because of the way he was used by the family. Sargent Shriver had met Kathleen Kennedy when he was at Yale. Then, after the war, Kathleen introduced him to Eunice. It was 1946, and Shriver was working for *Newsweek*, a fact Eunice apparently passed on to her father.

The Children Come of Age

Joe Kennedy was considering publishing the diaries and letters Young Joe had written before his death. He thought that either *The Saturday Evening Post* or *The Reader's Digest*, both publications where he had contacts, might be interested. Since Shriver was with *Newsweek*, and since he was friends with Eunice and Kathleen, he was asked to come to the Waldorf Towers where Joe had a suite.

Shriver told Joe Kennedy the truth, that there was no market for the writing. Most of it was dated, something Kennedy knew, and none of it offered such insight into the figures of the world that anyone would care to read it. Since Young Joe was dead and publication could no longer benefit his career, Joe senior was both a realist and apparently impressed with the thirty-year-old man. He offered Shriver the chance to go to Chicago and work for him at the Merchandise Mart.

Shriver was interested. He knew nothing about real estate, but he had a strong business mind, understood communication, and was honest. His job was to be Joe Kennedy's representative, to make certain everything ran smoothly, and to regularly analyze the operation.

The real estate work began to expose Sarge to a portion of the business world of Joe Kennedy, a world his children never saw. Joe had made the Park Agency his headquarters for running the business of the family. This was actually a converted suite in what had previously been the Marguery Hotel on Park Avenue.

The Merchandise Mart was to be the basis for working capital, though his holdings were vastly more extensive, as has been seen. Twenty-five percent of the Merchandise Mart went to Rose, assuring Joe of substantial capital. So long as he was alive, Rose's ownership meant nothing. They both knew he would run the business.

A second 25 percent was divided among the children. This assured that they would never have to work, though the work ethic was too strong for them to do otherwise. Years later the family liked to talk about their selfless public service, but the truth was that they often knew nothing other than the pursuit of power. When Ted ran for the Senate, a family comment as to why was, "He had to do *something*."

Twenty-five percent of the Merchandise Mart went to the Joseph P. Kennedy Jr. Foundation, a charitable organization that, in those days, primarily supported the New York and Washington Catholic archdioceses. The gifts from the foundation were usually quite generous and badly needed. They were also timed for maximum political and press mileage for one or another of the sons.

The remainder of the money was Joe's, a part of Joseph P. Kennedy

Enterprises—the "Park Agency." The Kennedy children were given whatever money they needed through the Park office. It was like having an allowance, only instead of going to Daddy, they had to call New York. The Kennedy grandchildren each received $1 million when they were born to be put in trust until they were twenty-one. Any unexpected expenses, any problems, any bills, everything went through the Park office. None of the family had any idea how much money they had or what anything cost.

BG: MRS. KENNEDY WANTED to be frugal, but she had no sense of money. She could be so tight that she did not want an aging freezer fixed in Palm Beach despite the fact that the massive Kennedy brood that descended every winter required a freezer. I had to arrange with the Park Agency to let me hire a repairman for around $100, much less than the cost of a new unit. Mrs. Kennedy was outraged, certain the family could make do with the small unit in the refrigerator.

One of the first times I learned what she was like was when she was outraged to discover two pieces of chicken missing from the previous evening's dinner. She had counted every piece of chicken before it went into the refrigerator, then recounted them in the morning. She quizzed me about the two pieces as though I were guilty and needed to confess. Actually they had been taken by her grandson Bobby Shriver, who had dared to consume the few cents' worth of food. I was outraged not only by Mrs. Kennedy's wrath, but also by Bobby's unwillingness to admit what had happened. I was probably angrier with him than his grandmother would have been had he said what he had done.

Ann Gargan told me how stingy Mrs. Kennedy could be, turning out all the lights in the halls and offices if anyone left them for even a moment. Some places were so dark at night that Joe said, "Christ, Rose, I could fall down the steps, break my leg, and run up a hospital bill of hundreds of dollars while you're trying to save a few cents on a lightbulb."

The staff of the New York office was fortunately the opposite of Mrs. Kennedy. Once I started working for her, I knew I might have to be in her home for long hours, seven days a week. I needed a complete change of scenery, so I talked with Tom Walsh of the Park Agency.

Tom told me to find an apartment within close commute, that the office would pay for it. I asked him in what price range I should look, and he told me that it didn't matter. He knew I would not go to extremes, and the staff wanted me comfortable.

I did learn that I had to be careful how I dressed and what car I drove. If I wore clothing that seemed to have been purchased at Saks Fifth Avenue or from one of the luxury shops along Worth Avenue, I was in trouble. The clothing could be from a deeply discounted sale or even a remainder shop, but if it was originally from an expensive store, Mrs. Kennedy noticed. She would immediately call the New York office to demand to know what I was being paid. She did not want me earning enough money to be able to afford clothing like that.

The same was true with my car. If it looked more expensive than she thought was right, a call would be placed to the New York office. She had her own standards of how anyone working for her could appear, and I had to meet them or she would try to have my pay reduced.

By contrast, I once made the mistake on the Cape of ordering a fifty-nine-cent bag of potato chips along with the lobster dinner Mrs. Kennedy was having. We were swimming in the pool when I mentioned this. She immediately said, "Oh, we have some leftover chips still in the kitchen. Go and cancel that bag!"

I got out of the pool, dripping wet, and went back into the house to call and cancel the order for the fifty-nine-cent bag of potato chips. And all this from a woman whose family holdings made them among the richest people in America.

Less than a year after going to Chicago, Shriver returned to Washington. At the Justice Department, Eunice had what seemed to be a make-work position for the daughter of a prominent political insider. A national conference on juvenile delinquency had been held, produced several task-force reports, and then supposedly hired Eunice to implement them. The lack of importance of the job was obvious as she had neither budget nor staff, and when Shriver helped her, he did so on her father's payroll.

Eunice and Sargent Shriver courted for six years before marrying. Eventually Jack trusted him as much as his father had (or was encouraged to use him by his father). Sargent was a key player in the 1960 election, made director of the Peace Corps, ambassador to France, was in charge of Lyndon Johnson's "war on poverty," and then, on his own, was asked to be Sen. George McGovern's vice-presidential running mate. The Shrivers would ultimately prove to be the most devoted parents among the Kennedys, their children, along with those raised alone by Jacqueline, being the most consistently successful in their chosen fields. However, later problems in their personal life caused an estrangement between Eunice and Sargent Shriver such that when they traveled to Palm Beach together, she stayed at the family compound and he stayed at the Breakers Hotel. But in those early years, Sargent was the most respected of the outsiders marrying into the family, and his wife-to-be was the strongest of the surviving sisters.

It was Sarge who suggested to Joe Kennedy that a foundation be established to help the mentally retarded. While the Special Olympics was Eunice's idea, it was Sarge who spurred the funding of such an organization.

Later, Stephen Smith would be added to the men who helped with the family finances. He married Jean, who had worked in the public relations department of the Merchandise Mart and as an aide to Father James Keller, the founder of the Christophers. This was a right-wing organization concerned with communism and corruption. When Jean returned to New York from Chicago, she met Smith, an executive in a successful transportation firm, which gave him the business background that ultimately led to his taking over the Park office. His family had made large sums of money, and he was reared in the midst of great wealth.

The Smith marriage would not prove happy. Steve Smith was a womanizer who made no effort to be discreet. He would go to restaurants and nightclubs where he was apt to be recognized.

Peter Lawford, who also did not believe in monogamy, was shocked by what he perceived as the physical and emotional abusiveness of his brother-in-law. He was quite supportive, at least according to his recollections, when Jean, frustrated and hurting, had an affair that almost led to a divorce.

Lawford talked freely of the affair during the last decade of his life, but he would never name the lover. He said that in the summer of 1966 Jean decided to fly to Paris where she would be with her lover. She would stay with him while a divorce was arranged. Then they would live happily together.

According to Lawford, the lover never showed, Jean returned to the United States "with her tail between her legs," and Smith took a separate residence for his affairs. The last years of Smith's life were difficult for Jean, though she kept up the façade of a normal marriage so that outsiders would not be aware of what was happening.

Author Larry Leamer was the first person to release the name of Jean Smith's lover. According to his research, it was famed lyricist Alan Jay Lerner, who delighted in women and romance, but not in commitment.

The Shrivers were married in 1953 and the Smiths three years later. But of all the men brought into the family, none was so notorious as Pat's husband, the actor Peter Lawford.

Lawford was a Kennedy man in perhaps the worst sense of that word. A womanizer, he once had a bet with Jack after he became president as to whether Jack, Ted, Peter, or some of Jack's friends from Harvard would have sex with a woman other than their wives in the Lincoln bedroom. Lawford was also the procurer of women ranging from starlets to Marilyn Monroe for Jack's pleasure, both in the White House and when Jack visited the Lawford home in Hyannis Port.

Peter Lawford was never impressed with the Kennedy family money. His father, Brig. Gen. Sir Sydney Lawford, was one of the great British heroes of World War I. His mother was Lady May Lawford, who had become pregnant while married to the general's aide-de-camp. For at least the last ten years of his life, Peter, who hated his mother, would tell how she was eight and a half months pregnant when she told her husband who the father of the baby was. He summoned her to his quarters, where he met her wearing full dress uniform, minus only his shoes and socks. He had braced a shotgun at such an angle that he could pull the trigger with his toes. When she faced him, he saluted her and blew his head off.

The story was dramatic and also untrue. His father, divorced from May, lived until 1947, dying an alcoholic.

Peter's childhood was never pleasant. He was dressed as a girl, complete with a bow in his hair, until he was nine. He would later be seduced by his nanny and a friend who taught him oral sex even before he reached puberty. He also lost the use of one arm when, as a child temporarily living with his parents in France, he accidentally put his arm through a freshly cleaned windowpane while reaching for a toy on the other side. The glass shattered, and when he pulled back his arm, the shards severed muscle, flesh, and an artery. Between blood loss and infection, he nearly died. Fortunately the doctors saved both his life and his arm, though the hand was left little more than a claw. His father had been terrified until Peter was well. His mother, who later entitled her autobiography *Bitch*, complained, "Couldn't you have done this another day, Peter? You knew I was dining out tonight."

The Lawfords moved to the United States during World War II. Much of their wealth was lost and Peter took a job as a parking-lot attendant in Florida, the lot ironically owned by Joe Kennedy. However, he had done some child acting in England as early as 1931, and he soon began appearing in American movies. He was handsome, physically fit, and could not serve in the military. He would always thrust his crippled hand in his pocket or loop his thumb through his belt so that his disability went unnoticed. Because the film industry was part of the propaganda effort in World War II, a clean-cut youth with a British accent was in demand.

Peter met Jack Kennedy when Jack was in Hollywood in 1944, recuperating and making his way through as many starlets as possible. Five years later, he and Pat found themselves at the same party in London. Neither meeting impressed Peter. He had not been in England when the family became somewhat notorious because of Joe's work as ambassador. And he had known so many rich and powerful people growing up that the aura they may have had for Americans was lost on him.

By contrast, Pat, like Kathleen, was a movie buff and starstruck. She had seen all of Peter's films. She was also tall, slender, intelligent, and not particularly attractive, traits that Peter desired in a woman.

The only thing wrong with Pat was her Catholic upbringing (though she had attended Rosemont College in Pennsylvania, a departure from the Sacred Heart experience of her sisters). Even after they were married, he complained because she would say her prayers before they would get into bed for sex. He claimed that she spent so much time praying, by the time she was done, he had lost interest in sex. He said it was like trying to make love to the pope.

Pat attended the Republican National Convention in 1952 as an "enemy observer." By chance, Peter was present with Henry Ford. Peter was apolitical, but when he heard Pat taunting the speeches, he began taking the opposite side, just to tease her. They had dinner together, then did not see each other until 1953 when both were in New York and happened to encounter each other while she was grocery shopping. After another dinner, they flew to Palm Beach together for Christmas, Pat staying in her family home, Peter staying at the Fords'.

Joe Kennedy made clear that he hated British men who were actors and wore green socks, all traits of Peter's. However, when Joe Kennedy had Peter checked out, he turned out to be a regular patron of expensive prostitutes, a man who apparently could not be trusted to be faithful. Joe Kennedy was relieved by the report, Peter being enough like Joe and his sons that he welcomed him into the family. The couple was married April 24, 1954, in a ten-minute ceremony in St. Thomas More's Catholic Church in Manhattan. Peter was Anglican, preventing them from being married in St. Patrick's Cathedral despite Peter's willingness to rear the children as Catholic.

After the honeymoon, the Lawfords moved to California and rented a home. Although they did not realize it at the time, it was the same house Joe Kennedy had used for his affair with Gloria Swanson. Ironically, when Jack Kennedy began having a sexual affair with actress Marilyn Monroe, as famous in her day as Gloria Swanson had been in Joe's youth, he often used one of the bathrooms in the Lawford house. Because of his bad back, he would sometimes use the bathtub for sex, lying on his back, Marilyn on top.

11

The Campaigner

Rose had never been involved with a national campaign when Jack Kennedy made his move for the presidency. The odds were against his success, at least so far as Massachusetts Democratic leaders were concerned. Kennedy was considered a lightweight in his home state, nice enough to make a career of the Senate, his record too shallow to survive national scrutiny. That was why early supporters for Kennedy as senator, such as Edgar Grossman, political realists all, were shocked to hear that the National Democratic Committee thought he could go all the way.

Jack was always his own worst enemy, but the times were right for him. The mood of the press was forgiving when analyzing the personal life of a politician. When Jack attended the Democratic National Convention in Los Angeles in 1960, he was caught by reporters sneaking out of a woman's apartment. It was obvious he was having an affair, though he used the fact that he was the friend of the building's owner, actor Jack Haley, as his cover. It was so transparent that Walter Winchell, the nationally syndicated columnist and radio commentator, decided to pursue the story, calling it in to his editor in New York. He was the only one, though.

Winchell's editor was shocked, not by the fact that a senator was caught cheating on his wife, but rather that Winchell would want to print the story. The senator was a married man, and in 1960, no one was about to embarrass a married man with a story about his philandering. For the public, Kennedy's faithfulness to Jacqueline would remain a cherished myth.

The Campaigner

Rose was never more alive than when she was campaigning. She understood it, was better at it than her children. She had long helped Jack, constantly passing him notes about his past performances and making suggestions concerning upcoming speeches. As a result, he was developing speech and debate skills that greatly enhanced his image. And Rose, at seventy, had more stamina and was more impressive than her son's support personnel thirty and more years her junior.

BG: I REALIZED WHAT campaigning meant to Mrs. Kennedy when I was with her during Teddy's campaign for reelection to the Senate in 1976. We had been to Boston's Ritz Carlton Hotel where she had spoken before approximately four thousand people in the massive ballroom. She was approaching ninety, yet her voice was steady and her eyes were alive with fire.

As we were driving home to the Cape, she said with a delighted smile on her face, "You see, Barbara, this is how it was when I used to campaign for my father. We would tour around the state doing this, but in those days we had people standing outside the polls handing out cigars with dollar bills wrapped around them." She paused, amused by the memory. "Of course, we aren't allowed to do that now." And then she giggled.

Joe Gargan, Rose's nephew and longtime friend of Ted's, acted as an advance man for Jack. He went into cities and organized various supporters, working with the local Democratic Party as well as volunteers specifically interested in Kennedy for president. But once the basics were done, Rose was often the next to move in, both giving speeches and working with her children in a variation of Coffee With the Kennedys as practiced in 1952.

Rose was always more aware of the women's vote than were the male politicians. She was not a feminist. She just remembered how her father's success had resulted in large measure from the involvement of women at a time when they lacked the vote. By 1960, approximately 3 million women were registered Democrats who were not expected to turn out at the polls. Rose both courted them and guided the strategy of both family and volunteers in a manner somewhat similar to how the Democrats would court registered but inactive black voters in 1964. The votes of these almost overlooked women voters could be the deciding factor in a close race. As it turned out, the race was so close, the extra women's vote Rose sought, generally ignored by other politicians, was critical.

Jack, humoring his mother when she insisted upon pursuing women the way she had for the congressional campaign fourteen years earlier, checked to see the gender breakdown of Massachusetts voters. To his surprise, women far surpassed men as registered voters. Yet the traditional leadership of both the Republicans and the Democrats had ignored this critical resource. More important, the pattern was likely to be repeated in every other state, making Rose's approach innovative.

Polly Fitzgerald, Jack's great-aunt, lived in Worcester and agreed to hold a tea during Jack's first campaign for Senate. She had been the recent president of the Ace of Clubs and was socially prominent. Her tea was so successful that she agreed to organize them statewide, Rose handling the speaking.

Polly Fitzgerald divided the state into identifiable communities, then sought one or more people in each community who were prominent. Almost always this was a man and usually a lawyer. Then he would find fifty women of importance for whatever reason—other lawyers, doctors, business executives, heads of women's clubs, or whatever else. Each woman would then be asked to get in touch with ten others. They were asked to go to the hairdresser's, gas stations, and anywhere else to talk up the gatherings. Eventually five thousand names were all carefully indexed on card files. The participants would bring their best dishes, tablecloths, and silverware. Then invitations were sent out: "Reception in honor of Mrs. Joseph P. Kennedy, Sr., and her son, Congressman John F. Kennedy."

By 1952 the hostility to Joe had faded. Few remembered the controversy surrounding his wartime actions. Even fewer still cared.

Rose attended thirty-one regional gatherings in 1952, each carefully planned. Prior to that Senate race, demographics were of limited importance. Partially this was because she knew the congressional district and its people. Partially this was because she thought she could play off her audience, shifting her talk slightly as was warranted by the reaction to her speaking.

In 1952 she developed the technique she would use eight years later on a national scale. She asked every organizer of a gathering every question she could imagine. She wanted to know the backgrounds, interests, and concerns of those invited. She wanted to know their income levels, the type of work they and/or their husbands did. She wanted to know their ethnic, racial, and religious heritage. Then she planned her speech and her clothing to be of greatest interest. Her limousine often carried clothing ranging from evening gowns to simple blouses and skirts, allowing her to change clothes between closely spaced speeches before radically different groups. Her accessories ranged from inexpensive babushkas to a mink coat.

The question in 1960 was how Rose would play to the heartland. In Boston, Rose had everything going for her. She was a beautiful woman who was the wife of the former ambassador to the Court of St. James. She was the mother of a congressman whose image remained that of a war hero. She was a Gold Star Mother whose loss was as deep as that of anyone to whom she might speak. She was the daughter of Honey Fitz. She was a grandmother with a large number of children. She knew when to say a few words in a foreign language that was the native tongue of her listeners or her listeners' parents. And she was extremely articulate.

Rose had proved her worth in other ways. She understood political image, so she began watching television, trying to see all of the speeches and interviews given by then senator Henry Cabot Lodge. Whatever she spotted that was effective, from the wearing of a patterned tie (Jack wore plain neckties prior to then) to a gesture, she made note of it and alerted her son.

Jack understood what his mother was doing. Years earlier, the father of Jack's opponent, Henry Cabot Lodge Sr., had run against John Fitzgerald. Jack's grandfather had lost, though Honey Fitz's support among the then nonvoting women was so strong, both Jack and his grandfather believed the old man would have won if women could have voted. Jack told this story at the various gatherings where his mother spoke, then said, "Ladies, I need you." It was an effective ploy.

Nineteen sixty would be a national campaign, yet the work that had been done with the statewide campaigns had obviously laid the groundwork for how to achieve success.

Jack Kennedy did not have street smarts, but Rose did. She did not try to duplicate the Nixon effort. Instead, she realized that the types of groups that had assured success in the Senate race would also work on a national level. She, her daughters, and as many other family members, Kennedy supporters, and political hangers-on as she could find began targeting parent-teacher associations, women's clubs, and similar groups. A growing number of women were in the news business, most of them responsible for women's stories. They were normally excluded from covering national political races, but Rose saw to it that they were contacted. She knew that they would get the word to the various clubs on which they reported.

Joe did his usual manipulation of the media wherever he could, though this time it was not the men who were of interest. When an October 1960 issue of *Look* ran a political story, the featured photograph was of the Kennedy women, not either candidate.

Jacqueline Kennedy was pregnant with her second child, a good excuse in her mind not to have to do very much. ("True" Kennedys never let pregnancy interfere with political campaigns or competitive sports.) But the various sisters and other in-laws were along for the ride.

Eunice was the most aggressive, the quiet, bright, quite beautiful Joan one of the most appealing. Jean and Ethel did whatever was necessary, and Pat was almost as strong as Eunice. In addition, Pat's husband, Peter Lawford, rallied some of the biggest Hollywood stars of the day.

Nineteen sixty was not the first year that Hollywood celebrities became involved in national politics. They had been involved at least since the era of Roosevelt. What made this race different was that the media to which they had access was greater. Dean Martin, Frank Sinatra, Sammy Davis Jr., Joey Bishop, Angie Dickinson, and several other "names" of the day actively campaigned for Jack Kennedy. And America's love affair with celebrity was such that their presence swayed some votes. Yet Rose remained as much or more of a celebrity than any of them, especially with the critical women's constituency most politicians previously ignored.

Rose seemed indefatigable as the first Kennedy presence in states holding primaries. She reached New Hampshire in February, making five speeches a day in order to set the tone for her son's arrival. She sensed the mood of the crowd, both for herself and for him. She also set the tone for aspects of the primary campaign.

For example, Joe wanted to promote his son's heroism. PT-109 made a great story, yet in 1960, America was a nation troubled by the prospect of war.

Rose, on the other hand, discussed Jack as a proud mother would discuss her son. She told of his childhood, always carrying the three-by-five cards on which she had recorded his growing up. She spoke of his early successes. And she told of his dislike of war, how gentle a man he was, this hero of war. She positioned him as a peace-loving man who would give his life for his country and almost did. He was not afraid to fight anyone at any time. Yet what went unsaid was that he would not be so foolish as to be involved in another Korea. Jack was a hero of what writer Studs Terkel would later call "the good war."

Rose understood how to pace herself because she had watched her father do it. Most politicians, including Jack Kennedy, would push themselves, proud about how little sleep they needed. The result could be humorous or disastrous—a misspoken word or phrase resulting from being too tired to think clearly. Yet long hours without rest seemed a test of manhood about which only they cared.

John Fitzgerald would work practically through the night, though he also knew he had to appear fresh. He followed a ritual of napping every chance he could get. Rose did the same, her tiny frame stretched out on the backseat of the chauffeur-driven cars taking her from speech to speech. She always seemed lively, alert, delighted to be wherever she was speaking. And because the people accompanying her were not napping, the more disheveled they became, the more vibrant she seemed by contrast. The impact was always strong.

The Kennedy women did an unprecedented job of ethnic campaigning. Rose spoke a smattering of German and was reasonably fluent in French. Jacqueline spoke fluent French and Italian. Pat took the Jewish constituency, not speaking Hebrew or Yiddish but having the cachet of having been to Israel when her actor husband filmed the movie *Exodus*. Bob and Jacqueline's brother-in-law, Prince Radziwill, handled Polish groups. And Eunice tried to impress the Lebanese with her silks purchased during a brief trip to Egypt.

There was only one minor slip in Rose's thinking. She spent eight days in Wisconsin during its primary. Since Hubert Humphrey of neighboring Minnesota was a strong challenger, Rose did her best to appeal to the state's German-speaking constituents. She introduced German words and phrases into her speeches.

This was a disaster, though she realized that soon enough so that most of her work was untroubled. Some of the German natives had fled Hitler and hated Germany. Others had come long before Hitler but faced extreme hatred during World War II. Some of the Germans did not want to think about their roots. Others did not want others thinking about their origins, fearing some sort of reprisal or shunning even though Hitler had been defeated fifteen years earlier. German groups in Wisconsin only wanted to hear speeches in English.

What is seldom discussed by the Kennedy family is what else was taking place in Wisconsin. Rosemary lived there, and any member of the family could have stopped by to see her. However, another year would pass before this occurred. Rosemary was not a political liability: she was a family failure, an embarrassment. The only blessing was that her life was healthier with the nuns of St. Coletta's than it ever could have been had she been kept in the family's homes.

Rose was exhilarated by the primaries. She delightedly announced to family and campaign workers, "I'll go wherever they want me to go and do whatever they want me to do during the campaign."

Because of the state's anti-Catholicism, Rose did not campaign in West Virginia. Prior to the West Virginia primary, a poll found Jack Kennedy had a 70-to-30 lead over Humphrey. That figure was reversed as soon as the people learned Jack was a Catholic. He and most of the men making speeches on his behalf were booed. The crowd was always hostile, certain he represented the pope.

In 1952, Rose had been honored by Pope Pius XII, a man she had first met when he was still a cardinal. She was given a scroll that told of her exemplary life and many charities and was honored as a papal countess. Since Francis Cardinal Spellman had delivered it, and since the story had made news in several cities, Jack's staff felt it would be resurrected, causing further problems if Rose visited West Virginia.

Ultimately the only successful campaigner in the state was Franklin D. Roosevelt Jr., whose father was beloved. The senior Franklin had successfully promoted legislation that gave miners the right to organize, bargain collectively, and ultimately earn a living wage.

Joe Kennedy also got involved in West Virginia, though behind the scenes. He had long ago decided to incur any expense necessary to get Jack elected. He did not care with whom he worked or how he got the job done. If something would add support, it was worth the money. For instance, when mass mailings of an endorsement of Kennedy by the younger Roosevelt were to be sent to registered voters, Joe paid to have them shipped to the post office in Hyde Park, New York, for mailing. They would then seem to have originated from the late president's home, a subtle but effective touch.

Franklin Roosevelt Jr. also defused some past hatred, stressing how close his father had been with "Jack Kennedy's daddy" (he rarely mentioned Joe by name). Since FDR junior's wartime service was greater than Jack's and had been spent on board a destroyer, he spoke of PT-109 as though the two vessels had worked together, a pair of cowboys riding into a Western (Japanese) town to clean up the bad guys.

Rose was skilled at defusing the Catholic issue the few times she actually encountered it. The question, from non-Catholics who often belonged to Protestant faiths that were wary of the papacy, was what influence the pope would have on a president. Rose always explained that the Vatican was located in Italy, a predominantly Catholic country, yet the pope had no influence in its politics. Then she pointed to France, another Catholic country, headed by Charles de Gaulle, yet one in which the pope had no influence in government affairs. Finally she reminded the person of the numerous Catholics in the American Congress, who never voted as a bloc and were often at odds with one another.

Ultimately all the efforts, including Joe's spending, proved successful. As Hubert Humphrey commented, in a manner similar to Lodge's reaction in the 1952 Senate race, "I don't have to fight one [Kennedy]. I have to fight a family of them."

The Democractic National Convention was held in the Los Angeles Sports Arena, and Jack Kennedy won the presidential nomination on the first ballot. Rose, according to security personnel and other observers, was completely unexcited. It was as though she knew her son would win, that it was his destiny. She understood more than anyone else in the family the vagaries of politics. She knew that Jack's womanizing had become well-known to the press, though they did not publish such stories, as has been seen. She understood how one's dirty little secrets could become explosive. Yet this race belonged to the Kennedys. She had no doubts.

By the time the general election campaign started in earnest, Jack was relying upon his sex appeal rather than encouraging the women whose support he needed. He refused to give women other than his mother and sisters any meaningful work in his campaign, regardless of how qualified they might be. Margaret Price was named vice chairman of the Democratic National Committee, but even though she was also head of Women's Activities, her job was little more than to take notes and make coffee. The millions of registered women voters were not considered important to the election. They certainly were not welcome in any position of power.

The family dynamics became clear as never before. Rose ignored the men and positioned herself for campaigning in key areas where she was certain she could be of value. Ultimately she went to fourteen states, making forty-six major addresses and numerous minor ones.

By contrast, Jacqueline, whom some would think Jack's greatest asset in office, was considered a liability during the campaign. She was a sophisticate at a time when the nation was more interested in the girl next door.

Oddly, by contrast, America's female journalists began a love affair with Jackie that the public did not share. Jacqueline had an aura about her that fascinated female and a few male reporters. Her difference excited them, and her coverage was uncritical.

The Kennedy women found that instead of attending only Coffee With the Kennedys types of events, as they had when working just one state, they did less campaigning and more coordinating on a national level. They acted as trainers, teaching other women how to hold the events that would bring out more votes. Their husbands used the long separations for philandering.

Joe Kennedy, for once, was faithful to Rose, who no longer cared about him. Through Jack she had achieved what she had once expected to enjoy when she first got married. Where Jack became so exhausted during the campaign that some of his speeches were barely comprehensible, Rose always looked as though she were starting on her first day of campaigning after a restful night's sleep.

The rest of the men on the campaign trail were often brazenly aggressive toward women. Ted, not yet in public office, took a date to a dinner where the friends were celebrities who were likely to be recognized. Peter Lawford joked with Jack about what the celebrities were doing when not supplying starlets for both of them.

Steve Smith cheated on his wife, though he apparently was circumspect before the election. And Sarge was the faithful one, though shunned by the brothers and sisters. He was not aggressive enough. He was not 100 percent dedicated to Jack. As Eunice became increasingly involved, Sarge, willing to do whatever it took to help, was viewed as too weak to be of much support.

Election night was focused on Bob's home in Hyannis Port. All the brothers and sisters, their spouses, and various campaign leaders were there. Many writers have downplayed the evening's freneticism, having the family nervously gathered around a small television set. But Joe Kennedy had paid for a new telephone system, one as sophisticated as that used by the Boston Convention Center. He wanted to keep close tabs on events throughout the country, especially in those areas where, it was later learned, his money and organized-crime contacts helped ensure victory. The race was going to be close, so close that CBS television briefly projected Richard Nixon the winner.

Jack was exhausted. Eunice, seemingly almost as strong as her mother, would collapse when the election was over, her condition diagnosed as Addison's disease, identical to her brother Jack's.

At 7:15 P.M. the popular vote was such that computer projections indicated a 100-to-1 probability that Richard Nixon would win over Kennedy. However, the West Coast polls remained open, and by 8 P.M. returns showed a slight lead for Kennedy.

Jack was unconcerned about the popular vote, as was Joe, who, with Rose, went back and forth between their home and Bob's. The electoral vote was what mattered. Jack could ultimately lose the popular vote and still win the presidency if the states' electoral votes wound up the right way.

Lyndon Johnson, who was not present, telephoned when Ohio, a key electoral state, was obviously going to Nixon. Jack had made six different stops in Ohio, his hand and arm becoming swollen from shaking so many hands there. Thus he was less than thrilled when Johnson facetiously commented that he had just heard that *Jack* was losing Ohio, but that *we* (Jack and Lyndon) were winning Pennsylvania, another key state for electoral votes.

Around 11 P.M. the voting patterns changed. The East and Midwest had given Kennedy a 2-million-vote lead. The returns from the West and Southwest were going Republican. Ultimately the lead for Kennedy would dwindle to approximately 150,000 votes, a statistical dead heat. However, the electoral vote count was more certain, and by 3:30 A.M., Richard Nixon, exhausted, emotionally drained, announced to the press and his followers that it appeared almost certain that Jack Kennedy would be the next president. Two hours later, with Michigan's votes almost all counted, Kennedy appeared to have 285 electoral votes (Michigan had 20). He only needed 269 to win. The waiting was over.

Later the morning after the election, Rose and Joe, along with the rest of the family, were chauffeured to the U.S. armory in Hyannis. It was both large enough and secure enough to handle the excited mob, the broadcast equipment, and the other press needs.

Rose never mentioned what happened next, though the incident undoubtedly troubled her. But Rose knew what she had accomplished, and her actions quite possibly made the difference in the returns of several key states.

Jack Kennedy ignored his mother on the stage. She was introduced, of course. She smiled and waved, looking radiant, and the crowd applauded loudly. However, in one of the most emotional moments of the victory speech, Jack put out his arms to his father. The older man, by then pale and sick with exhaustion, only a few months from a crippling stroke, hesitated.

Then Joe stepped toward his son and the two men embraced. An emotional moment for both, it totally excluded Rose.

Later, Rose would remember the events differently. She would treat that morning, including the embrace, as of limited importance, an election won, yet little different from others. Instead, she said that the moment when everything truly fell into place for her was when she saw on television a news report of Jack paying a courtesy call on Dwight Eisenhower. The older man showed the younger man what would be his new home. This rite of passage moved Rose deeply. And again, it was experienced from afar.

12

Years of Change

The anger was not obvious until the day of the stroke. Rose had been hurt too deeply and too often. As a Catholic, she would never divorce. As a woman in love with shopping, she was delighted that her husband was rich. Her staff handled anything unpleasant that might come along. During and after their stay in England, she had been able to parlay Joe's importance into more respect than she had previously imagined possible. And now she had her own private rooms in every house the couple owned, would stay in a different hotel from Joe in every city to which they traveled.

For his part, Joe had his women, had encouraged his sons to have theirs. The Kennedy males were philanderers, something Rose generalized to all men. It was a way of making peace with what she knew was taking place whenever Joe left town. But he had flaunted his activities by despoiling Hyannis Port with Gloria Swanson, just as James Curley had despoiled Josie's home with Honey Fitz's Toodles. He had destroyed the most beautiful of their daughters.

And then there had been the moment when Jack had stood before the adoring throngs to accept their congratulations for winning the presidency. Jack had ignored her, the snub effectively diminishing her months of work. He ignored the entire Fitzgerald genius for politics, which had brought him almost as far as Joe's money.

Just as Jack did not mention Jacqueline the night he won the nomination, so on election morning the embrace had been for his father. Only his father. Rose had been shown her place by both her men.

BG: I STILL REMEMBER the first time I saw Rose Kennedy. Jack was accepting the Democratic National Convention's first-ballot nomination for president. A massive spotlight was aimed at the front of the stage to allow him to experience the cheering throngs before him. But instead of Jack standing in the spotlight, it was his mother, Rose. She was beaming at "her" audience. However, it wasn't her moment, and to my amusement, Jack gently but firmly took his mother and moved her aside, reclaiming what should have been his moment from the start.

If there were any lingering doubts that Rose was being pushed aside from the seat of power and glamour, they were dispelled on inauguration day, January 20, 1961. Father Anderson Bakewell, S.J., was holding a special mass to seek God's blessing for the new administration. The mass was early, allowing the participants plenty of time to prepare for the ceremony. Rose planned to attend. She had told Jack that, but even if she hadn't, he knew she was a Child of Mary. He knew the importance of daily mass, especially this mass, to his mother.

Rose entered the church, looking to see if anyone else in the family was there. No one was, but she hoped Jack would come. He was her son, and it was only right to start the inauguration with God's blessing. And if he did arrive, he would sit with his mother as the family did when going to mass together. That was why she took a seat where she would be visible.

Jack entered alone. The church was small, four-fifths filled with parishioners, the back lined with photographers, but Rose was easy to spot.

Jack ignored his mother, though. He walked alone to an end seat and sat down. In a manner so subtle none of the Kennedy watchers noticed, he had declared his independence from his parents. Only Rose sensed the change that morning, a change she had known was coming from the day Jack won the election. Joe would not realize what was happening until he discovered he had less access to his sons and the seat of power than Jack's daily bimbos.

Rose had emotionally abandoned her son when he felt he needed her the most. Increasingly she was being treated as she had treated others. Yet she was not introspective. If anything, she blamed Joe, the man she still professed to love yet with whom she was barely civil.

Later, Rose would deny the growing estrangement. She said of the incident, "I didn't sit with him because I was bundled up with a lot of funny-looking scarves and things, but I was delighted to think that he had gone [to mass]." What she did not say was that she was too proud of her appearance and her reputation for being on the various best-dressed lists to go in public the day of the inauguration with "funny-looking scarves and things." It was not her style.

She did not get angry at Jack, would not get angry with Jack. He, at least, was The President. Rose would come to visit the White House the way she visited the King and Queen. She could never think of her son as betrayer. Only Joe.

Rose added the fact that she was the mother of the president of the United States to her growing number of eccentricities. When she went driving, she would often have her chauffeur stop whenever they saw a hitchhiker in the uniform of one of the armed forces. Her sons had been in the Navy, and she seemed to think that anyone in the military would not harm her. They were good boys, serving their country, listening to their mothers.

Once the driver stopped and the youth got in the limousine, sitting beside the chauffeur, Rose in the backseat, she would ask him if he knew who she was. He would invariably have no idea. The woman was obviously rich, but beyond that fact, nothing was certain. Finally she would delight in revealing that she was the president's mother. She never had any sense that her actions might be dangerous. She was being helpful by giving the boys a ride, delighting in her little prank.

For his part, Joe had come to ignore Rose, turning to his niece for companionable friendship. That niece, Ann Gargan, her sister, Mary Jo, and her brother, Joe, were the children of Rose's sister Agnes. Their mother died of an embolism at the age of thirty-nine when Ann was two, and their father died when Ann was ten. The latter death was unusual, so typical of the tragedies faced by both the Kennedys and the Fitzgeralds. The father had been an undersecretary of the armed forces commuting between Washington and Boston. He suffered a heart attack during one of his trips, dying on the train in an area where no one noticed him for two days. He was discovered because of the foul smell of the decomposing body, a horrible shock to everyone. The Kennedys took his three children into their home in the summers, partially rearing them, and putting them through school.

The Gargans were the poor relatives, and the gifts always came with strings. Joe Gargan was at times treated like hired help. He became a lawyer, yet never fully developed his practice. If the Kennedys wanted him to work on a campaign, help with their property, or do something else for them, he did it. He might resent it. He might question the morality of the actions, as he would come to do when Ted, his closest friend among the Kennedys, accidentally killed a woman at Chappaquiddick.

BG: JOE GARGAN, LIKE TED, feared the wrath of his aunt Rose and would do anything she said. He told me that when he and Ted were seventeen, she would make them take a nap every afternoon, as though they were little kids. And there was no faking. When they were supposed to be asleep, she would look into the room and make certain their heads were on their pillows.

He said, "We just did as she told us. There was never any question."

Ann was as mischievous as Ethel Skakel had been while attending Catholic schools, such as the Sacred Heart Academy in Newton, Massachusetts, and Marymount in Tarrytown, New York. She delighted in practical jokes, such as pinning notes to the nuns' flowing black habits when they passed during study hall. Other students would remove the notes so Ann would not get caught, and all of them delighted in Ann's communication system.

Ann also took Waterman's blue-black ink and put it in the holy-water font. Nuns coming from mass would absentmindedly dip a finger in the font, then make the sign of the cross. Only later, when they noticed each other, did they realize that the cross was inked on their foreheads.

Ann was a rebel, but not in her devotion to God. She liked pricking the pomposity of the teaching nuns, but she longed to share in their lives. At nineteen she entered a convent, hoping to become a nursing nun.

She would probably not have become an RN as many nuns wishing to participate in a healing ministry chose to do. Instead she saw her mission as assisting those with scientific skills. It was an odd commitment for a young woman who had no interest in science. Her love was of bringing comfort to others, and she wanted to do so through the church.

Ann was just two months from taking her vows when she developed what was diagnosed as multiple sclerosis. She left the order, and Joe Kennedy was determined that she would have the best care money could buy. He sent her to the Lahey Clinic. He sent her to Switzerland. He also showed her numerous small kindnesses, such as cutting her meat when her lack of muscle control made such efforts embarrassingly difficult. And eventually she grew stronger, all symptoms disappearing. Perhaps her illness was not multiple sclerosis as originally diagnosed. Perhaps she was one of the lucky individuals who responded to unusual treatments. Whatever the case, she decided that her uncle Joe had blessed her with new life. She vowed to devote herself to pleasing him for however long he remained alive.

The staff viewed Ann as a cross between a faithful lapdog and the loyal servant who walks ten paces behind the master, carrying his briefcase. Yet no matter how odd the relationship seemed to others, Joe apparently appreciated it.

As Jack assumed the presidency, Bob was appointed attorney general and became his closest family confidant. Joe was seemingly squeezed out of daily affairs. However, Joe actually telephoned regularly, said Rose after Joe's death, implying the type of behind-the-scenes power he had always desired.

Rose was content to be the mother of the president, a position that regularly brought requests for interviews and photographs. But Joe saw no value to having power if you could not use it, and his sons were not letting him be a part of the White House. He talked regularly; they listened, then acted on their own. Joe never fully achieved his dream.

One theory was that the sons did not want to think that they were puppets of their father. But the truth was that Joe had assumed too much with his boys. He had never prepared them for his life and world. He had never taught them about his business ventures, his associates— both disreputable mobsters and some of the most respected names in business. He had never explained the family fortune, the trust funds, and the other factors that would assure that the money would be nurtured and increased for future generations. He assumed they would either instinctively know what to do or would stand back and let him tell them how to use their power. He also viewed the White House as his own, his son a surrogate for his wishes. He had just not expected that his sons would gain the backbone to turn away from his fantasies of power, manipulation, and revenge.

Jack and Bob wanted nothing to do with their father when it came to running the country. They were probably aware that Joe wanted to use the White House to crush his enemies and, perhaps, to reward his friends. Certainly other men had done that. But the sons wanted Joe down in Palm Beach, another wealthy old man playing golf, eating in restaurants, enjoying old age where he could not bother them.

Joe and Rose had separate lives in Palm Beach. The servants said that each might give them orders, often for different things that had to be done at the same time. Neither consulted with the other.

Even their golf games were different. Rose had a fast, aggressive game that was as likely to begin in the middle of the course as it was at the first tee. She would barge through other players, her tiny figure moving with such intensity, she looked like a dust devil twisting through a Southwestern town. Though her whirlwind lacked force, it was such an awe-inspiring sight that everyone tended to move out of her way.

Rose also played with three balls simultaneously. If she wanted to get in nine holes of golf, she could complete them with just three holes. An eighteen-hole game required just six holes. The three balls allowed her to compress her time on the course while getting the exercise she desired.

When playing golf in Hyannis Port, Rose had another idiosyncrasy. She did not realize that Joe paid the golf club for both of them to use it. Instead, she took delight in what she thought was cheating the club out of greens fees. She would sneak onto the course at the fifth hole, playing her three balls through to the eighth, then leave the course. Had Joe not been making payments for both of them, she was right about getting away without getting caught.

Joe was a competitive player who saw the game as a place for gossip and information. He played one ball, going a full nine or eighteen holes. He regularly started at eight o'clock each morning he was in Palm Beach. However, he only played with friends or family members other than Rose.

Even with golf, Joe had an eye for women. He was in Cannes, France, in August of 1961, playing golf with a twenty-two-year-old beautiful blond "caddy" named Françoise Pellegrino, who later admitted that she had been Joe's caddy for the previous five years. He was "very generous" with her, had paid for English lessons and sent her a case of champagne for her birthday. A deeper relationship was implied, though nothing was investigated more thoroughly so as not to offend the president. (The now defunct *New York Daily Mirror* headlined their version of the story "Pa Joe's Nifty Caddy.") However, both to laugh at Joe and to take advantage of the publicity, a new golf course being built in Miami announced that it would hire girl caddies.

BG: MRS. KENNEDY WAS SEEMINGLY forever in denial. A biography of Joe had been written during this period titled *The Founding Father,* and it came out in 1964. One of my first jobs for Mrs. Kennedy was to go through the book and transcribe her margin notes. She had carefully written down everything she thought was inaccurate. Later she was outraged by Lord Longford's book on the Kennedys because he had called Joe "predatory towards women." There would be no criticizing Joe no matter how much she was hurt by his actions.

On December 19, 1961, Joe decided to play golf with Ann Gargan. Before teeing off, he commented, "I really don't feel too well today, but it must be the cold I've had." They decided to play just the back nine, and by the sixth hole, he was beginning to feel uneasy. He seemed to be having a mild reaction to something bad he had eaten, and though that did not match the symptoms of his cold, he thought little of it.

Joe did not realize that he was far sicker than his queasy sensation led him to believe. To her horror, Ann suddenly realized that her uncle was wandering around the course as though lost. He seemed drunk, though he had had nothing to drink, no medications that would disorient him. She gently guided him back to the golf cart, drove him to the car, and brought him home. There he found Jacqueline and his granddaughter Caroline. He told them not to call any doctors, then was helped to bed.

BG: MRS. KENNEDY HAD NO time for illness, as if it were an intolerable weakness.

I remember one time when I came down with the flu while working. I was dizzy, nauseated, and had to lie down. A couch was in the maids' room across from my office. By leaving both doors open, I could rest on the couch and still be able to answer any telephone calls. Mrs. Kennedy discovered where I was, came in, and had me take dictation while I was flat on my back. The letters weren't important. They could have waited until I felt better. But she had no compassion. She had no patience for illness.

The debility of old age was also something she was certain her well-exercised body could avoid. She delighted in remaining agile when those around her were losing some of their physical skills. For example, one day while we were sitting together in her room, she mentioned that she had had lunch with the Duchess of Windsor the previous spring. Mrs. Kennedy made nasty remarks, saying that she thought that the Duchess's last face-lift had resulted in a little too much tightening. Mrs. Kennedy joked that it must have slightly damaged her brain, making her a little "dippy" when she talked. Then Mrs. Kennedy said, "She is ten years younger than I, and she staggers around." To emphasize the point, she impishly got up and began teetering, tripping over herself, delighted that she had not, would not, experience such ravages. What was even funnier is that she almost fell over herself as she discovered she was not quite so well coordinated as she bragged.

Tragically, she might have been right. Had heroic resuscitation methods not been used following her stroke, she would have been physically active until death. As it was, she went into a fetal position and showed little life other than breathing for the last decade that her body still functioned.

Rose had been shopping, and when she learned Joe said he was ill, she applied her own litmus test. She asked Ann if he had been able to walk into the house himself. When told he had walked, though only with Ann's help, that was good enough for her. She did not check on him. She decided that all he needed was a nap.

The lack of concern was surprising because Joe and Rose had been warned that he was a candidate for a stroke. He had seen doctors several times over the previous few months, and each time they had prescribed anticoagulants for him. He refused to take them, setting himself up for what was to follow.

Rose did check on Joe after lunch, though, and something was so wrong, his face so ashen, that even she decided that a doctor had to be called. The physician immediately realized what was happening, that Joe's condition was serious—possibly a stroke, possibly his heart. An ambulance was called, Joe was placed inside, and Ann jumped in to sit beside him. They sped to St. Mary's hospital with a motorcycle escort, and when they arrived, the chaplain administered the last rites of the Roman Catholic Church. Joe might possibly not last the afternoon.

Rose was alerted to the administering of the last rites, but she had a routine to follow. She went to the Palm Beach Golf Club to play three holes with three balls.

To Rose's dismay, her chauffeur came racing toward her in another golf cart as she was hitting ball after ball. Almost breathless, he informed her that she was needed at the hospital. Papers had to be signed. Joe's problem was serious and they needed Rose. Mr. Kennedy could no longer talk. His right side was partially paralyzed, his mouth uncontrollable, saliva constantly dripping. His right leg and arm were paralyzed. And Joe was unable to remember anyone, including family members.

But Rose could not be interrupted. While her horrified chauffeur tried to hurry her along, Rose insisted upon going into the pool for her daily swim. This was her routine, and Rose had no intention of interrupting that routine for Joe. She had spent many a lonely night while he followed an all too familiar routine in a distant city where he would dine with and often sleep with a beautiful woman. She had waited faithfully for Joe while he conducted business and adultery hundreds or thousands of miles from her for what might be weeks or months at a time. She had waited much too long for him. He would now wait for her. If life-saving procedures had to be delayed until she arrived, that was not her concern.

Finally, after a shower, a change of clothing, and the end of her day's primary routine, she allowed herself to be driven to the hospital. Because of the prominence of the family and the seriousness of the stroke, the police closed roads and diverted traffic to speed Rose on her way.

Once in St. Mary's she was informed that he had suffered a blood clot in an artery of the brain—technically, an intracranial thrombosis. An arteriogram was performed, and the thrombosis was found in the left cerebral hemisphere. It was inoperable.

Ironically, the damage from Joe's stroke left him with much the same appearance as Rosemary. The partial facial paralysis, the tendency to drool, the partially crippled body, the inability to make intelligible statements—all made him identical to his daughter. Rose had avoided seeing Rosemary. Joe had refused to see her. Now, though Joe could still think clearly, he had experienced damage identical to that of the prefrontal lobotomy.

At first Joe lay in Room 354 of St. Mary's, a hospital to which he had donated the money to build the third floor of the south wing. The room in which he was now a patient had a bronze plaque stating: "In Memory of Joseph P. Kennedy, Jr. Donated by Mr. and Mrs. Joseph P. Kennedy, Sr."

Richard Cardinal Cushing of Boston visited Joe in the hospital, then met with the press. He said that he had told his longtime friend, "Keep up your courage. You're going to be all right." He said that Joe Kennedy replied, "I know I am." In truth, from the day of his stroke until his death, Joe Kennedy, like his daughter Rosemary after her lobotomy, never again carried on an intelligible conversation.

BG: I LATER LEARNED THAT Mrs. Kennedy seemed to handle any major crisis by choosing physical activity over direct involvement with the person in trouble. When Eunice had a mild stroke the summer of 1977, fell off a pier and then was pulled out of the water and taken to a hospital by friends, Mrs. Kennedy began walking right after she was told what had happened. She was oblivious to the fact that she might be needed, and when it became important to find her, I had to be dispatched to track her down. I was the person most familiar with her exercise patterns, and I finally located her in Jackie's backyard.

It was Mrs. Kennedy's birthday that day and I had sent her flowers. Instead of discussing Eunice or her needs, apparently because it would bring up emotions she did not want to show, Mrs. Kennedy attacked me for spending money for flowers for her. She told me that I should have saved the money for something I might need.

That same year, I believe in the winter of 1977, Eunice called to say that Rosemary had had convulsions at St. Coletta's. The convulsions occurred because Eunice had decided her sister did not need some medication that had been prescribed for a long time. Her judgment was flawed, as she learned by Rosemary's violent physical reaction after the drugs were stopped against the will of the medical staff.

Mrs. Kennedy came into my office after talking by telephone with Eunice. She asked me if I would go swimming with her. It was

226

the middle of the afternoon and I was working, but she wanted companionship and wanted to exercise to deal with the crisis. However, once we got to the pool, Mrs. Kennedy said she didn't want to talk. She just wanted to swim.

Jean Kennedy Smith showed up, holding young Kym. Jean was concerned because it was the wrong time of day for her mother to be swimming. I explained what had happened, including that Mrs. Kennedy said that Rosemary had been taken off the drug she needed. I didn't want to say who'd decided that, but my tact was unnecessary. Jean snapped, "Well, who did that? Eunice."

Rose Kennedy and her daughters found themselves in an odd sort of limbo. Joe Kennedy was the powerful leader of the family. He dominated their thinking, their planning.

The Kennedy children had deliberately been made weak and dependant by Joe. Whether or not they had jobs, they had no concept of money. They had no idea what it took to live. They did not know how to use basic home appliances, from toasters to washing machines. They were spoiled, naive, and as much as Rose dominated their emotions, ultimately everyone had deferred to Joe. He was the person who would pressure them on everything from marriage prospects to working on political campaigns. He was more intimately involved in their private lives than the vast majority of parents of adult children.

BG: FROM WHAT I LEARNED, the sisters seemed to turn away from their competitiveness against outsiders and begin fighting among themselves after they lost Joe's guidance. There was a viciousness to them that sometimes seemed more appropriate to small children fighting in a sandbox.

For example, Rose taught all the children to be prompt. She was outraged if a child was so much as five minutes late for dinner or an appointment. After they lost Joe, they began taking this to an extreme against each other.

I remember many a time when the sisters were going on one or another of their boats. Eunice, Ethel, and Ted all had boats that you reached by taking a launch to where it was moored. Eunice or

Ethel or Pat would tell one or more of her sisters to be at the launch at a set time. Then, at the exact second set, the sister waiting at the launch would start across the water. Frequently the other sister was running across the beach toward the launch, like a frenzied office worker who, late leaving work, has to race to catch a bus as its doors are closing. Each seemingly took secret pleasure at frustrating the others.

Usually it would be Eunice taking the launch to the boat as Pat came racing across the dock. But one time, Pat agreed to drive Eunice to Boston. Eunice was delayed, calling her sister to tell her and saying that she would be no more than fifteen minutes late. Pat was not on a tight schedule, and Eunice could reasonably expect her to wait. Instead, Pat drove to Eunice's house, and when she did not see her sister outside waiting, she kept driving, not even bothering to stop and ring the bell. It was just mean.

Eunice had different problems with Ethel. Ethel liked to buy things but had neither love for what she purchased nor pride in ownership. She might buy a dozen sweaters, identical except for their color, just because she felt like owning them all. They might become lost, damaged through improper handling, or ignored. She had no respect for anything after its purchase.

Eunice knew this, yet Eunice was foolish enough to loan Ethel a favorite white cardigan she had probably purchased in Paris. It was expensive, and Ethel knew Eunice cherished it. Still, Ethel mislaid it. She had no idea where it was or what had happened to it, nor did she care.

The anger among the sisters and sisters-in-law was constant. It never seemed to get out of hand when I was there, but I learned from the previous secretary that the fights could be intense. Pat, especially, was extremely foulmouthed.

Pat was also devious. A woman named Mamselle had been her children's governess, then gone to work as Mrs. Kennedy's cook. She was in her seventies, lived with her sister in an inexpensive condominium, and her health was such that she needed to retire. However, she also needed some sort of retirement supplement, a fact that Christopher Lawford, by then an adult, brought up to his mother, Pat.

Mrs. Kennedy would have been outraged, but Tom Walsh of the New York office agreed. He called me to have me determine her real needs. What was her home worth? Was it paid for? Did she have any savings? Any special sources of income?

Mamselle had nothing like that, as I told him. He decided that $200 a month, in addition to anything else she received, would be fair.

Mamselle was deeply moved by what she thought was the generosity of Pat. The money made the difference between barely surviving and being able to retire with dignity. She wanted to send a note to Pat, thanking her, as well as one to Mrs. Kennedy. Since I had been told that the money eventually came from Mrs. Kennedy's account, I persuaded Mamselle that such a gesture was unnecessary. In that way, she would not be thanking the devious Pat, who had nothing to do with the money, nor Mrs. Kennedy, who would undoubtedly have stopped the arrangement since Mamselle had "only" been her cook.

I didn't go to work for the family until after Joe's stroke. Once Mrs. Kennedy was in charge, she was outraged by paying so much money to the staff, and she certainly had no interest in their social security or other retirement benefits.

Old Joe had created a monster in the form of his highly competitive daughters, suddenly without direction. They seemed to hate the world, and since their world was so self-centered, that meant they were constantly bickering.

Some of the staff members said that Eunice was not changed by Joe's problems. Despite her public charities, she has never been a very nice person.

I remember the first day I met her. Mrs. Kennedy and I were in her bedroom, discussing a letter, when suddenly Eunice burst into the room. Her unkempt hair was freshly washed, and she was wearing an old T-shirt along with a pair of shorts. I don't remember her question for her mother anymore, but I do remember that it was relatively unimportant and could have waited.

I smiled, expecting to introduce myself or be introduced to her. Instead she looked blankly at me for a moment, as though measuring my worth in her life. Then, still without saying a word, she scratched her crotch with her hand in cross between a rude gesture and a dismissal. Her eyes focused on her mother then, and when they were done talking, Eunice left the room. Other than for her scratching her crotch, she never acknowledged my presence. I guess I had been found wanting, as, I would later discover, was most everyone she did not wish to impress.

The only one who was nice was the youngest, Jean. She grew up with Ted and didn't feel the need to dominate everyone and everything the way the others did. Many times she would sneak into my office, then make me promise I would not tell her mother as she gave me tickets to a show, fresh cut flowers, or some other thoughtful gift. She knew that Mrs. Kennedy would see such human kindness as improper. "The Secretary," as I was usually called by Mrs. Kennedy, and the rest of the servants in the home received their pay. We needed nothing else, except, perhaps, the used bras she invariably offered me from time to time.

During the months that followed Joe's stroke, Rose continued her life as she had before. This time, when she turned down invitations, Joe was her excuse and no one argued. They saw her as selflessly dedicated to his care, though the truth was that he could not stand her.

BG: I WILL NEVER FORGET the look of rage on Rosemary's face when she saw her mother the first time I was in the home during a visit. She screamed at Mrs. Kennedy, her devastated mind seeing her mother as a horror. No matter what had happened in the past, my heart ached for Mrs. Kennedy. However, I learned from the staff that this was not her first experience with family hostility.

I was told that the first time the partially paralyzed Joe returned home and Mrs. Kennedy walked into his bedroom, he became intensely agitated. He began yelling at her, angrily waving his still-functioning left arm. She was forced to retreat from his wrath.

It was all so sad, so seemingly needless.

Ann Gargan was both a blessing and a hindrance for Joe. She had no understanding of a stroke victim's needs. She also seemed not to comprehend that Joe never wanted to stop working. Bored with business and turned away from the seat of power he had coveted, Joe had returned to making movies after Jack became president. Robert J. Donovan had written the book *PT-109*, an exciting account of heroism at sea with a few key facts deliberately ignored. Joe Kennedy decided to produce the project, buying the film rights for $120,000, then paying $2,500 to each of the surviving crew members and any crew member's widow in exchange for the right to portray the men in the film. Jack Kennedy approved the script and was delighted to learn he would be portrayed by Cliff Robertson. However, the film was so innocuous that everyone saw through the charade of changing history to suit the White House. *Look* magazine described the film's quality as "just this side of *The Bobbsey Twins.*"

A movie deal was also negotiated for Bob based on his book, *The Enemy Within*, the story of corruption in the Teamsters union. Joe helped negotiate the deal with Twentieth Century–Fox.

But the pace had slowed slightly. Joe owned a farm in Osterville, on Cape Cod, where he regularly went horseback riding. And there was the golf at Oyster Harbor Golf Club when he was on the Cape. But he felt frustrated by not being so intensely involved with business as he had been, and that frustration showed in an increasingly fiery temper. He was hostile to Rose, and when he flubbed a shot on the golf course, he would often curse and fling his club in anger.

Once he had his stroke, Ann Gargan became destructively protective. Joe had almost full use of his left side. He had full motor skills for feeding himself. Yet Ann was feeding him his meals, determined that he should not have to do anything for himself. He had led a long, full life in her estimation. He had cared for others. Now it was his turn to be pampered. She had no sense that, unless he pushed himself, using his good muscles to the fullest and working his weak side to recover whatever could be restored, he would be a cripple until death.

The strong-willed Ann Gargan met her match in the equally strong-willed private-duty nurse, Rita Dallas, RN. She would work with Joe Kennedy, both in his homes and in Horizon House, the treatment program in Pennsylvania where he would learn to walk. She was not afraid to risk Ann's wrath when the young woman was acting out of love, not good medicine.

Rose was unsure how to handle herself following Joe's stroke. Her routine had been changed in ways she had never thought possible. Death was not difficult to adapt to. The person was gone from your life. There might be the pain of loneliness, but a routine could be restructured around his or her absence.

Joe was neither dead nor alive. He had more potential than Rosemary, and it was imperative that he be kept at home to achieve whatever recovery might be possible. There was a staff to care for him. There would be no more showgirls, no more humiliations for Rose. Yet the cycles of their lives were radically altered, and each day that he became either better or worse, she had to alter her plans. If she got involved.

Rose had trouble with her new role. She seemed to see herself as mistress of the house, the person suddenly in charge, and she wanted to do a good job. Instead of pinning notes all over her clothing, she took a large diaper safety pin, attached it to her blouse, and used it to hold all the notes she wrote to herself. Then, as she completed a task, she would pull the note from the diaper pin and discard it. By the end of the day she took great pride in wearing the note-free diaper pin as a badge of honor. It was her reward for doing all that she had scheduled for herself.

Rose also tried to better manage the household budget. She discovered that the nurses were making regular trips to the kitchen to grab a cup of coffee. Their shifts were long and hard as they exercised Joe and helped him restore his muscles. They used coffee to keep going, yet Rose was outraged by the possible cost. She did not know what anyone spent for the coffee, but she was aware that coffee prices were rising. She asked Rita Dallas to keep the nursing staff to one cup of coffee per person per shift. Instead, Dallas had a hot plate installed in the nurses' station so they would not go to the kitchen so frequently. Since Rose had no interest in seeing Joe, she never knew.

Rose tried to maintain her routine as much as possible, ignoring her husband entirely. She could mentally wall off the sections of their home where he was receiving care, then return to her schedule of golf, swimming, walking, shopping, travel, and the like. However, Rita Dallas felt Joe needed to be returned to a normal environment as much as possible, and this meant having breakfast with his wife.

Joe Kennedy was desperately trying to retain some semblance of normal life. His secretary would come for dictation. He would telephone the New York office and call Jack at the White House. His sons would tell him what was happening in their worlds. The men in the New York office would listen to him, then promise to handle everything. And his secretary would fill her book with shorthand. Yet what none of them ever told Joe was that he was completely unintelligible. He could communicate no and yes. He could yell and have what amounted to a temper tantrum. But from the time of his stroke until he died, he never spoke coherently.

According to Rita Dallas, Rose was not pleased the first morning Joe was to be brought to breakfast. She took dinner in his room and thought that was enough of a change from her routine. Joe tended to drool from the paralyzed side of his face, and she thought that seeing it at breakfast would be unpleasant and embarrassing for him.

It was difficult to tell whether Rose was concerned for her husband's well-being or for her own. She seemed to have assumed that he would soon die, talking of life after his death. She bought a mourning dress and arranged to have it packed whenever she moved from home to home. The dress would stay with her the rest of Joe's life, even though years would pass before his death. Even Ann Gargan discussed what was presumed to be an inevitable event in the near future, saying that she would probably never again return to Florida. She hated the place.

Joe was delighted the first day of what seemed more like normal living. He used his left hand to groom himself, carefully brushing and combing his hair in a hand mirror held by the nurse.

Joe's nurse could not stay by his side in the dining room. The hired help did not eat with the family, even if the help was an RN whose job might mean the partial or full recovery of Joe Kennedy. At breakfast would be Rose, Joe, and Ann Gargan, who wheeled him to his place. Rita Dallas was relegated to the doorway between the dining room and the library, a position from which she could see what was taking place.

A stroke victim might have any number of problems. Joe had become dexterous with his left hand and would have no trouble feeding himself. But food might shift to a side of his face where chewing was difficult, causing him to swallow wrong and choke. Though this was unlikely, the RN had to be near just in case.

Rita Dallas later learned that Joe Kennedy thoroughly disliked his wife's rules. When he was ambassador to the Court of St. James, he frequently encouraged the paid staff to eat with the family. The nannies and governesses were invariably impeccably mannered, one of the reasons they were hired to rear the children. Watching them eat was always a lesson in proper etiquette, and Joe relied upon their presence at meals as a lesson for the children.

Rose was a snob, though. If you were paid, you did not dine with the family. She would not break her rule, not even for her husband's health.

Ann created the problem with what seemed like an innocent prank. Rose buried her nose in the morning newspaper. She always read the papers and would not change just because of her husband's presence. She was so tiny that she was completely hidden from view as she read whatever news she thought might interest Joe.

Slipping underneath the table, carefully avoiding touching her aunt Rose, Ann maneuvered to where Joe sat. Then she carefully mimicked every gesture of her aunt.

Joe Kennedy seemed to laugh, and then, in the manner familiar to all caregivers of stroke victims, the laughter turned to uncontrollable shaking, laughing, and crying. Joe could not control physical reactions to emotions. He could not control anything. By the time his nurse rushed to his side, he was bent over weeping. Ann was clinging to him, horrified by what had happened. Rose, who knew nothing of the cause, was horrified, certain she had done something terrible, yet confused by what had occurred.

The family member with the most understanding for Joe's emotional ordeal was Jacqueline. The first lady would visit regularly, encouraging the man she called Grandpa, including being present at his earliest efforts to walk. She instinctively understood what his wife, daughters, and niece had to learn—that the deformities of a stroke victim could be psychologically depressing.

One day, Rita Dallas found that someone had wrapped Joe's deformed right hand in a scarf to hide it. She unwrapped it, knowing that its appearance would be less depressing than thinking that others wanted it hidden. Jacqueline would kiss the deformed hand when she greeted him. And when he seemed unusually depressed from being so helpless, she would lay her head on his lap so he could stroke it with his good hand. She understood that by his seemingly comforting her, he became more comfortable with himself. He was always calmer for her presence, unlike his reactions to all the other Kennedy women, who failed to understand his emotions.

Ted Kennedy made his bid for a government job the year of the stroke. As the family joked, he had to do something, and a Senate seat seemed ideal. Then the Kennedy men would be in the White House, the Justice Department, and the Senate.

One wonders what would have happened to Ted Kennedy had he had the courage of his older sister Kathleen. While coordinating campaigns throughout the Southwest, Ted had fallen in love with the region. He thought he would like to move there, buy a small-town newspaper, and become a publisher. He had the wealth to set up the business, the income to cover himself in lean times, and he could enjoy the business rather than doing other people's bidding.

No one tolerated Ted's moment of independence, though. His father insisted that he return to Massachusetts, to use the base the family dominated. There was no sense in his trying to prove himself. The Kennedys had done that for him. He should take advantage of his name and circumstances, not pioneer new ground.

Reluctantly Ted returned, taking a job as Suffolk County's assistant district attorney. It was not a make-work position, though many viewed it as little more than political patronage for him. He worked hard, but everyone knew that he was being groomed for his boss's job or something higher. No one knew what until Joe, just prior to his stroke, made clear what Ted's future would be.

Ted lacked the experience to run for the Senate. He lacked the interest. In addition, he had a few scandals in his past, including having been expelled from Harvard years earlier for cheating. However, unlike his brothers, Ted had the courage to face his own actions. After the expulsion he enlisted in the military, served his time without seeking his father's intervention, then went on to law school. He would become a notorious womanizer and overzealous drinker, but he was never again involved in an academic scandal.

Unfortunately for Ted, his last name was Kennedy. Joe had made his pronouncement before his stroke, and now he would never again be able to discuss the matter. Bob and Jack did not want Ted to run, but since it was inevitable, they were determined he would win, whatever that cost.

The cost was high. Steve Smith was sent to manage Ted's campaign, thus giving him extra training for more involved political roles in the future. Jack summoned *Boston Globe* reporter Bob Healy to the White House to try to get him to suppress a story he had written about Ted's cheating at Harvard. Jack privately complained to friends that cheating on exams was the worst thing you could do if you wanted the support of WASPs. He joked that they only respected you if you stole from stockholders and banks.

Rose was up to the challenge of defusing some of the criticism. She would never again campaign the way she had for Jack, but she still knew when she needed to make an appearance. And she still had better instincts than her children or their advisers when it came to Boston mudslinging.

Taking on the issue of the Kennedy dynasty in office, she was quoted as saying, "I agree with those of you who are opposed to my son, or at least I can understand. Jack was 'too young,' as I recall. So was Bobby 'too young.' But they're doing pretty well, aren't they? Matter of fact, I wanted Teddy to go into the Church. But the trouble was that he wanted to start out as a bishop."

By acknowledging the feelings against Ted, and by making a joke that reinforced the image people disliked—the too aggresive young upstart reaching too high—she defused the hostility.

Rose did not concern herself with Ted's national image, which was terrible in those days. The *New York Times* was especially vocal in its editorial criticism of the Kennedys trying to create a dynasty. They stressed Ted's lack of experience. They made clear that any other man with his background but a different family name would never get past the Senate primary.

What Rose understood was that the Kennedys owned Massachusetts, partially through what they had done, and partially because they dominated the corruption. Some voted for Ted because they wanted to do something for Jack. Some voted for Ted because they knew full well he would have the full weight of the White House on his side when he tried to gain benefits for the state. Some voted for Ted because they thought Rose made sense. And ultimately Ted won both the primary and the election.

Rose also spent more time at the White House, sometimes with Joe, sometimes without. She was usually given the Lincoln bedroom, which she made clear to all who would listen was not up to the standard of the bedroom she had enjoyed in Queen Victoria's private chambers. She also occasionally hosted or acted as cohost for events where her presence added to the royal image of the Kennedys—the queen mother in residence.

Rose and Joe were in Hyannis Port in November of 1963. He had begun to deteriorate, the paralysis worse than in the past, his voice gone. Rose spent little time with him, relying upon Ann Gargan to be the family connection. Death she had handled, would handle again sooner than she imagined. Weakness, illness, and slow deterioration leading to death were quite different. She wanted no part of them. It was not as if she feared for her own future so much as she seemed to want to distance herself from what she perceived to be an imperfection.

Jack and Ted were becoming close, and Jack liked to reinforce the relationship for the voters of Massachusetts. During a speech earlier that year, he commented that Teddy was concerned with winning the election on his own and not being judged by the family name. Jack said, "Teddy wants to be judged on his own; so he is thinking of changing his name . . . from Teddy Kennedy to Teddy Roosevelt."

Jack had last seen his parents on Sunday, October 20. He had gone to his father, put his arm around Joe's shoulders, and kissed him on the forehead. Then he walked to the helicopter that awaited him, paused, and returned to kiss his father once more. He told Rita Dallas to take good care of his father, then left. In hindsight, those who witnessed the event thought he might have known that he would never see the old man again.

The morning of the assassination was beautiful in Hyannis Port. The weather was cool but lacked the bite of winter. Most of the flowers were still in bloom, and the air was clear, blue, a perfect day. After Rose returned from mass and breakfast, she and Joe took a ride in their station wagon to view the scenery. As usual, after Joe was returned home, Rose continued on to play nine holes of golf in her condensed version of the game.

Joe napped after lunch, and Rose decided to go to her room for a rest. Only Ann was active, listening to the radio with the volume so loud, Rose became angry. She went to Ann, demanding that she shut off the noise, only to be told of a bulletin that the president had been shot.

Perhaps as an emotional defense, Rose was not worried, she later claimed. Jack had nearly died several times. Although his Addison's disease was being kept from the public, the deterioration caused by both the disease and the type of treatment available to him at the time were expected to take his life in no more than a few years. If he could retain his strength through another election campaign and win, he might die in office, much like Franklin Roosevelt. And, of course, there had been the horror of the sinking of his boat and the desperate fight for survival that followed. In Rose's mind, if Jack had been shot, he would recover.

Rose returned to her room, agitated yet determined to show self-control in front of the family and staff. Then, a few minutes later, Bob telephoned from Washington to say that Jack was in serious condition and not expected to live. Shortly after that came word that he was dead.

A telephone call came from Lyndon Johnson, who had immediately been sworn in as the new president. Johnson always hated the Kennedys. He had been Senate majority leader, far more powerful a man than Jack Kennedy. He also was a power player, rumored to have as many mob connections through New Orleans's Carlos Marcello as Joe was alleged to have through Chicago's Frank Costello. Yet when Johnson called, he was compassionate, not talking to a member of a political family but rather to a mother in shock, a woman who had lost a son. He did not know what to say, yet realized that his floundering did not matter. Nothing was right, nothing would ever be right again for Rose. "I wish to God there was something I could do," Johnson told her. "I just wanted you to know that."

Lady Bird Johnson was next on the line. Lady Bird had campaigned with Rose in 1960, and unlike the animosity between the men, the two women experienced mutual respect. Rose found Lady Bird warm, intelligent, and extremely caring. Neither woman would later remember what they said to each other during their brief talk, though Rose recalled that Lady Bird ended with the words, "We must all realize how fortunate the country was to have your son as long as it did."

BG: BECAUSE OF MRS. KENNEDY'S age and position in life, Lady Bird Johnson treated her with the utmost respect, calling her "ma'am" as a proper lady of the South was trained to do. When discussing it later, Mrs. Kennedy asked why Lady Bird would use that term. When I explained, she accepted the idea but was still puzzled. She told me that she thought the word *ma'am* was only used by domestics when addressing their employers.

Other family members were learning of the death in different ways. Rosemary had allegedly been watching television when the show was interrupted with the news. At least that was the story that was told later. However, she was in such a poor mental condition that if she had been propped in front of the set, she would not have comprehended what was being said.

The Shrivers were notified, though only of a wounding, while having lunch at the Lafayette Hotel. After they left, they heard the news on the street.

Rose decided not to tell Joe when he awakened. She wanted his physician to come from Boston, and for Ted and Eunice to come from Washington. Jackie would not be there, of course, and Bob would have to stay with Jackie. Pat was flying in from California, and the arrivals of the others were being coordinated. Rose wanted as many of the family present as possible.

According to one story of what happened, Ann Gargan unplugged all the television sets in the house, convincing Joe of an electrical problem. He wondered why Ann was there at all since she was supposed to be leaving to visit some friends in Detroit. But she said that the gardener had been in a minor accident and she planned to stay a little longer until she knew everything was all right.

According to another story, Ann, intensely excited, rushed into Joe's room and said, "As you see, I haven't left yet. There's been an accident—" At that point Rita Dallas stopped her, saying that Rose wanted Ann to wait until one of the sons arrived. Rose was terrified that something would happen to Joe right then, and she thought he would handle the news better with Bob or Ted present. "My car got banged up," Ann quickly covered. "That was the accident. That's why I can't go. So I'm staying."

Finally, having alerted everyone in the manner she wanted, Rose put on her aging black coat and went outside. The beach was cold, the tourists long gone, the wind bringing a chill to the air that was not felt farther inland. The sun was still bright, the day still beautiful, yet nothing would be the same again. Once more the family had been robbed of its position, this time by a crazed gunman whose motives remained unknown.

Rose walked for miles, eventually being joined by her nephew Joe Gargan. Sometimes they talked. Sometimes they were silent. Yet with each step, Rose was trying to remind herself that the family must continue.

As had become usual, Rose avoided telling Joe. That burden fell to Eunice when she arrived. She had been delayed because she had been checking on the others affected by the shooting, especially Gov. John Connally, who was wounded.

There are two stories about what happened. The first is that Joe was told nothing the day of the assassination. Rose awakened early the next day, as usual, attending the seven-o'clock mass at St. Francis Xavier Church. Then she returned home to breakfast with Joe, keeping the *New York Times* from its usual position by his plate.

Ted and Eunice also attended mass, returning at nine-thirty after their father had exercised in a covered, heated swimming pool that had been built on the estate to assist with his therapy. Together they went to his room where Joe motioned to Ted to plug in the television set. Ted did as asked, then suddenly pulled the plug, looked at his father, and told him that Jack was dead.

The second story, later related by author Larry Leamer in his book on the Kennedy women, did not mention the mass or Joe's swim. Instead, Eunice, accompanied by Ted, tried to speak, at first almost blithering, talking about Jack having an accident, being okay, being dead, being in heaven. It seemed she was trying to find words to express the unexpressible, at the same time seeking reassurance that somehow there was order, there was logic, that Jack was in heaven.

Joe turned from Eunice to Ted, who said, "Dad, Jack was shot." Then as both children embraced their father, weeping, Eunice quietly sobbed that Jack was dead.

Rose remembered something similar to the Leamer story, though she included Ann Gargan, the doctor, a nurse, and "perhaps one or two others" as present.

Joe read the newspaper story, then lay back on his bed, brushing the paper onto the floor. He had been given a sedative and was soon asleep.

Reporters had established a vigil outside the Kennedy compound, and they surmised the timing. A flag, always raised in the early-morning hours, was flown daily from a flagpole on the front lawn. That day, to raise the flag would be unseemly. It needed to be at half-mast, yet to put it there before Joe was told would have been to alert him to the death. The staff chose instead to wait for Ted and Eunice to tell their father. Just before ten o'clock in the morning, the reporters watched the flag slowly rise to the top of the flagpole where it waved in the breeze. Once fully unfurled, it was immediately lowered to half-mast.

Joe was physically able to go to the funeral, which was held the following Monday. However, he stayed in Hyannis Port, watching on television, Father John Cavanaugh, a longtime friend and former president of Notre Dame University, by his side. They watched together, Father Cavanaugh helping him through his grief.

There was a procession of family members from the White House to the cathedral, but Rose chose not to join them. She attended an early mass, taking Communion, so she would not have to go forward at the cathedral. Finally she was driven with the others to the grave site in Arlington, after which she returned to the White House. By evening she was back in Hyannis Port.

If there was a moment when Rose Kennedy became beloved in the hearts of millions of Americans, it was the day of Jack's funeral. The various Kennedys were remembered for different reasons on that day.

Perhaps most vivid for those who were present, watched the funeral procession on television, or saw the pictures in newspapers and magazines throughout the world was the image of John junior. Little more than a toddler, he stood with his mother, his hand coming up in a salute as the caisson bearing his father's coffin passed by. He had no understanding of death or what was happening to the man with whom he had once played hide-and-seek in the Oval Office. He did not know that in the coffin being pulled on the caisson was all that remained of the man whose name he would bear. Yet his gesture touched the hearts of all who saw it, a little boy saluting his dad, the commander in chief of the world's most powerful nation, just before he was laid to rest.

Others remember the quiet dignity of the veiled Jacqueline. The public watched endless replays of the assassination, and its aftermath. Later she was photographed, her dress stained with blood, at the swearing-in ceremony of Lyndon Johnson, an essential part of the transition in a democratic nation.

Rose represented something else. The day Jack Kennedy was laid to rest, Rose was every suffering woman in America. She spoke with Ethiopian emperor Haile Selassie, one of the dignitaries attending the funeral, a man whose own son had died a few years earlier. "It's wrong for parents to bury their children," said Rose. "It should be the other way around."

Selassie, feeling his own grief, said, "It's a violation of nature."

It was as though Rose Kennedy was being taunted by life. She was like a person in hell where everything she ever wanted was briefly hers to touch, to taste, to smell, then was abruptly withdrawn. She had loved the young Joe Kennedy, not for what he was but for what she fantasized him to be. She had loved him with a passion reserved solely for those too young to have experienced all the vagaries of life. She had loved him "forever" as she was certain in her heart of hearts he had loved her.

Joe was both the forbidden fruit from the tree of knowledge her father had warned her to avoid and the sly serpent whispering falsehoods in her ears. He had briefly brought her to heights of emotional ecstasy, then stripped her of dignity, security, and self-worth piece by piece. He had used women—chorus girls, movie stars, and anyone else he could seduce—as the knife too dull to slash yet providing a thousand cuts whose pain was ultimately much deeper than anything Rose could once have imagined enduring.

Rose feared for her oldest daughter, a woman of great beauty yet seemingly of limited intelligence and little sense of life. Yet even as she worked to change Rosemary, that beauty, too, would be taken away, the essence of her being destroyed, and a living shell returned.

Rose had raised her oldest son, the namesake of her husband, to be the leader of a dynasty that would bring honor and glory to the family. And Joe junior had died in war.

Rose had reached the pinnacle of society through both wealth and the appointment of her husband to the post of ambassador to the Court of St. James. She had slept on Queen Victoria's bed. She had been snubbed by the Brahmins of Boston when she had her coming-out party, then watched as her daughters were accepted by the Anglican King and Queen of England. Yet as she reveled in hard-won respect, Joe was making misstatements and bad judgment calls that brought the family disgrace.

Next came Kathleen—the lively, rebellious girl known as Kick. Rose's second-oldest daughter had ingratiated herself with the oldest, most prominent families in England, families whose histories included hostility to the Irish. Where Rose had been finally accepted by royalty, it was as though her daughter had become royalty. Until she took a married lover. Until she died in a plane crash.

And now Jack. Rose was the mother of the president, the matriarch of Camelot, envied, honored, and then torn apart by the events of a history she did not want to live. One day her children would recite the catechism of 1960s historical events to her grandchildren the way she and Joe had done when teaching their children about the assassinations and upheavals of World War I.

She had been tantalized, seduced, and then savaged. Again and again she had buried the dead, lost all that she valued.

Rose Kennedy had been an object of derision to some, especially to her staff that witnessed the "frownies," the notes pinned to her blouse, and the other eccentricities. She had been the queen mother to others, the beloved or reviled woman who led an American dynasty.

Yet with the assassination, as the tiny figure stood all in black, a wide-brimmed hat and veil covering her face, she was transformed into something else. She was an aging woman with a dying husband who had buried as many dead as mothers who must rear their children in active war zones. Money had bought her fancier places to grieve, but they had not prevented the endless flow of tears.

Rose Kennedy had become an old lady in pain. She would survive more than thirty more years, the lifetime of Kathleen before her untimely death. Rose would have expensive homes, the luxury of a chauffeur, a maid, a cook, and numerous other trappings of the wealthy. Her face would grace the pages of *People, Newsweek, Time,* and the ultimate chronicler of American celebrity, the *National Enquirer.* She would be classed as an American version of the Queen Mother. Yet what would assure her place in the hearts of Americans was much simpler than that.

In the death of her son, Rose Kennedy was stripped of the trappings of glamour and wealth. She became a woman of the world, though not because of her travels and sophistication. Instead, she became as one with the women in Bangladesh mourning the death of children whose stomachs are bloated from starvation. She became as one with ghetto mothers whose children are victims of the random violence of city streets. She became as one with the mothers of Northern Ireland whose children are murdered in the name of politics and religion. She became as one with the mothers of nations where children die in the midst of the strife of civil war and revolution.

All women may be said to be united in the pain of childbirth. But the lucky ones know only the frustrations of nurturing, sheltering, and educating the children who will one day grow to adulthood, achieve middle age, and mourn the loss of the women who brought them into the world. They will not experience the "violation of nature" mentioned by Haile Selassie.

For some, though, a wound will fester in the heart, the pain of a loss that forever unites them as sisters. The lowest scullery maid and the wealthiest of the highborn, if each must bury a child grown to adulthood, share a bond far stronger than their differences. And so, in her grief, Rose Kennedy found the love and acceptance she had never experienced in her lifetime of social striving.

13

To Begin Anew

On Friday of the week Jack was buried, Rose drove to Dorchester to see her mother, then ninety-eight. (She would die in 1964.) She was too frail to be told of the loss of her grandson. But Rose wanted to see her before returning to Palm Beach. There were memorials to attend, telephone calls to answer, yet the familiar routine that had sustained her for more than seventy years would sustain her through grief.

Rose handled death better than Joe. With Jack dead and Bob preparing to leave the attorney general's office, Joe had no further access to power. He would never again hear his son's voice briefing him on affairs of state. He would never again see the president's helicopter land in his yard. He had lost everything he ever wanted, and even if Bob or Ted could achieve the White house, he seemed to sense it would not be the same. He would either not live that long or not be healthy enough to contribute.

Thousands of letters came to Rose Kennedy as she and Joe were in Palm Beach for Christmas. Americans felt the need to express their grief.

Rose began answering some of the letters, turning most of them over to her daughters as well as the New York and Washington staff members. Joe could not help, so Rose began focusing on responding to friends.

Rose also appeared at a few of the memorial services. Cardinal Cushing held a solemn high mass in Boston's Holy Cross Cathedral in the late president's honor. The Boston Symphony Orchestra played Mozart's Requiem in D Minor during the mass, Erich Leinsdorf conducting. This was an especially moving part of the mass since Mozart had died during the writing of the Requiem, leaving it as unfinished as Jack's first term in office.

There were other events, other travels, including the renaming of the Paris Quai de Passy as the Avenue du Président Kennedy. Such renamings became frequent in many parts of the world. The John F. Kennedy Library had to be started as well. Although originally planned as a simple archives and reading room related to his presidency, with his death the library was expanded to a full research facility and museum.

On June 19, 1964, Ted Kennedy had his baptism of pain that seemed to be a ritual for the Kennedy sons. He was flying in a private plane with Indiana senator Birch Bayh and his wife, staff member Ed Moss, and a charter pilot. The plane crashed, killing the pilot and Moss. The Bayhs were relatively unharmed, but Ted suffered a severe back injury.

BG: JOE GARGAN TOLD ME that when the doctors examined him, they realized that his injury and his position on the gurney were such that if he was not flipped over onto his stomach, then placed in a special support device, he would die right there. At the same time, if the move was not made correctly, he would be left a paraplegic or worse.

The hospital had the suspension device, but neither the equipment nor the personnel needed to move so seriously injured a patient. Joe, who is approximately six feet four, quickly rounded up several friends of similar size, all of them quite strong. They stood with their palms up, their hands side by side, then slid them underneath Ted, carefully flipping him onto the support device. Their timing had to be flawless; any man who shifted even the smallest part of Ted's body at the wrong moment was likely to cause the senator partial paralysis. Fortunately their effort was successful. Had they waited for equipment from another hospital, the delay would have resulted in irreversible damage.

Ted was forced to remain in bed for six months, most of the time in traction. Like a good Kennedy male, he spent part of the time collecting reminiscences and newspaper clippings about Joe Kennedy Sr. for a memorial book entitled *The Fruitful Bough*. But with Joe unable to shepherd the book through any of his friends, it became a family vanity publication meant to put the old man in the best possible light. Ted also took up oil painting, most of his quite good work being of boats and other marine scenes.

However, Bob would take the spotlight. Insiders had been speculating about his relationship with his sister-in-law Jacqueline, with whom he had been spending extensive time. The two were seen together throughout New York City, dining, going to social gatherings, and the like. Jacqueline had moved into the Carlyle Hotel, where the Kennedys had long maintained a suite, a convenient location for Bob.

The truth was far less dramatic than even some friends wanted to believe. Bob Kennedy was not the saint Rose thought when it came to his marriage. He was also not the open womanizer his brothers had been. He had an affair with actress Marilyn Monroe during the last few months of her life, an affair that also involved Jack, who was the first to date her. And he had been known to have casual relationships while working for the Justice Department. But Jackie was a friend, someone with whom he could share feelings he was uncomfortable sharing with Ethel.

Bob had engaged in a flurry of self-destructive activity shortly after the assassination. Interviews with his staff conducted not long after the murder indicated that they felt that Bob was testing danger, to see the limits of life. He went white-water rafting, for example, and though he was normally safety conscious, not letting anyone, including himself, go on the water without a life jacket, he did not wear his during that period. If he went into the water, he might die without the vest. The staff members interviewed at the time felt that rather than hoping for accidental death, he was reaffirming his being alive. He wanted to walk with death and thumb his nose at it.

Bob, the Kennedys' middle child, had never felt himself quite accepted. More aggressive than Jack, pugnacious like his father, small in physical size relative to his brothers, he seemed to feel close to no one, constantly having to prove himself. He married a woman who fit perfectly into the family, yet he was quieter than Ethel in private, more in tune to Jackie's emotions. To a degree they both felt a little like outsiders. They were also both devoted to their children, the memories of Bob's older children such as Kathleen vividly recalling activities with their father, not their mother.

The Kennedy sisters, along with Ethel, ridiculed Jackie's handling of Jack's death. Eunice derisively called her "the widder." Yet they may have been jealous of the way Jacqueline was treated by the public, of the close relationship she had with "Grandpa Joe."

What they did not understand was the horror of it all. Jack had mocked Jacqueline with his womanizing. Some of the Secret Service agents who had worked the White House detail called Jack a "ten-to-two" president. He liked to have one woman in the early morning, another in the afternoon. He did not flaunt his affairs in front of his wife, but he did have the Secret Service help him coordinate them so Jackie would not be in the same area at the same time.

Jackie had become a political asset, and Jack had to keep her content for the race for reelection. Fortunately she loved the glamour of the White House, the chance to work with the arts and to expose the American people to the rich, colorful history of the building and its interior. She did not want to lose the White House, and she may not have wanted to lose Jack. There was much about him that she loved, and while she hated his womanizing, she had known the same behavior from her father. She also did not have to experience the humiliation that Josie Fitzgerald endured with John Fitzgerald's Toodles or that Rose endured with Joe's Gloria Swanson.

Then there was the horror of the shooting, the shock that caused her to reach out and try to retrieve Jack's brains to somehow keep him alive. Her designer suit was covered with blood.

Bob understood all this. They could and did share much. He became like a protective big brother, as did Peter Lawford, who was by then estranged from the family. However, while Peter was a friend with whom Jackie shared her experiences by letter and telephone as she began traveling again, she could help Bob as much as he was helping her.

Lem Billings, Jack's closest and longest-term friend, told Jacqueline Kennedy biographer C. David Heymann, "At a certain moment when Bobby Kennedy, reaching the depths of his depression, expressed doubts about remaining in Washington and continuing in public service, Jackie sat down and wrote him a letter—a most feeling letter, in which she implored him not to give up, not to quit. She told him she needed him and that the children, especially John junior, needed him as a surrogate father, as somebody they could turn to, now that their own father was gone. And another thing—and this the most vital in the long run—was how much the country still needed him. It was time, she wrote, to honor Jack's memory—not continue to mourn it. They would both, herself included, be negligent in their responsibilities to that memory if they collapsed. Jack would want them both to carry on what he had stood for, and died for—she through the children, Bobby through public service."

Bob came to agree with his sister-in-law, and in 1964 he ran for Senate in New York. He had spent much of his life in New York State, and though most people considered the Kennedys to be Massachusetts incarnate, Bob could legitimately lay claim to being a New Yorker. For twenty years he had gone to school in Riverdale and Bronxville. Ethel spent less time in New York, though she had briefly lived in Larchmont and Rye. However, to solidify the second-generation relationship with the state, Pat Kennedy purchased a co-op on the East Side of Manhattan in July, and Bob and Ethel bought a twenty-five-room estate in Glen Cove, Long Island. The house, on five acres of land, included a forty-foot swimming pool and a large playhouse for the children. Yet most of their time would be spent in a suite at the Carlyle in Manhattan or on their estate in Virginia.

Jacqueline Kennedy also adopted New York City as her home, though she did so because she wanted to spend the rest of her life there. She purchased a fifteen-room—five bedrooms, five baths—cooperative apartment at 1040 Fifth Avenue at the corner of Eighty-fifth Street. The apartment, previously owned by the administration defense secretary Robert McNamara, had a view of Central Park and the Metropolitan Museum of Art.

Rose was originally going to stay away from the campaign trail. There was too much pain, too many memories. However, she gradually changed her mind.

Ethel did not wait for her mother-in-law to begin her own version of Coffee With the Kennedys. She worked from the family's Glen Cove home, the walls carefully decorated with photographs meant to link Bob with Jack's legacy. Her prepared speech stressed the spirit that Jack had given the country, a spirit that caused Americans to be more concerned with those less fortunate. The implication was that Bob would carry forth that spirit if elected.

Chartered buses brought spouses of dignitaries to the homes, an approach reminiscent of her grandfather-in-law's use of women for his Boston campaigns.

Rose began working with Bob during his campaign as she realized he was having trouble relating to people. His image wasn't clear. To some, he was a wealthy carpetbagger, entering a state just in time to try to win an election. To others, he was a spoiled rich boy who could not understand the poor. To still others, he was a tough conservative who had gone head-to-head against corruption in the Teamsters union, attacking the leadership without hurting the rank and file. And to still others, he was the symbol of caring for the poor and downtrodden.

The Kennedy sisters had trouble conveying a solid image of Bob, other than to paint him as carrying on his brother's legacy. Only Eunice was comfortable going into low-income areas to talk with people. Pat and Jean were much more comfortable in the wealthier cities of the state. But Rose understood how to sell a candidate, wherever he went, so she gave Bob advice in addition to her own campaigning.

Bob needed to appear happier to be with each group before which he spoke, his mother reminded him. He had a tendency to withdraw emotionally because he hated campaigning. Rose not only sent him notes telling him how to change his actions and appearance, she also began appearing with him occasionally, putting on a show. She would tease her son about whatever seemed appropriate—the family, his being ill at ease in the public eye, or something else. Then, when he was relaxed, she would start talking politics with him. It was like a late-night television interview show with Rose as the comedian/host, and it worked brilliantly. Bob became humanized as never before.

Despite the success of her support, Rose realized that Bob was probably frustrated by her constant suggestions, knowing that what she was really saying was that he did not know how to campaign effectively. Finally, afraid that her endless notes and calls might alienate her son, she wrote a letter meant to restore his sense of humor: "This may be the last time I'll write a letter like this, because I remember Socrates, who used to give a lot of advice in Athens, was finally given hemlock to drink!"

Rose went anywhere she thought she could do some good. The day of her fiftieth wedding anniversary, she ignored Joe to sell Bob in the upstate city of Newburgh.

The efforts paid off. On election day, Bob took the state by seven hundred thousand votes.

Bobby's decision to challenge Lyndon Johnson for the White House four years later has remained controversial to this day. Those who have studied his campaign strongly question Bob's courage and his motives. By 1968, Lyndon Johnson was in trouble. The antiwar movement was growing in momentum, and he was facing an open rebellion from Minnesota senator Eugene McCarthy.

Bob Kennedy had made no secret of his dislike for Johnson. Bob had treated him like an outsider when he was vice president and could not hide his disdain for him once Johnson succeeded Jack. Other Kennedys maintained cordial ties to the White House. Sargent Shriver worked closely with LBJ, and Johnson was actively sympathetic to Eunice's work with the retarded. He even named her to the President's Commission on Mental Retardation.

Jackie supposedly was also close to the White House. Johnson was genuinely concerned about the lives of Caroline, John junior, and old Joe. Some writers have said that the Johnsons contacted all of them on a regular basis. And both Johnsons were sympathetic to Jackie's interest in historic renovation and preservation of the art and interior of the White House.

Senator McCarthy had actually gone to see Bob Kennedy before challenging Johnson. McCarthy believed that if Bob Kennedy ran, he could win, could unseat Johnson, then end the war. Toward this end McCarthy consulted with Bob in November of 1967, only to be turned away. Bob told him he had no intention of running, and if Gene should make his move, he could count on Bob's support.

To even McCarthy's amazement, he won 40 percent of the vote in the New Hampshire primary, mortally wounding the Johnson presidency. By the end of March 1968, Johnson would announce that he would not seek a second full term as president.

Bob Kennedy had talked privately of running for president even as he was assuring McCarthy he would not. Some of the men closest to Jack were advising against such a move, as was his brother Ted. Even Bob knew that Joe would have spoken against him had he been better able to communicate, for the timing was off, the party too divided.

Public statements have indicated that the Kennedy women supported Bob. Eunice avoided the fray because of her connections with the Johnson White House. But a number of authors have said that Ethel was intensely enthusiastic, Jean and Pat offering both personal support and their money. Bob had not consulted with Jacqueline, though he knew he would have her support if he asked.

BG: MAMSELLE WAS PRESENT when the family met to discuss Bob's running for president. She was not in the room, but the arguing was so loud, she overheard everything being said. She remembered a different situation from that presented to the public. She told me that no one, including Mrs. Kennedy, wanted Bob to run for president. They were certain he was going to get killed, that he was taking a risk for reasons that no longer mattered. The presidency seemed a death sentence, not a viable goal.

On March 15, 1968, Ted Kennedy was sent to Minnesota to tell Gene McCarthy that, because of his having shown Johnson his days in office were probably numbered, Bob would now break his pledge to Gene and run. Both Bob's actions and his making Ted contact McCarthy, who had personally spoken with Bob five months earlier, were less than honorable. However, Ethel, like her mother-in-law, put her own spin on the delays. She was quoted as saying, "That shows you how great Bobby is. He heard out all the arguments, then he made up his mind and did what he thought was right."

Bob, knowing the truth about himself, delighted in his wife's words. He commented that no matter what he did, Ethel always thought he was right and his critics were wrong.

Memories have blurred concerning Bob's run for the presidency. The tendency is to remember a national outpouring of support, a united front against both Johnson's past and the Republicans. In truth, Bob Kennedy could not have been more divisive, and Joe realized it. The Democratic Party was horribly split. The betrayal of Gene McCarthy, who had had the courtesy to clear his run with Bob, angered many, including those who disagreed with the Minnesota senator. The failure to support the incumbent Democratic president angered others. And the fact that Bob had not paid his dues other than being the surviving oldest Kennedy son angered still others. Other men were considered more deserving, more experienced, and better able to lead.

Rita Dallas was present when Bob broke the news to his father. He visited his parents the day before he announced his candidacy, and the nurse thought it obvious that Joe was not happy about the move. Only Rose seemed supportive, though whether she believed in the rightness of the timing and the move or only longed to be in the spotlight again is unknown.

Ethel remained the most enthusiastic of the Kennedys, with Jacqueline almost as delighted. This came to a head one evening when Bobby, Jacqueline, Ethel, and others were examining the primary polls. Lyndon Johnson had formally announced his decision not to run for reelection

on March 31. At the same time, Democratic support for Bob was growing rapidly. "Looks like we're going to make it," Bob said happily.

Jacqueline, thrilled, said, "Won't it be wonderful when we get back in
the White House?" She had embraced the Kennedy family when she
was first lady, having an open-door policy toward the various siblings, in-
laws, nieces, and nephews of her husband. She saw the taking of the
White House as Rose did, as a family affair no matter which Kennedy
couple "ruled."

But Ethel had come to hate Jacqueline. She worried that her husband
might have had an affair with her. Even if he hadn't, she had always
hated her sister-in-law, and the idea that a popular former first lady
might intrude on her moment in the spotlight was outrageous. She
angrily retorted, "What do you mean *we?*"

Rose developed a personal, unwritten handbook for campaigning.
First, she would regularly advise Bob concerning any problems. Her
notes and calls to him included warning him to talk slowly, his speech
often much too rapid to be effective. She made certain that his grammar was correct during his prepared speeches. She told him when to get
a haircut. She also helped him find ways to soften his image as being
ruthless, focusing on his handling of tough assignments such as his
probe of labor racketeering, which had resulted in threats against his
family. He was a man dedicated to fighting for the public good, or so
she wanted his image to be. In that way, he would be more likely viewed
as intense rather than ruthless.

The rest of Rose's rules were meant for herself and the others campaigning on Bob's behalf. For example, if talking to a crowd after a
formal speech was taking too long, the speaker should not be rushed
away by campaign aides. Instead, someone should come up and stress
that there was another engagement and he or she should not be late. Or
the person should say that a family member was waiting. Whatever
tactic was used, it was always meant to assure that the people left behind, unable to shake the candidate's or the other speaker's hand, felt it
would be rude for the person *not* to leave. Just saying it was time to go
implied that the candidate thought the people waiting to shake his
hand were not important.

Rose developed ways to reduce the chance of having a sore right hand
after shaking hundreds or thousands of hands at various events. She
learned what shoes to wear for standing in the long receiving lines. She
also developed tricks such as strategically placing an armchair or a couch
right behind where she would be standing. Then, when her feet became

tired, she could half-lean on the arm and reduce the weight on her feet. The shift was so slight that few realized what she was doing. Those who did notice were impressed that she had found a way to stay and talk with them when she was obviously tired.

Rose also learned to avoid standing in receiving lines with local politicians and local candidates when speaking around the country. Some of her critics saw this as her trying to stay above lesser men than her son. Others saw her as being a loyalist only to Bob, not to the party as a whole. But in truth, she had learned that local candidates always had large numbers of family and friends in the audience. The receiving line would stop, sometimes for several minutes, as acquaintances talked. This added an hour or more to a stop that needed to be briefer in order to keep a realistic travel and speaking schedule.

Rose made certain that she, Bob, and the Kennedy siblings working on the campaign were always punctual. Just as she realized that the gatherings of women in poor communities wanted to see her in fine clothes as a sign of respect for them, so she saw punctuality as a sign of respect for the audience. Being late implied that the group that caused the delay was of greater concern.

The only time a certain testiness crept into Rose's handling of her primary campaigning was when Kennedy money was to be spent. Joe Kennedy could no longer authorize funds. Rose was more aware of the family involvement through voluntary contributions within the family and the financing from the New York office. The trust funds had been established so that contributions could be made where Joe or his aides thought expedient, then the children would be notified by letter of the contributions "they" had made. She may not have known the extent of Joe's past vote buying, but she knew from early childhood that vote buying was a part of politics. When one reporter too many pushed her, she remembered saying, "It's our money and we're free to spend it any way we please. It's part of this campaign business. If you have money, you spend it to win."

The campaign was not going as well as the family had hoped. Rose's efforts were effective, but her heart was not in it. She knew that Joe would never have allowed Bob to go for the presidency when he did. His actions were premature. She and Joe seemed almost alone among the Kennedys in realizing that being sentimental for a return to "Camelot" was not adequate reason to run.

Jacqueline was also uneasy. She understood better than any of the other Kennedys how hostile some Americans could be. She felt that Bob was facing the same type of political climate that had resulted in Jack's assassination.

Still the family campaigned. Ethel had ten children and was pregnant with her eleventh.

Bob was not dominating the Democratic primaries as he had hoped. On May 28, 1968, Bob lost in the Oregon primary to McCarthy. Jack had never lost a primary. Still, there was the big prize, the California primary on June 5.

BG: BOB PLACED A CALL to Ted when he lost in Oregon. The news media were going crazy with the story. There were headlines about Bob everywhere, and the nightly news ran feature after feature about Bob and the loss. He had expected to win the state, and Ted couldn't resist teasing him. When Ted's receptionist asked who was calling, Bob said, "Just say it's Bobby."

Ted got on the phone and impishly asked, "Bobby who?"

California was Bob Kennedy country. He spent so many hours campaigning throughout the state that when he reached Los Angeles, he was physically ill—exhausted, vomiting, and dizzy. Even worse, when Bob and his son David took a few hours off to relax in the ocean, the water was too cold and rough for casual swimming. David got caught in the undertow along with his father, who fought not only to save himself but also his son. They were tossed about in the waves, swallowed enough water to be a little sick, and were bruised by the violence of the turbulence. But they were fine.

On June 5, Rose had been watching the election returns from Hyannis Port, keeping both a television and a radio turned on so she would miss nothing. By eleven P.M. Eastern time, Bob was steadily moving ahead and seemed the likely winner. However, with three hours' difference between coasts, it seemed more sensible for Rose to go to bed rather than wait to hear the final results.

Rose awakened at six A.M., turning on the television as she dressed for mass. She heard then that Bob had been taken to a hospital, though she did not know why. She hoped that there had been a minor accident during a victory celebration. She had no idea he had been shot until Ann Gargan came into her room and told her.

Rose insisted upon going to mass and was joined by Monsignor Thomson, their pastor. They rode to church together, praying. The rest of the day, having learned exactly what had happened, she busied herself in the house, cleaning, rearranging possessions, doing anything to keep distracted, accomplishing nothing except getting through the day. At one point photographer Ted Polumbaum saw her walking on the broad driveway behind the house. She wore a light pink coat, white socks, oxford sport shoes, and sunglasses. She was carrying a tennis ball, bouncing it mindlessly as she paced back and forth on the drive, stopping only to pick it up when she dropped it.

Later that day, Rose went to the Hyannisport Club, where she took her three balls to the fifteenth tee and played her usual three holes. Her actions were mechanical, the routine seeming to help ease the horror of what was taking place. By the next morning, June 6, Bob was gone.

Bob's death was particularly traumatic for his son David. He was supposed to have been in bed in the hotel, but instead was watching his father's triumph. He watched as his father was shot. Then he watched the replays as the news was repeated again and again. No one was present to take David away, to talk with him, to help him. Eventually Sen. John Glenn of Ohio, famous for his pioneering work in space, came to see him. But Glenn was not family.

Had the Kennedys not been reared to be so insular, to see themselves as somehow separate from the rest of the world, Bob's children, Ethel, and the family as a whole would have received intense counseling. They would have been allowed to grieve, to be angry, to express their feelings about life and death. They would have had a chance to heal in as constructive a manner as possible.

But these were the children and grandchildren of Joe and Rose. They had spent a lifetime seeking respect. They were going to be models for the nation. So they tried to do the impossible. They were their own best friends, their own counselors, their own confidants. And in trying to act in so impossible a manner given that they were all hurting, the family completely fell apart.

BG: CAROLINE WOULD LATER tell me that she was determined to go to a different college from anyone else in her family. She was always with the Kennedy cousins and she was determined to experience life away from the extended family.

Ethel's eleven children were robbed of their father and needed a full-time mother. They would run to drugs and alcohol, becoming self-destructive in ways no one could imagine.

But that would all be in the future. For the moment, the Kennedys put their hopes in Ted, The Senator, as Joe's guidance was soon to end.

BG: I DON'T KNOW WHAT Ethel's house was like before Bob died, but after his death it became total chaos. Both domestic help and secretaries came and went as though through a revolving door. Almost no one could tolerate working for her and her family. In one summer, six cooks were hired, then quit. In just two years, thirty-five eager, experienced secretaries were hired, each quitting in turn.

Jacqueline found her sister-in-law's chaotic lifestyle rather humorous. She had a little-known love of painting and liked to give her work as gifts. Her style was skillfully primitive, and the picture she gave Ethel was delightfully satirical. The picture was of Ethel's house with children everywhere—hanging out the windows, climbing over the roof, and running all about. A car was parked in front of the house, the new cook walking onto the front porch, her face eager, smiling. She was perfectly dressed, her clothing neat, her hat primly on her head, and she was carrying her purse and suitcase. In the back of the house was another car, this one waiting for the previous cook, who was angrily making her exit. Her hair was in disarray, her hat askew on her head, and her clothing hurriedly jammed into her suitcase as though nothing mattered except making her escape.

I once read in *People* magazine that former staff members called Ethel "Mommy Dearest" because of her harsh disposition. But I remember Mrs. Kennedy being jealous of Ethel. Despite the Kennedy men's tendency never to be monogamous when given a chance to cheat, Bob was more devoted to Ethel than any of the other Kennedy men, including old Joe, had ever been to their wives.

With such high staff turnover, Ethel couldn't use employment agencies and other traditional sources for getting help. Instead she utilized the local cooking school near her McLean, Virginia, home. Working for a Kennedy was an excellent reference for them. However, only the rare individual lasted as long as six weeks, especially when she took the cook with her to the Cape.

One young fellow talked with my son, Kevin, about the stress he was under and how he was able to keep the job as long as he did. He said that every night after work he would leave and head for the bars, staying until three-thirty in the morning or until closing, whichever was earlier. In the morning, after too little sleep, he would take a shower, ending with a long cold rinse of his head to try to numb himself for work. He complained that there was no set routine for meals. Everyone ate what they wanted, when they wanted.

Just as bad for a professional was that the laundry was adjacent to the kitchen. Clothes, maids, and kids were constantly under his feet.

The only consistent aspect to his days on the Cape came at noon. He was to prepare what Mrs. Kennedy always referred to as Ethel's "movable feast," hampers filled with fried chicken, two or three kinds of sandwiches, deviled eggs, a variety of cheese, potato salad, beer, wine, a variety of cold drinks, a sweet dessert, and fruit. The hampers would be taken to the boat to be eaten during the daily outing by various members of the four families and their guests. It was the same seven days a week.

Even Ethel's two spaniels participated. If in the confusion they were left behind, the barking dogs would race to the water, leap in, and paddle after the boat until someone stopped, doubled back, and pulled them in.

The Chappaquiddick incident in 1969 dealt the Kennedy dynasty a blow from which it would never recover. Many believe an illicit rendez-vous was taking place, while others think Ted was being faithful—to his girlfriend, Helga Wagner. His wife, Joan, pregnant with what she thought would be their fourth child, was never a consideration. However, as she had twice before, following the births of Kara, in 1960, and Ted junior, in 1961 (Patrick was born in 1967), Joan miscarried. The timing, shortly after the incident of the night of July 18, 1969, indicates that the loss was directly related to the extreme stress Ted created by his actions.

The "Boiler Room Girls" were a core group of female loyalists who had spent long hours working on Bob Kennedy's campaign for the presidency. Had he lived and won, they would likely have been offered jobs in the new administration. Thus there was the pain of both losing the senator and losing the chance to be a part of a world perhaps as glamorous as that which became part of Jack's myth.

Six of the Boiler Room Girls, Ted, Joe Gargan, Paul Markham (a former Georgetown Prep classmate of Gargan's who eventually became U.S. attorney for Massachusetts, in part through Kennedy patronage), along with chauffeurs John Crimmins and Ray LaRosa (the latter only an occasional driver), and advance man Charles Tretter, a lawyer by profession, all gathered at Chappaquiddick. They had met before, drinking, talking, perhaps having sex, perhaps not. (No one would ever say. Given the womanizing of at least some of the men, the idea cannot be dismissed. And given the prolonged grieving of many Kennedy loyalists, the meeting could just as easily have been part of a series of wakes.)

BG: JOE GARGAN WAS WORKING as assistant vice president at the Merchant's Bank and Trust Company of Cape Cod when he arranged the party. A Boston man named Larry Laskey, who had been in the motion picture business, went to the Cape to semiretire and started the bank where Joe worked. The Kennedy family opened accounts there, Laskey apparently being related to a man with the same name (different spelling) with whom Joe had worked in Hollywood. Stewart Granger, George Jessel, and other old-time stars regularly stopped by to see him as well.

I was briefly employed by the bank around 1970 or 1971, and the staff was still talking about Chappaquiddick. They knew I had been with the Kennedys the morning the body was found, but they also knew that I did not know what preparations had been made for the party.

The staff told me that, before the party, Joe Gargan had ordered a large quantity of rum and vodka, which was either ordered by one of the staff on Joe's behalf or brought to the bank for storage prior to his taking it to the island. No one had any intention of remaining sober, something borne out in what happened.

I don't know what Ted planned to do with Mary Jo Kopechne, but it probably involved sex. Books on the case have quoted testimony that Mary Jo left her purse in the rental house when she left with Ted.

I've been in the same situations a few times, and no girl would leave her purse if she expected to be away for long. I don't believe they were going back to the mainland.

Probably they were drinking and decided to do something— make out, have sex, something. The house was crowded and Ted probably said, "Let's get out of here and go for a ride somewhere."

You have to understand that the island was rural with lots of areas to pull over and do whatever in the car. That's what people did when the mood struck, and that was probably what Ted and Mary Jo were doing to get some privacy. Ted had a big Oldsmobile. It was a logical thing to happen.

The senator was a terrible driver. That's why he usually had someone drive him. He just couldn't handle a car and had no sense of direction. He'd stop for a light, then start to turn, going over the curb because he did not move forward enough to stay on the pavement. It makes perfect sense for him to have gone into the water that night, given how bad a driver he was, the drinking, the whole thing.

But I'm convinced Mary Jo thought they would be returning. Otherwise she would never have left her purse behind.

Eventually the most frequently heard story was that Ted, drunk, tired, confused by the darkness, and a poor driver under the best of circumstances, missed a turn. He wanted a paved road but ended on Dike

Road, a dirt road a quarter mile from the cottage. He claimed that when he realized his mistake, he could not turn around, even though the road was deserted. He said that he was traveling between twenty and twenty-two miles per hour when he struck the Dike Bridge, was launched thirty-five feet in the air, flipped over, and landed on the car's roof in the water.

Ted managed to free himself from the car, then said he dived repeatedly trying to save Mary Jo. Finally he went back to the cottage where he met Joe Gargan and Paul Markham, who went to the bridge to help. Eventually Ted swam back to Edgartown and returned to his hotel. That statement no one disputes.

BG: JOE GARGAN TOLD ME his version of what had happened. I already knew that the story of Ted's swimming back to Edgartown made sense. I don't know if it was too late for the ferry, but the swim would have been faster. Ted was a strong swimmer who regularly covered much greater distances.

Joe told me that everyone in the cottage was sleeping when Ted came in the house and whispered to Joe and Paul that he needed help. The two men went outside with Ted, who told them what had happened. Ted was going to take the ferry back and get help. Joe and Paul Markham were to get her out.

Joe's first shock was seeing how bad the accident was. He dived down, not knowing if Mary Jo was still in the car since Ted had gotten out. The window was broken open, the glass remaining rather jagged. Joe went through the opening, cutting himself on the glass, and found Mary Jo. She was definitely dead. He returned to the surface, certain Ted would be sending help. He and Paul returned to the cottage so Joe could dry off and to wait for whomever Ted sent to handle things. (The Edgartown side had better rescue services and equipment.) There was nothing more they could do.

The local police chief conducted an investigation. His final report included:

Chief [Dominick] Arena first received word of the accident at approx. 8:20 A.M. when a call from Mrs. Sylvia Malm was made to the Edgartown Police Station concerning a report received by her at her home from 2 boys who had been fishing on the Dike Road Bridge that they spotted a car in the water upside down. The invest. officer arrived at the scene and upon observing the car for the first time found it almost completely submerged, part of the left rear tire was above water—the invest. officer entered the water and swam to the car but because of the strong tide each time he went under he was unable to determine whether or not anyone was in the car. Assistance was then requested from the Edgartown Fire Dept. scuba squad and one John Farrar came to the scene and was able to enter the car and with the assistance of the invest. officer remove the body from the car. The victim was a young lady, dressed in white blouse, black slacks, and sandals; she was dead when removed. Dr. Donald Mills, MD, of Edgartown, an associate Medical Examiner was notified and came to the scene and pronounced the victim (Miss Mary Jo Kopechne, 28, of 2912 Olive St., Washington, D.C.) dead of accidental drowning. Her body had been found in the rear of the car. Her body was ordered removed to the Martha's Vineyard Funeral Home.

Rose later recalled that Ted had flown in from Washington on Friday, the eighteenth, so he could skipper a boat called the *Victura*, previously owned by Jack, in the annual Edgartown Regatta. He was staying on Martha's Vineyard, and after the race, he went to the Chappaquiddick Island cottage Joe Gargan had rented. She said that Ted had never been there before, but that they would be joined by some of the men and women who had worked on Bob's presidential campaign. There they would have a "cookout."

Rose's memoirs talk of Ted's arriving in Hyannis Port the afternoon following the accident. She said that he was "sick with grief over the death of the young woman," as well as being disturbed and distracted. She thought he was in a state of shock, especially since he had nearly drowned and was not yet fully recovered from his injuries in the plane crash.

Laurence Leamer would also mention that Ted did not arrive until the afternoon of July 19, 1969. Ann Gargan was quoted as saying that Ted came that afternoon, and that Ann had broken the news shortly before Ted's arrival. According to Leamer's book on the Kennedy women, Rose had already been to mass and played her usual three holes of three-ball golf. She was preparing for an afternoon church garden party at St. Francis Xavier when alerted to what had happened.

BG: TED WAS BACK SUNDAY morning. I don't know if he drove or flew from Edgartown, but no matter how he came, the trip would have taken between thirty and forty-five minutes.

I had been typing at home and had some letters to take over for Mrs. Kennedy's signature. I knew she would be going to mass, so I arrived right after she finished breakfast. This would have made it approximately ten o'clock in the morning, and certainly no later.

I heard a little of the story on the radio on the way to the compound, but there were no meaningful details and I didn't connect the senator with what had happened.

As I arrived, Ted was coming out of Ethel's house, on the front porch. He was wearing a white collar around his neck, one of those braces meant to keep the neck from moving too much. I didn't know if he was having some problems from the injuries from the plane crash or if a doctor had prescribed it that day. But you couldn't miss it because he was wearing a navy blue suit.

He was laughing as he came out, and when I drove around to the back to place the letters on the secretary's desk, I saw that Pat and Mrs. Kennedy were just finishing their breakfast. They were talking and laughing. Obviously, nothing serious was taking place, just business as usual.

When I left the house, I walked along the wooden ramp area that went from the driveway to the house. The ramped area adjoined the covered swimming pool and had been installed for Joe's wheelchair. I looked down toward the ocean between the pool and the house and saw either two or three men, I forget which, walking along the beach, all of them wearing suits. One was Ted, and he was serious, gesturing with his hand as he talked.

I later learned what had happened. We were all working intensely because the family received thousands of letters and telegrams, some supportive and some hostile. I'm sure Mrs. Kennedy read the newspaper accounts, but she was not the type to sit down and discuss matters with her children. She may never have talked with Ted about it.

Mrs. Kennedy later said that the whole thing was disgusting. She didn't blame people for feeling the way they did toward Ted. She said that he should never have gone off alone with the girl. Joe Gargan should have watched out for him, should have known better.

And from then Rose had a typical Kennedy rationale. Kennedys do nothing wrong, and when they do, it is always someone else's fault. In this case, Joe Gargan should have protected Ted from his drinking and womanizing, even though the senator was an adult with a mind of his own.

But Rose could not admit this to herself, any more than she wanted to risk hearing a story from Ted that was different from the way she wanted to view the incident. She arranged for her lawyer to remove Joe Gargan from her will, the ultimate dismissal of anyone who met with her displeasure. She later reinstated him, though she must have changed her will for one reason or another ten or twelve times during the years I worked with her. Money was control, and disinheritance was the worst punishment she felt she could give someone.

Mrs. Kennedy was also derisive of Ted's womanizing so publicly. She liked to quote her husband, explaining that The Ambassador always stressed that there was nothing wrong with taking beautiful women to the Stork Club every night where you would be seen. But if you wanted to go to the Stork Club, you couldn't be in politics. When you went into politics, you had to be smart about womanizing.

What I never heard was any sense of the terribleness of the death Ted caused. Had he not been so politically connected, he would have been charged with and convicted of involuntary manslaughter, along with other crimes. Instead there would be payments to the Kopechnes and a dramatic televised speech by Ted. Then the drinking and womanizing continued.

Tragically, the Kennedys ultimately proved not to be loyal to Gargan in a crisis. After Chappaquiddick he was largely dropped from the family circle. Ted refused to let him work on his campaigns again because the family feared that his presence would result in reporters asking questions about the death of Mary Jo Kopechne. Ted, alone, could handle anything; Ted with Joe Gargan would be vulnerable to additional attacks best avoided. The idea was nonsense, as history would show, but the family was more comfortable throwing Gargan away than continuing with the closeness of the past.

Later Joe Gargan would talk freely. He had been an alcoholic who decided to regain his life. He sought help for his drinking, as Joan Kennedy would do. But for the moment, each of them suffered. Joe was temporarily made a "non-Kennedy" for not better covering Ted's actions. And Joan Kennedy, who publicly stood by her husband as though she believed in the innocence of the "cookout," had a miscarriage. The stress was too great on her pregnancy.

The aftermath was handled by Stephen Smith. He had become the damage-control specialist for the Kennedys, working to preserve the family's good name at any cost. Other Kennedy loyalists gathered, including Ted Sorensen, Robert McNamara, and Richard Goodwin. Dun Guiford removed the body, William vanden Heuvel went to see the Kopechnes, and Burke Marshall was alerted in case there were legal problems. Fortunately for them, DA Edmund Dinis was a Kennedy loyalist who could be counted upon to go slowly. This led to a twelve-day delay for an inquest into Mary Jo's death, plenty of time to make certain the results would not be too embarrassing, for by then there would be little or no chance for an autopsy.

Bernie Flynn, the Dukes County district attorney's investigator, was actually convinced that Ted had not even been driving that night. However, a Kennedy does not cover for anyone else. Joe Gargan might have been asked to claim he had been behind the wheel, and Joe would probably have taken the fall for that night if asked. But Ted would certainly not jeopardize his career and the façade of a good marriage for anyone on the island.

In the end, Ted Kennedy's negligence was found to be the probable cause of Mary Joe Kopechne's death, and he was guilty of leaving the scene of an accident. He received two months in jail—suspended—and was given a year's probation.

Joan Kennedy would continue to appear with her husband in public, but their marriage was over for all practical purposes. Ted was creating too much stress for her.

Ted Kennedy told his father what had happened, even though he did not talk with his mother. He kept stressing that the death had been an accident.

Even Rose sensed, though did not directly say, how bad things had become. She knew that her father, and later Joe, used Eddie Moore to cover for them. A man playing the games of her father, husband, and son could get into trouble, big trouble. They needed someone to act as a fixer, to plead, bribe, or do whatever else was necessary to keep the taint of a scandal from haunting the men for whom they worked. And if necessary, men like Eddie Moore would take the fall.

Joe Gargan had Eddie Moore's position in Rose's mind, though Joe was not an Eddie Moore. He was family, a friend, and though he would go to great lengths, his drinking problems were partial proof that he was uncomfortable with the amorality of it all.

Joe had begun growing weaker after Bob's death. With the news of Chappaquiddick, the old man lost his will to live. Those around him said that his eyes appeared as if he were crying endlessly. But Joe was essentially mute, increasingly helpless.

Jacqueline Kennedy had married Aristotle Onassis the year before and to an increasingly critical public seemed to be reveling in the creature comforts his great wealth could buy her. Yet she regularly came to see Joe, and always sensitive to the psychological impact of his debilities, she would kiss him on his sagging, paralyzed face, hold his gnarled hand. She called him Grandpa. She brought him unconditional love.

On November 17, 1969, the family knew that Joe Kennedy had little time to live. A vigil began, Jackie spending the night by his side. Ted also stayed with him, sometimes dozing on a chair beside his father, a blanket wrapped around him so he could get some rest.

By nine o'clock the night of November 18, death was a few hours or even minutes away. Joe's vital signs changed, changes subtle enough that only trained professionals could read them. Rita Dallas and the doctor alerted the family, many of whom did not begin to arrive until around 10:30 P.M.

Pat came first, followed by Eunice and Sargent Shriver. Then came Jacqueline, racing barefoot to the house. She had not bothered to dress when called, knowing only that she wanted to be present at the end. Ted had never left his father, and Joan now joined both the men. Steve Smith was there, and Ethel.

Only Rose did not come. She was not sharing the death vigil. She would come for the last breaths of life, not before. Instead, according to Ann Gargan, she went swimming, keeping her routine as normal as possible until the last instant.

Rita Dallas carefully monitored the fading vital signs. Then, shortly after 11 P.M., she told Ted it was time to get his mother. Rose entered the room, pressed a rosary into her husband's hand, and was silent until Eunice began the Lord's Prayer. Rose and each of the children said a line of the prayer, Rose speaking last. Within seconds, Joe Kennedy breathed his last. Although she had not had a husband since the stroke, for the first time in her life Rose Kennedy was on her own. No more strong men would dominate her decisions, trying to guide her actions. Rose Kennedy would face whatever the rest of her life might bring, and she would do so alone.

14

The Later Years

The wealth that Joe Kennedy left behind was one of America's largest family fortunes, though neither Rose nor any of the surviving children had any sense of its size. Unlike others with great fortunes, Joe never prepared any of them to handle the assets they would one day inherit. His children lacked even the most basic common sense when it came to the cost of living.

Once, Jack was telling an employee of his father's that the man's large family needed no more than $5,000 a year. To Jack, this was a fortune capable of buying every luxury. He was shocked when his father, both annoyed by his son's arrogance and amused by his naïveté, explained to him that Jack was already spending $50,000 per year on what Joe defined as "incidentals." Jack never again brought up the subject of money.

The basic income for Rose and the children came from trust funds established in 1926, 1936, 1949, and 1959. These were not irrevocable, nor were they meant to assure the children's independence. The money was designed to be tapped by old Joe for whatever he desired. He wanted to have a cash cushion, estimated at $100 million, should he make mistakes with his investments.

In later years, whenever anyone in the family made a political move, one or more of the funds were tapped to help pay for it. Stephen Smith was the primary controller of all this, but he acted as old Joe desired.

The Chicago Merchandise Mart and the newer Apparel Center were major sources of funds. In addition, there were businesses such as Ken-oil Corporation, Moheen Oil Corporation, a Coca-Cola bottling-company and distributorship partnership, extensive real estate, extensive securities holdings, the Park Foundation, the President John F. Kennedy Library, Special Olympics, Inc., and the Robert F. Kennedy Memorial.

Many of the Kennedy holdings were secret, often hidden in corporations whose real partners were not publicized. Kennedy wanted to obtain and retain as much money as he could so that he could manipulate others. In 1977, the *New York Times* tried to pierce the veil of secrecy, and though it could only estimate the total wealth, two facts showed much about the founding father. First, the estate taxes levied against Joe Kennedy when he died totaled only $13,330.90. By contrast, Senator Kennedy's taxable income for 1975 was $417,542, and while his final tax bill was unknown, it had to run considerably more than his father's estate taxes had been.

The trust funds seem to have been at least $30 million each for the nine children. Estimates of $300 million or more are probably the most reliable. An additional trust was in Rose's name, and more money was part of the Joseph P. Kennedy Foundation. Given the real estate investments, the business ventures, and other investments, the lowest estate figure is probably $500 million. The highest is a billion dollars. All the figures are educated guesses, because Joe Kennedy hid as much wealth as possible.

Whatever the ultimate numbers, the Kennedy family could not possibly outspend the family assets. That was why Joe Kennedy, when still alive, would willingly spend his money on the staff. It was not unusual for him to walk into the kitchen and tuck a $50 bill in the cook's apron pocket. However, knowing that his wife had no conception of their wealth ($50 was the *maximum* she would ever spend on a Christmas gift for any of her children), he always whispered, "Don't tell her."

BG: I was hired by Mrs. Kennedy before Joe died, and I would be her assistant until after a stroke had ended her ability to communicate. In the beginning, she was still a vibrant woman, but she was cheap even then. To this day I sometimes find myself working in near darkness, forgetting that Mrs. Kennedy is no longer my employer. She would turn off the light in my office when she walked in, informing me that there was still sunlight. It did not matter if the room had but one window or if the sun was casting heavy shadows or what I was doing. Total darkness warranted electric light. Anything less was a judgment call, and it was always best to err on the side of penny-pinching by turning off lamps or overhead lights.

At times Mrs. Kennedy was generous to me, though she usually thought better of it. Gifts were often requested back the next day. She had apparently found a better use for them than spoiling the staff.

Mrs. Kennedy did donate to a local thrift shop run by the Church, always demanding a receipt for tax purposes. The value was so little that her accountants pleaded with her not to bother. It probably cost them far more in time to handle the additional paperwork than the small deduction was worth. But she fancied herself being frugal. She never understood how meaningless some of the thrift-shop items could be. After one week's "gifts" included two old girdles and a lone sneaker with the word Teddy printed on it, I decided to inspect the donations first so I could remove those that would be embarrassing.

Each fall Mrs. Kennedy would write to fashion designers for sketches and samples of material for hats, afternoon dresses, cocktail and dinner gowns, and coat ensembles. However, though she loved the special treatment she received, she made few purchases after Joe's death. In one four-year period, I remember her buying just two or three ensembles for daytime wear, and a royal blue coat with lynx collar for evening wear. She had two or three more dresses made for her in Palm Beach. Even the impulse items from Saks and Lily Pulitzer were relatively simple cotton frocks.

The only time she changed was when a writer for the London Times criticized her for wearing the same blue winter coat with lynx collar and hat that she had worn in the past. By then Mrs. Kennedy was proud to have been named one of the best-dressed women in the world, and with that honor came the expectation of an ever-changing wardrobe. Her activities had declined to such a degree that she felt it unnecessary to constantly be shopping. Still, stung by the Times' criticism, she had some clothing custom made for her in Paris.

Oddly, Mrs. Kennedy felt that her daughters should save money on their clothes. She mentioned that if they would wear black-and-white instead of multicolored outfits, they could save money. She said that clothing in black and white was not memorable. You could wear the same outfits repeatedly without anyone noticing. She said that her daughters should go to the most expensive stores and look for the current black-and-white designs. Then they should go to the cheaper stores where they could find designer copies for less.

Mrs. Kennedy was apparently proud that the black-and-white TV in her room was less expensive than the others in the house. I walked in and realized that the set was actually color. Someone had turned the adjustment knobs and she never realized the truth. She was amazed by the simple correction.

The cook was told to save the crumbs at the bottom of the cookie jar for sprinkling on Mrs. Kennedy's pudding at the next day's lunch. And I was amazed to see her throw down the stairwell whatever toast was left from her evening snack. The cook had orders to retrieve it, then give it to Mrs. Kennedy as part of her breakfast.

Like Jack, Mrs. Kennedy had stomach trouble that prevented her from eating certain foods. She knew the airlines would make a special meal if requested in advance. Thinking she would save money when she flew (always tourist class), she would cancel the meal and have the cook pack her a lunch of chicken sandwiches, her favorite cookies, and a thermos of milk.

She also took taxis wherever she went, though even then she was frugal. If someone was going in a similar direction, she would try to share the cab to cut the cost. I remember one day after arriving back in New York, Mrs. Kennedy approached a woman who agreed to share the ride. As they drove through the city, Mrs. Kennedy told the woman who she was. The other passenger was so surprised, she actually fainted. The driver had to stop the car to help revive her.

At one point, the Hyannis Port house needed a new roof. Holes could be patched, but it was all deteriorating so rapidly that a replacement was the most practical way to go. However, after getting estimates from a number of companies, Mrs. Kennedy told me that she would just pay for patches.

The Park Agency agreed with me that a new roof was critical. I waited until Mrs. Kennedy left for Palm Beach for the winter, then arranged for the work to be handled by the lowest bidder. By the time she returned, the shingles would have weathered enough that she would never notice the difference. Unfortunately, that winter a story about the family appeared on the news one evening in Palm Beach. A helicopter crew had taken a recent aerial picture of the Hyannis Port compound. The shingles had not weathered. A full replacement had obviously been made, and Mrs. Kennedy was outraged.

Yet another time Mrs. Kennedy discovered that the Chrysler Corporation was giving a $200 rebate with the purchase of a new car. She immediately bought a Chrysler, not because she needed one but because she thought she was getting a bargain.

Mrs. Kennedy sometimes had trouble keeping help partly because the nonsalaried employees would only be paid when she was in residence.

For example, Mrs. Kennedy would arrange for a three-week trip to Europe because staying that long reduced the airfare considerably, though never so much as to cover the cost of the additional meals and hotel bills. She looked at each item of her trip separately, never analyzing all she was spending on being frugal.

The day Mrs. Kennedy would be driven to the airport, the staff would line up on the front porch of the Hyannis Port house. Usually this meant the chauffeur, the cook-maid, her nephew Joe Gargan, and me. She would kiss us goodbye one by one, get in the car, and drive off down the driveway. As soon as she was out of sight, the cook-maid would rush to the rear of the house where her car was waiting, door open, motor running. She got in and left, determined not to stay at the compound one minute longer than she was paid to be there. Jennette, the maid, had her wages stopped from the moment Mrs. Kennedy left the drive in the fall until the moment she returned the following spring.

Just as Mrs. Kennedy made endless notes to herself she pinned on her clothing, so she wrote notes to the staff. My memos were written on the torn-off backs of envelopes in order to save money.

Eventually the family tore up envelopes and other material for a valid reason. One of the staff was regularly going through the trash to look for letters signed by the famous. Then she sold them to autograph dealers, earning enough money in one year to buy a new car. I was amazed that Mrs. Kennedy did not do the same, going through an intermediary. I guess that though she was cheap, she had standards.

Mrs. Kennedy always read the *New York Times* and either the *Boston Herald* or *Boston Tribune*. She would tear out articles that interested her. Then she would copy quotations, phrases, current sayings, and any other short item that interested her. She would make endless lists like this, then have me type them on thin paper so she could fold them and keep them in her purse.

I knew Mrs. Kennedy studied her lists late at night before going to sleep, though I thought that was the extent of it. One evening on my way home, I was driving down Scudder Avenue. She was sitting on a hill under a tree, unconcernedly studying one of her lists, completely oblivious to the traffic, the gawkers, or anything else around her.

I was also asked to go to the stationery store just before we went to Palm Beach for the winter. The current year-calendar refills were on sale for half price. She would place them in her holders, then use them the following year. The days were wrong, of course, but she never made a mistake because she corrected the refills with the current year calendar she received free from her church.

Once I came upon some notes concerning some recent expenditures while Mrs. Kennedy was in Paris. Hats at Paulet had cost $230. Among the designers, Sherrer had received $1,146, Courreges $70, and Dior $450. She had also spent $15 for a masseuse, then taken the receipt and contacted the New York office to see if the $15 might be a legitimate tax deduction.

Another trait of Mrs. Kennedy's was to give someone what seemed to be a gift, then request it back hours, days, or years later. For example, she and I found an old silver-plated spoon in the attic that she did not want. She called her decorator, Bob Luddington, to ask if the spoon had any value. When he said it was a worthless souvenir she must have picked up somewhere, she gave it to me as a present. Then, that night, she called me at home to ask for it back, having decided that she must have some use for it.

More outrageous was the white mink hat she gave to her sister-in-law. The woman wore the hat for several years, then one day Mrs. Kennedy sent her a letter saying she needed it and asking for its return. It was also not unusual for Mrs. Kennedy to give a blouse to one of her relatives, then call them two years later saying, "Do you remember that blouse I gave you? I need it back. Please return it."

The trip between Hyannis Port and Palm Beach used to be made with a moving van. Every six months a van would pull up to be loaded with the possessions that seemed necessary for Rose Kennedy and any staff that might be traveling with her.

The secretary who worked for Mrs. Kennedy before I did told me that one winter the movers sent a massive van to Hyannis Port. Mrs. Kennedy looked out her window and saw clothes on wheeled racks much like those in Manhattan's garment district, along with television sets, record players, and numerous other items being placed on the truck. She was convinced she was paying for far more truck than was necessary. Without waiting for an explanation, she ordered that from then on, everyone traveling would load what they needed into their individual cars.

The next move taught Mrs. Kennedy how many personal items she had. Her car was packed full, then a U-Haul trailer had to be added. Then, on the thruway, the trailer came loose and went into a ditch. Television sets and other breakables went crashing. After that, Mrs. Kennedy began buying two of everything so there would always be what she needed in both houses.

The third generation was getting older and becoming increasingly troubled, but Mrs. Kennedy seemed oblivious to the way the children's lives were unfolding. Her concerns about them seemed rather superficial when compared with the drug and alcohol abuse problems many of them would experience.

The grandchildren took advantage of their grandmother in a way the sons and daughters had never dared to try. Sydney Lawford used to get money for gas from Mrs. Kennedy. Then she would pocket the money, drive to Bareman's where the family was known, and charge whatever gas she put in the car.

Maria Shriver would show up for the weekend without her family but with a boyfriend in tow. This was in the days before Arnold Schwarzenegger. In the morning, when she knew Mrs. Kennedy was out of town, I would find her sitting in Mrs. Kennedy's place at the head of the table, having the maid serve the boy and her. She would never have dared to take this imperial role had her grandmother been in town.

I laughed about the whole scene when I was alone with Nellie the cook. Nellie looked at me, raised her eyebrows, and said, "She'll never die wonderin'."

I had to laugh when I saw Maria on the Arsenio Hall show years later. She told the audience that due to her strict Catholic upbringing, she had not kissed a boy until she was in her twenties.

Maria also tried to manipulate me to do her favors. She knew that I had access to Mrs. Kennedy's car, and she tried to get it from me for trips to Fort Lauderdale or Miami, all of which I refused. She knew her grandmother would not tolerate such use, but like her mother, she wanted me not to say anything. When I flatly refused, she said, "I'll never ask you for a favor again."

Much to her frustration I responded, "Will you please put that in writing?"

By the summer of 1974, the Kennedy women were trying to establish some order in their lives, which had once been so controlled by old Joe. Teddy was the titular head of the family, and he tried to come to Massachusetts every weekend if possible. Yet he was having personal problems that went beyond the troubles he had created with his womanizing.

Our suspicions were first aroused when no one could reach Joan Kennedy. If I asked about Joan when talking with the senator or a member of his staff, I was invariably told that she was "visiting friends in California." Mrs. Kennedy was given the same story.

The children's nanny was in full-time residence, answering the telephone and handling any social activities in either Hyannis Port or Washington.

Finally Eunice felt that her mother should know the truth. Joan was in a residential facility for treatment for alcoholism. To her credit, Eunice explained that alcoholism is a disease and had to be treated as such. Mrs. Kennedy thought differently, of course, seeing the drinking as nothing more than a needless weakness: "She's so beautiful, and she has everything . . . two beautiful homes. Even her own secretary." The drinking made no sense since her daughter-in-law had looks and physical possessions, the attributes Mrs. Kennedy sometimes seemed to use when determining her own happiness during her years with a philandering husband.

Joan returned briefly to Hyannis Port at the end of the summer. Her priority was not to help her husband's political career, though. Their son, Teddy junior, had to have his leg amputated because of cancer. He was undergoing radiation therapy, and their other son, Patrick, had asthma so severe that it was life threatening. Joan's priorities were getting and staying sober and helping her children.

The cook told me that Ted held a dinner party at his home in Virginia, using the nanny as hostess. She wore Joan's clothing, and the implication was so outrageous, Ethel, one of the guests, was heard to exclaim, "What's *she* doing here?"

Early the following year, entertainer Carol Channing came to visit Mrs. Kennedy in Hyannis Port. There were to be drinks served on the porch, with Joan included, or so Mrs. Kennedy thought. However, Ethel came to my office and said, "Does Gramma know that Joan has previous plans and will not be able to join us?"

I later learned from Arthur, the gardener, that the "previous plans" were something else entirely. He had stopped by the senator's house to get something and encountered Joan alone in the kitchen. She was apparently on an eating binge, food all over the kitchen and mayonnaise in her hair. Arthur, extremely upset by what he had seen, said, "Gosh, she used to be such a good-looking woman."

Often when Joan arrived in Palm Beach, she intended to have a normal visit. However, Mrs. Kennedy felt Joan should be kept busy, such as having her sort through all the books in the library to separate out the signed editions.

Ted and Joan would be assigned separate bedrooms—usually the lake bedroom and the president's bedroom. The latter was where Jack used to stay. It had a separate entrance from the rest of the house, so the Kennedy men and some of the women liked to get the room for their affairs. They could sneak lovers into the house without fear of being seen by Mrs. Kennedy.

"They don't sleep together in Washington," Mrs. Kennedy explained. She added that Joan also did not get up in the morning to help the children go to school. What she did not say was that most of Joan's actions were meant to help her avoid having to see her husband. In fact, once he arrived on the Cape or in Palm Beach, she would closet herself in her room.

Wherever Joan Kennedy went there seemed to be misadventures. For example, one Friday afternoon I went to meet her at the West Palm Beach airport. I went to the gate where her plane had landed, then watched all the passengers disembark. Finally, just as I was about to leave, Joan came out, a stewardess holding her arm. I feared that she was drunk, but she was all right.

We went through the terminal, then out to the car. I opened the trunk, setting off the alarm. Then we discovered that we could not turn it off.

Airport security heard the noise and an officer came to investigate. Then a second man came to help. Eventually what seemed to be half the guard force came by, everyone trying to help us shut off the alarm. In the end we had to drive through West Palm Beach, the siren announcing our presence, until we reached Bareman's Texaco station on Royal Poinciana Way. There the alarm wires were removed from the bottom of the car, and Joan and I were given a lift to the Kennedy mansion in the front seat of their tow truck.

Mrs. Kennedy was just leaving for her walk when the truck arrived. Afterward, when I explained to her what had happened, she just giggled and said, "You have a time of it, don't you?"

The family members were constantly pulling apart. In 1975, with Ted considering a possible run for the presidency, the siblings were no longer united. Sargent Shriver thought he would like to take a run for the Democratic nomination for president. He was a dark horse, but he was still well-known from the Kennedy administration. He had been the head of the Peace Corps, and his wife was known for her work with the retarded through the Special Olympics program. He was an outsider at a time when the nation had been shocked by revelations of corruption inside the Nixon White House. Most important, on June 4, when he privately discussed the matter with Ted, the senator told him that he had no intention of running.

The children were still trying to live as they had when Joe was alive, but the patriarch was dead. They wanted the matriarch to assume his mantle, yet she had no interest in such matters.

Prior to the meeting between Sarge and Ted, the children had tried to reason together. No one made a move without the family gathering to discuss it. Then they would go to Rose, who might or might not have been present at their meeting, to see if they could get her approval. If they could, then they would act. If not, they were supposed to abandon the idea, but actually they did whatever they wanted. It was like a company meeting where the CEO was just a figurehead.

At the same time, the Kennedys felt that one of the second generation should be the leader. This role was assumed by Ted, who had been forced to be increasingly involved with the families of his siblings as first Jack and then Bob had been murdered.

The trouble was that if Ted was the leader, then Ted had to have a clear shot at the presidency. Ted was a realist about his chances on a national scale. He was questioning whether he would ever want to run since war and assassination had left him the only surviving brother. The hostility he received after the death of Mary Jo Kopechne made him realize that he might never have a chance at higher office.

The Kennedy family thought Ted would run in 1980, something the senator was not certain about. Rose definitely did not want him to yield to the pressures of family and supporters. She feared his death, understood that a person seeking to go down in history had only to place a bullet in the last surviving Kennedy brother. He had become the patriarch for the family, the surrogate father for Bob's and John's children.

Rose had also been shocked by an incident that same year when Ted had been pelted with eggs and tomatoes in Boston. Other politicians had been treated the same way over the years. But never a Kennedy. And Boston should have been the most supportive area.

In a somewhat earlier sign of a mood change in the country, the press was no longer willing to hide scandals among the powerful. Judith Exner, who had been both Jack's mistress and the girlfriend of mobster Sam Giancana, wrote a book entitled *My Story*. She revealed her long-term affair with Jack, and the Palm Beach newspaper everyone calls "the shiny sheet" ran her picture on the front page, along with a story.

Mrs. Kennedy read the article, then commented, "I saw the Exner woman's picture on the front page this morning with her large breasts. I just don't see how all that could have been going on in the White House with all the staff and other people around."

Mrs. Kennedy did not realize that her son was surrounded by loyalists who would do whatever was necessary to cover for him. The public did understand, though. The volume of mail dropped off noticeably after Jack lost his sainthood. Yet his mother did not want to face that.

The issue of women's breasts would come up again. Mrs. Kennedy was always upset by the provocative way she felt her granddaughters dressed. One time, after seeing Maria Shriver in a halter top, she sent a letter to Sarge demanding to know how Maria could be permitted to "show her breasts."

The question was what would happen if Shriver was successful. Ted could not challenge his brother-in-law's second term, yet Sarge had no "right" to go against the family. Ted realized the possibilities only after he had cleared the way for Sarge to make his move in 1976, and he was bitter about it. He did not like having a brother-in-law kill his options.

In 1976, Ethel announced that she would not support Sarge. And the men running his campaign, including Cyrus Vance, John Kennedy's army secretary, refused to approach Jackie, whom they considered a liability following her marriage to Onassis. Finally, privately, Eunice stated that the women in the Kennedy family would not campaign for Sarge.

Mrs. Kennedy was the one exception. She authorized three checks of $6,000 to Sarge, $6,000 to Eunice, and $3,000 to Bobby Shriver junior for Sarge's political expense accounts. The total was $15,000, which I assume is the amount to which she referred in an August 1976 letter to Tom Walsh at the New York office—"We gave Eunice, Sargent and Bobby checks for $15,000 as a contribution to his campaign."

Mrs. Kennedy allegedly funneled up to $50,000 to the campaign, though I have not been able to confirm these rumors. I do know that Joe Gargan said that money for Sarge came from Rosemary's trust fund. Whether this was the $15,000 I knew about or a different sum, I have no idea. I do know that Mrs. Kennedy was relieved when Sarge dropped out of the campaign and hoped he would not seriously consider a different option, that of running for governor of Maryland, as he had unsuccessfully done earlier. She said that she was sick of contributing to his campaigns.

Money had become a big focus of Mrs. Kennedy's life. She began using money as a weapon. It was as though, with Joe gone, she felt that money was her only control over people and she wielded it like a club.

Sometimes Mrs. Kennedy was blunt, as I saw her being with Kym Maria Smith, one of Jean and Steve Smith's two adopted children. The Smiths had two sons, Steve junior and William, and adopted daughters Amanda Mary Smith and Kym. Kym was Korean, and for some reason Mrs. Kennedy was uncomfortable with the sisters. Perhaps it was racism. Perhaps she thought that Jean should "make" her own children. Mrs. Kennedy never explained herself. However, there came a day when Kym was visiting her grandmother and Mrs. Kennedy stared at her, then said, "Be nice to me, child. Someday you will inherit my money." What she did not say was that the adopted girls would receive less money than their biological siblings. The older Smith children, like all the biological grandchildren, were to receive $300,000. Amanda would be given $200,000 because she looked "American." Kym was left only $100,000.

Of course, the will was actually a vehicle that varied with Mrs. Kennedy's emotional state. She had no sense of how much she was worth. She had no sense of what she should be giving, whether based on love or a feeling of duty.

At the same time, Mrs. Kennedy could be quite generous. She was supporting much of her family in ways that caused the New York office some concern because they could not tell who was in need and who was merely using the wealthy old woman. For example, each of the Fitzgerald brothers received between $20,000 and $25,000 per year. Each grandniece and grandnephew received an annual Christmas check that began at $4,000 but was cut back to $3,000. The money was supposed to be for their college education, but she was doing it at a time when the annual checks were adequate to cover an entire year of education, and the money never stopped. The first economy was cutting the gift back by a thousand dollars per year. The second economy was ending the gifts when the children reached twenty-one. And the third, instituted shortly before she would suffer her final debilitating stroke, cut the money to $500. As it was, the nieces and nephews were able to afford the finest private schools available, something that ultimately upset Mrs. Kennedy because she had come to Joe's opinion that children should start their education in public school.

One of the nieces had to go on welfare for a while. Mrs. Kennedy helped her get off by giving her between $10,000 and $15,000 per year at a time when that was enough money to adequately raise a family of four. Yet the money seemed such a small amount to her that she asked me if it was enough for one person to live on.

Not in the Kennedy manner, of course. But Mrs. Kennedy did help those closest to her to the point where Eunice was bitter about what her mother was spending. When Mrs. Kennedy, then well into her eighties, was flying to Paris, I started to arrange for a limousine to meet her at the airport. She could afford the extra comfort, and with the adjustment to the time difference, I thought the limousine made more sense than her trying for a taxicab. She would hear none of such "extravagance," at which Eunice commented, "Mother's saving all her money for her relatives, so they can ride around in limousines after she's gone."

The situation with the constantly deteriorating Palm Beach house made a little sense. She said that the problem was that the house was not hers. According to Joe Kennedy's will, the house belonged jointly to the children with the stipulation that Rose Kennedy be allowed to remain in it for her lifetime. She decided that it wasn't her responsibility to repair or renovate what was not hers (the Hyannis Port home remained a showplace because it did belong to her). Giving some credit to her children, it may have been that they worried they would seem to be anxious for her death by making improvements while she lived there. They may have thought their mother would think the children wanted to sell it, a likely possibility given the way she sometimes thought.

And so the house deteriorated. The children and grandchildren continued descending on it like locusts. The place got worse and worse. And nobody seemed to care.

By January of 1976, Mrs. Kennedy seemed to have overcome her worries about Ted. She missed the excitement of campaigning. Ted was still wavering, though more likely to refuse to run. Joan was extremely unstable, and women close to her had begun to talk to the national press. They had revealed that her problems went beyond having to deal with her husband's drinking and womanizing. He had never treated her with respect, never let her be a part of a normal family life. Instead of her being allowed to care for her children, staff people were hired. Out of either weakness or foolish love for Ted, or both, she had allowed others to usurp her role as mother.

Joan had realized that she was not important to Ted, not important to her children, not important to anyone. She was at an emotional breaking point and might leave the senator. When her emotional state was combined with the memory of Chappaquiddick, which would never go away, the idea of a Ted Kennedy bid in 1976 was ludicrous.

Joe would have agreed. But Rose didn't have Joe, and at eighty-five, she had no idea how many more campaigns she might experience. On January 4, 1975, she was quoted in the *New York Times* in a manner that left Ted wide open for a party draft:

"I have made Ted promise me repeatedly that he would not run for President. I told him that his family needs him too much, that John's children and Bobby's children need him as the father they no longer have." That was her official family line. Then she gave the reporter the signal she wanted to send to party members:

"But even though he has given me his promise that he will not run, I realize there are considerations that could make him change his mind. He may feel it is something he has to do or the party may feel he must. And if that is his decision, I would support him. I'll campaign for him, anywhere he wants me to. You know, I'm quite a campaigner."

Nineteen seventy-six was not to be a Kennedy year. Sarge was being backed by Richard Drayne, who had been Ted Kennedy's press secretary for more than a decade. Washington senator Henry M. Jackson was being backed by former Kennedy loyalist Jesse Unruh. Georgia governor Jimmy Carter was making a strong showing in his bid, and if there was going to be a spoiler, it would likely be Hubert Humphrey. Even worse, Mrs. Kennedy had said in an interview that she would help Shriver if he ran. Ted Kennedy just lacked support, and that situation would only get worse in the years ahead.

Much of Mrs. Kennedy's life was in the past. It was rarely mentioned that she continued to keep in touch with Billy Cavendish's family long after both he and Kathleen were dead. Kathleen's former mother-in-law, the dowager Duchess of Devonshire, was a regular correspondent. The two women were constantly sharing intimate stories of their families despite the religious differences that had once made the two women suspicious of each other.

Jack was also important to Mrs. Kennedy. However, to her delight she found that she could take advantage of the love the American people had for Jack. His memory became yet another way for her to save money, this time with tips.

Mrs. Kennedy had a large stack of cards specially printed to postcard size so they would fit comfortably in her purse. The front had a picture of President Kennedy. On the back were several of his favorite Scripture passages, as well as a line from his inaugural address: "Ask not what your country can do for you; ask what you can do for your country." She would then autograph the cards and hand them out instead of a tip, no matter how much money was involved, no matter what the needs of the person receiving the card. She would always smile and say, "Save this, someday it will be worth money."

I don't know if she believed what she said. I do know that the recipients never knew what to say or how to react. And she must have saved herself hundreds or thousands of dollars in well-earned tips.

[During the last two years I was with Mrs. Kennedy, she stopped autographing items sent to her. Stamp collectors used to write all the time, and prior to those last two years she did fulfill their requests. But there came a time when she asked me to sign her name for her. I suppose the collectors will hate me for saying this, but unless the first day cover or other item they own was post-marked more than two years prior to her major stroke in 1978, it was not signed by Mrs. Kennedy. Only the postcard "tips."]

I felt that the entire family was deteriorating during those years. The grandchildren were experimenting with sex and drugs, Caroline going so far as to grow her own marijuana in the midst of plants her mother had at home. Bobby Kennedy junior almost died of an overdose while flying over Colorado in a commercial airliner. And Ted's actions seemed to give the wrong message.

For example, one Friday the senator showed up in Palm Beach with his girlfriend of the moment. He was joined by Christopher Lawford and Joe Kennedy II, each with a date of his own. They all danced together, trading girlfriends among themselves as they did. Later the senator might have gone off with his girlfriend or the girlfriend of one of his nephews. I happened upon him later walk-ing along and wearing only a towel wrapped around his waist.

Rita Dallas wrote that shortly after she started working for Joe, Mrs. Kennedy told her that Joe had brought the children up to be "natural." Then Mrs. Kennedy handed her some clean towels and asked her to take them to the sauna where the senator and some friends were enjoying themselves. The maid had refused to do it, no explanation given. "You're a nurse and it shouldn't bother you," Mrs. Kennedy added before Dallas went to the sauna.

The nurse wrote that when she stepped into the sauna, all the men, including the senator, were naked. They took the towels from her, leaving her uncertain what to do. But before she could leave, Teddy spoke to her by name, apparently having been told that she was the new nurse. She added:

"He was prancing around jovially full of fun and laughter. Draping his arm around my shoulder, which was stiff with shock, he made a flamboyant point of introducing me to his friends. Never before, nor ever since, have I been introduced to a naked man. Propriety of such nature is seldom called upon."

Swimming and nudity seemed to be two regular activities in the lives of the Kennedys. Mrs. Kennedy made swimming a major part of her life. I still remember the first time we went along the ocean path, then entered the cold bay water. Once we adjusted to the temperature, I found myself talking and giggling along with this famous woman who was obviously enjoying herself immensely in the water. Here we are, I thought, Rose Kennedy and I, bobbing around happily like two corks, in the cold Cape Cod water. It would have been fun to have known her when she was younger for this was a side of her rarely seen by outsiders.

There were many incidents in the weeks, months, and years to follow. One cloudy afternoon in Palm Beach, Mrs. Kennedy came and asked me to go in the swimming pool with her. I told her there was a storm forecast, but she said she wanted to go in anyway. I could see she was determined since she was wearing a bathing suit and had already donned her caps.

I went down to the pool later because I felt she shouldn't be in swimming alone. So I sauntered around the pool fully dressed while she paddled from one end to the other. She said, "Come on in. Don't be a ninny."

I said, "No, Mrs. Kennedy, there is thunder and lightning. Water attracts lightning. If it should strike the pool you'd be electrocuted."

She said, "Don't you want to be here to hear my last words?"

Another morning I arrived at work only to have Mamselle greeting me with "Babella. Babella. Hurry! Gramma is in the ocean swimming alone. Come take care of her."

I hurriedly donned my swimsuit and rushed down to the beach.

There she was, bobbing around with her layers of swim caps (she wore two, one on the front of her head, one on the back—"I have such an enormous head," she explained) a straw hat, an eye shield, sunglasses, and a chiffon scarf tied around all this.

I looked up and down the beach and I could see no one around. It was only 9:00 a.m. The ocean was very calm, with no white caps.

I dunked myself in the water hesitantly because I had been reading the book *Jaws* the night before, and my memories of the opening scene where the shark attacked the girl were still vivid in my mind.

"The water is delicious," she said. So there we were bobbing around talking and enjoying the morning when all of a sudden a swell came up along the beach. Then a big wave. I looked over and Mrs. Kennedy was gone! I was only a few feet away and I rushed over and reached under where I had last seen her, put my arms under hers and pulled her up with all my strength. She came up sputtering and grasping at her false teeth and the hat, I could see, was floating away, with the chiffon scarf trailing behind it. Her glasses and eye shield had disappeared, though fortunately I was able to grope around and locate them. I looked over and she was half-sitting in the shallow water, floundering and shivering. I took her by the arm and led her up to the beach where we had towels to cover us. After she had recovered somewhat she said, "Too bad there was no one on the beach to see this. Your name would be in the paper that you had saved me."

When I first went to Palm Beach with Mrs. Kennedy, there were problems with her pool. Her friend Mary Sanford had two pools, a large one outdoors and a small indoor pool that was in the middle of a modestly-sized room. The room included a changing area that was just part of the open space. There was a toilet, a sink, a shower, and a place to sit while changing in and out of your clothing. Privacy was afforded by closing heavy curtains.

After we had been in Mary's indoor pool for a while, Mrs. Kennedy told me she had to go to the bathroom. She climbed out of the water, walked to the changing area, and left the curtain wide open as she took off her suit. Then she sat on the toilet, naked, as I watched from the water.

My friends had all been envious of me when I got the job as Mrs. Kennedy's assistant. They had talked about the glamour of the Kennedys, about their fabulous lifestyle, about the travel and excitement. "Oh, Barbara, you're so lucky!" they had said.

And there I was, treading water while facing a naked old lady sitting on a toilet. Ah, the glamour of the idle rich!

Nudity never seemed to bother Mrs. Kennedy. I remember when we were in Palm Beach in the spring of 1977 when Mrs. Kennedy was in her late eighties. A cocktail party was scheduled for Gloria Guinness, and Sargent Shriver was handling the details.

Sarge had no idea that Gloria Guinness did not drink, and he also did not want to look at the realities of the Palm Beach house, which was ill equipped for entertaining. There were no fine linens, and little good china. There were no sherry glasses, for example, yet sherry was one of the drinks of choice in their social set.

The Kennedys maintained a full bar in the den of the Florida house, but Sarge wanted to set a temporary bar in the living room. He insisted upon a white tablecloth, though only a clean white sheet could be found in the house.

Still Sarge kept barking orders at me as well as the maid/cook, who had too much food to prepare to deal with him. He didn't seem to realize that slavery had been abolished a hundred years earlier.

Sarge came to my room where I was changing clothes for the evening, the final outrage. I was irate over his rudeness and demands, and so I stalked down the hall to Mrs. Kennedy's bedroom.

The door was closed, so I knocked. When I said who was there, Mrs. Kennedy told me to come right inside.

I entered, angrily saying, "Mrs. Kennedy, Sarge has to go!"

Then I saw her. She was staring in a mirror, a wide-brimmed hat on her head. The rest of her body was totally naked. "Oh, I can't get involved now," she said, adjusting the hat more to her liking, oblivious to the rest of her body.

I mentioned the unusual incident to the maid, then discovered it was not that unusual. The maid told me about finding Mrs. Kennedy in the attic standing naked before a mirror and trying on hats in the middle of the night.

The third generation learned from the parents and grandparents. It became no surprise to see the senator with only a towel wrapped around his waist, or Christopher Lawford "dressed" in the same manner, coming into my office.

At the same time, Mrs. Kennedy was prudish. She had a ritual at bedtime. Mamselle would leave her a small tray containing slices of French toast and a thermos of hot milk in case she was hungry before she went to sleep. Then she would read books, staying away from fiction. She preferred biographies and books on current events. Novels contained too much sex, or so she believed.

For example, Mrs. Kennedy asked me to find her a copy of *Jaws*. The grandchildren were talking about the Peter Benchley book that was eventually made into a popular horror movie, and she wanted to see what it was all about.

Mrs. Kennedy read only as far as a sex scene. The next morning, outraged by what she encountered, she handed the book to me and stated, "Burn this. It's trash!"

The one surprise was the Hyannis Port maid, Jeannette. For some reason she intimidated Mrs. Kennedy the way Mrs. Kennedy intimidated everyone else. Jeannette had her own rules for her employer to follow, and they were rarely broken. For example, Jeannette had afternoons off. She watched soap operas on television, and no one was permitted to disturb her, including Mrs. Kennedy. Jeannette was also a cook, but only for Mrs. Kennedy. She refused to be bothered with anyone else.

But the oddest moment I experienced when watching their relationship came when I happened to walk by the kitchen shortly after Mrs. Kennedy had gotten dressed and stopped by. She was on her way out to an important appointment, but she was talking as though she didn't want Jeannette to think she was a bad little girl. "I didn't have time to straighten my room yet," Mrs. Kennedy said sheepishly. "I'll do it when I return."

The enormity of the Kennedy clan was both trying and amusing. I remember one day my sixteen-year-old son, Kevin, was with me at Hyannis Port when Jackie came by. She knew I had children, knew they were sometimes with me. But I was not present and Jackie did not want to embarrass herself by admitting that there were just too many growing children to keep track of them. She began talking with Kevin, asking him about school and other activities. She assumed he was yet another Kennedy child.

No one wanted to admit that the dynasty could ever disintegrate, that the matriarch could become old. Yet Rose Kennedy was aging rapidly. She bought the latest makeup to stay in style. She watched her health, eating food for its nutritional value, such as her daily banana in order to assure adequate potassium. She campaigned for Ted's reelection to the Senate in 1976 and was considered by his supporters to be a critical tool for when he ran for president in 1980.

The campaign appearances became few in number, but amazingly potent. Her speeches on Ted's behalf, and a letter she handwrote, then had duplicated for his constituents, dramatically moved the voters. Her style was remarkable, honed from when she was a little girl. For example, my dictation book includes a speech she gave in September 1976 in the Sheraton Hotel in Boston:

My dear friends:
It is a very great pleasure for me to be here today and see so many of my old friends. I know you have brought many of your friends with you, and all of us together want to help to send Teddy to a smashing victory on November 6. I am delighted to be back here in Boston again. It was here that I was born, went to public school, and graduated from Dorchester High School in 1906. If any of you read the papers in those days, you would have seen my father was mayor of Boston and gave me my diploma. Again in 1914 I was married in the Cardinal's Chapel by Cardinal O'Connell, a very happy and memorable day for me.
My little family started here, attended public schools, and lived many happy years here until we moved later to New York.

So you can see that Boston is full of happy memories for me, and I am delighted to be back again today.

I want to talk to you a little bit about our candidate. I am going to tell you about the way he was brought up and some of his qualifications. I often quoted to my children the verse of Scripture from St. Luke: "Of those to whom much is given, much is to be expected." I urged all the children [to remember] the fact that they had been given exceptional advantages and so they should in turn try to help others less fortunate. I think my older sons followed this precept quite conscientiously and know that Teddy is concerned. He has worked very hard to insure that all the people from Massachusetts will be able to receive good-quality health care as a right, not as a privilege. He has known rich people who pay very low taxes commensurate with their wealth, while people whose incomes are lower pay a larger proportion. He is working very diligently to eliminate this abuse and move to a system that is more equitable.

I know from my own experience that he has great concern for the deprived and for the unfortunate. At home when Bobby passed away and his eleventh child was born, Teddy accompanied Ethel to the hospital. He tries to be present at the graduations of those children whose fathers are absent, and he is the first one to bring me the news when someone in the family has had an accident. He is very conscientious about it and I know I can always depend on him for the news of the latest developments in the family.

And so my friends I hope that you will cooperate with us all and give him an overwhelming vote on Tuesday . . .

One parting word. . . . I think it is wonderful for you to campaign at the age of thirty-six or forty-six and even sixty-six, but when you get to be eighty-six, don't let it happen to you.

Yet her campaign appearances would be few in number. Mostly she contributed direct-mail letters to selected areas, such as the following letter, meant to appeal to the elderly. The results would help keep Teddy in power, yet no matter what anyone wanted, Mrs. Kennedy had become old.

> Dear Friends,
>
> I have been pleased to be able to celebrate my 86th birthday this year. As someone still young in the way I view the world, I share many of the same concerns you do about the way society tends to ignore older people. As President Kennedy said, "We need the wisdom, the skills and the experience of our older citizens." Continuing this tradition, my young son, Ted Kennedy, has always given high priority to the needs of older Americans.
>
> I am proud that he authored the Hot Lunch Program for the elderly, that he was the chief sponsor of cost of living increases in Social Security payments, and that he has continued to work for better housing and health care for the Senior Citizens of Massachusetts and the rest of the nation.
>
> For these reasons, I am writing to ask that you remember Senator Kennedy in your vote in the Democratic Primary on September 14.

I realized that my days as Mrs. Kennedy's assistant were coming to an end as I saw her increasingly incapacitated. I had cursed her constant turning off of lights in my office and other frugalities. But by the mid-1970s she was no longer interested in counting pennies. The New York office could handle everything.

Mrs. Kennedy's eyesight was failing, and her hands began to shake so much that she could no longer write notes to herself or others. I limited the mail she saw to two or three letters a day, which had to be read to her, but even these were too much. They produced great anxiety in her.

The family that had been the focus of Mrs. Kennedy's world was overwhelming her. She had come to hate the chaos, the out-of-control surroundings where kids, dogs, drugs, and sex seemed rampant.

I remember finding Mrs. Kennedy in the maids' dining room one morning after a massive Thanksgiving feast. The previous evening everything had gone as smoothly as a Kennedy gathering can go. She was surrounded by massive amounts of food, a dozen members of her family, and enough help to handle the meal. Yet she was sitting at the table the next day crying uncontrollably.

The guests had created havoc. There were broken lamps and glasses. Towels had been carelessly left by the beach and the pool. Someone had sneaked into the kitchen during the night to eat more turkey. Though there was plenty of help to clean everything and the loss meant little to a woman of her means, the world was no longer within her control. The chaos of her life was no longer something she could handle.

The pain was made even more poignant one afternoon in Hyannis Port when I was leaving for home at the end of my work day. As I did routinely, I stopped to say goodbye. She looked at me solemnly, then said, "You're lucky. You can leave when you want to. I'm stuck here."

Pat's brood was probably the worst. They generally did nothing but abuse the house, while the Smith family always brought their own staff to handle the cooking and cleaning. One time when David Kennedy wanted to come alone to visit, Mrs. Kennedy went so far as to suggest that he delay his coming until the Smiths were scheduled to arrive. There would be extra staff to clean up.

In Hyannis Port Ethel caused enormous problems. Her life had no discipline. Her home was frequently in disrepair, especially the front porch, which was rotted, sagging, and filled with children climbing onto the roof. Many an unwary visitor was "attacked" from the roof with water-filled balloons.

The back entrance looked like the receiving entrance for a hotel. There were huge boxes of groceries from the market, children telling the cook what they wanted to eat (and when, as meals, except dinner, were taken as desired), and massive piles of dirty clothes waiting to be washed.

Ethel's children were reared with what seemed to be the best and worst parenting. She let the kids go wild, but she continued Bob's tradition of always having everyone sit down for dinner together. Other meals were chaos. Dinner included all the children, governesses, visiting relatives, secretaries, and famous guests, who might include singer Andy Williams, television newswoman Barbara Walters, actress Farrah Fawcett-Majors, talk-show host David Hartman, athletes Rafer Johnson and Bruce Jenner, and numerous others. The conversations were stimulating, and in that one part of their lives, there was a closeness.

Daytime was frightening, though. Ethel had eight dogs, which she ignored as much as she generally ignored her children. They roamed the streets, much to the disgust of the community. They also reverted to a more primitive state, becoming dangerously aggressive. One of them knocked Mrs. Kennedy to the ground, ripping her clothing and bruising her. Fortunately she wasn't seriously hurt, and I was surprised it happened only once. Ethel was oblivious to what the rest of us thought was her responsibility to either train the animals or restrain them, neither of which she did.

The worst problems with Ethel's brood went unnoticed by Mrs. Kennedy. She would send them memos concerning matters she felt were important, such as telling David Kennedy not to drink so much Coke. She felt it would damage his teeth, and she knew that bright, white teeth were important in life. She never suspected that a soft drink was not a problem. David was a heavy user of coke— cocaine. And his grandmother was oblivious.

Mrs. Kennedy once wrote to Caroline complaining because when the other young people arrived in Palm Beach, they often did not start their activities until 1 A.M. They would go from nightclub to nightclub, drinking, eating, and dancing until the places closed, then sleep through the day, which Mrs. Kennedy felt was a terrible habit.

Ethel was much like her mother in avoiding problems. When David Kennedy was arrested on drug charges, Steve Smith arranged for him to be sent to a California hospital for treatment. But Ethel Kennedy wanted nothing to do with such matters. She no longer seemed to care about David. She certainly was not going to sign him in to a hospital. In the end, Kathleen Townsend, his sister, had to handle the arrangements as legal guardian.

None of the grandchildren were saints. Bobby's kids were the roughest, but I still remember the day I heard a strange noise outside my office. I went to the window and there was John F. Kennedy Jr. urinating on the outside office wall. He had to urinate and walking an additional ten feet to the lavatory just inside the door was too much trouble for him.

Mrs. Kennedy kept in touch with the grandchildren by letter but increasingly avoided them in person because of the chaos. She wanted peace, though that would elude her even as her body and mind deteriorated and she had the money to buy whatever lifestyle she desired.

Many times Mrs. Kennedy was not lucid. She would seem to be lost in memory or talking about something far afield from the original conversation. At other times she could be roused to articulate, focused outrage, such as during the summer of 1976 when she responded to a James Reston column in the *New York Times*. The letter she dictated read:

> Like his brothers and sisters, my son Jack was reared in a home with a deep and abiding faith. He practiced his faith constantly until his death. Although not demonstrative in his practice, he attended Mass and understood the meaning and the value of daily prayer. . . .

The fire that had once burned so brightly was becoming little more than a smoldering ember with sparks of flame occasionally brightening the sky. Mrs. Kennedy was apparently having a series of "pencil" strokes in addition to the complications of the ever-growing family whose antics she had grown to accept. There was a difference between dealing with nine children and twenty-nine grandchildren. Her memory was worse than in the past, and now she could not read her notes, could not see if her face still needed a frownie. "One consolation in all this," she said to me one afternoon around Labor Day, "I'm leaving this very soon!"

There was no way to reply. Mrs. Kennedy was deteriorating rapidly. She needed a nurse or a second maid, not an assistant.

That year for her birthday, there was a large clambake. A light plane flew over the event trailing a banner reading, "Happy birthday, Mother."

With so much confusion at the party, Jackie was heard to say, "The family should have their own activities and leave Grandma out of it."

In September of 1979, Rose Kennedy had an operation for a strangulated hernia that prevented her from attending the October 20, 1979, opening of the John F. Kennedy Library. Taking advantage of the publicity, Ted Kennedy began allowing himself to be interviewed by selected members of the news media. The Kennedy Library dedication, the plan to run in the Democratic primaries, challenging President Jimmy Carter as Robert had challenged Lyndon Johnson, all seemed positive steps toward another Kennedy presidency. And Ted would win a few primaries, revealing the popularity of the Kennedy name.

But times had changed for the new patriarch of the Kennedy clan. No one was gentle in his or her questioning. Even the friendliest reporters understood the mood of the country. They asked about Chappaquiddick. They asked about Joan, who was living apart from her husband. They asked about the womanizing, about his drinking.

Older leaders in Massachusetts Democratic Party circles talked of Ted having a "safe" Senate seat, of his being a growing power where he was. Certainly Ted was becoming an elder statesman, establishing a far superior record than his brothers. Yet none had the desire to do for Ted what they had done for Bob and Jack.

There was a new generation of voters as well. Many had little or no knowledge of Jack Kennedy. They had no feelings about carrying on his legacy. They did not know his legacy. All they knew was a fat old man who drank too much had killed some woman in his car and was the brother of a president who was murdered before they were in first grade.

Winning a few primaries was not good enough. Ted no longer had the drive. His mother was barely lucid. And always the specter of assassination and other violence loomed over all their heads. Ted campaigned while wearing a bulletproof vest, and the Secret Service made certain an armored car met the senator at every stop.

Ted lost the Illinois primary decisively to Jimmy Carter. His votes were half the incumbent's in Iowa. And though he would win New York, among others, the primary balloting proved that Ted could not take the nomination.

The Later Years

January 21, 1977

Dear Senator [Ted Kennedy]:

I would like you and the other members of the family to know my feelings concerning the situation with your mother here in Palm Beach.

It is my opinion that she needs a nurse-companion and that she no longer needs a secretary. During the past year my duties have dwindled to chauffeuring, taking care of her personal needs and trying to keep the household running smoothly. This has become increasingly difficult due to her fast-declining mental and physical condition.

She is in agony due to her inability to sleep and her nerves during the day are such that most of her activities consist of ordering things and returning them and calling strangers to run unnecessary errands. She needs constant supervision and should not be left alone. I am not a doctor, but it seems to me that an antidepressant or relaxant would help to make her life more pleasant and this, of course, should be administered by someone trained to do so.

> *Sincerely,*
> *(Mrs.) Barbara J. Gibson*
> *Secretary to*
> *Mrs. Joseph P. Kennedy*

The dirty little secret in Rose Kennedy's later years was her drug addiction. Not that anyone thought of her in that way because, unlike so many of her grandchildren who delighted in "recreational drugs" such as cocaine, her drugs were "properly" prescribed. She was addicted to sleeping pills.

Mrs. Kennedy would go to bed at 11 P.M., lie there a bit, then decide that she could not sleep, taking her first sleeping pill. Given the tolerance Mrs. Kennedy had developed, the first pill would take almost an hour to work. However, just as she was becoming drowsy, she would decide that the pill had been ineffective. After all, she was tired but not unconscious. She would then get herself a second

295

sleeping pill, though the strong prescription meant it was not safe to take more than one.

The nightly overdose was usually not a major problem. She would be groggy in the morning until she had eaten and begun moving around. However, one morning at eight-thirty I received a frantic telephone call from the maid, Jeannette. Mrs. Kennedy would not move, and only Jeannette and the gardener were present. They didn't want to call the doctor because one of the emergency services would have been dispatched. Jeannette and the gardener felt that the problem was not life threatening, and that Mrs. Kennedy would be embarrassed. However, they were frightened by her lying in bed, not responding to efforts to awaken her.

By the time I arrived, Jeannette had Mrs. Kennedy balanced on the side of the bed as she tried to dress her. Jeannette was holding panty hose, struggling unsuccessfully to get them on Mrs. Kennedy's legs. Mrs. Kennedy was talking semicoherently, obviously thinking that she was in New York, not Hyannis Port. She was convinced that a taxi had been called to her hotel to take her to mass, and that was why she had to dress.

Eventually we got Mrs. Kennedy dressed and fed, had her drink some coffee, and got her walking. I tried to talk with her about the dangers of her prescription-drug misuse, but she would hear none of it. I finally reminded her that it was spring, a time when the public would be remembering the anniversary of Jack's birth. If she died of an overdose of sleeping pills, no matter how innocently she had taken them, the public would think she had grown despondent, committing suicide. I said that such a death would sully his memory, and to a degree she seemed to think that made sense. However the overdosing continued, both in Hyannis Port and later in Palm Beach.

I felt that the family needed to know what was happening, so I called the senator in Washington. He believed me when I explained the problem, even though he had never seen it. However, he lacked the courage to confront his mother. Instead, when the family was in Palm Beach, he arranged for a party where Mrs. Kennedy's New York physician would be present. Although ostensibly a guest, he was actually being paid to examine Mrs. Kennedy to see if there was a problem.

The "examination" was a farce. Ted decided that his mother looked fine and avoided further involvement.

I kept talking with the children, trying to find someone who cared. Pat had her own problems with pills, but Jean Smith was sensitive to the situation and told me to take her mother's pills and dump them down the toilet. I did, and when Mrs. Kennedy found out, I told her that Mrs. Smith had told me to do it.

Mrs. Kennedy was irate. She said, "I won't be treated like a child." Then she ordered me to call her daughter, something Jean expected. She had her maid tell me that she was out of town, though I knew the truth.

Unfortunately our efforts were for nothing. Mrs. Kennedy had a secret cache in her traveling case, which she used until new prescriptions could be filled.

Given such a history, it was natural that David Kennedy, Bob and Ethel's son, would get involved with drugs. His use would prove more deadly, though.

David, Ethel's fourth child, was born in 1955. He was shy, had a mild speech impediment, and was closer to his father than the other boys.

Ethel had never been mother of the year except by sheer number of children. She seemed to live on the tennis courts while pregnant and engaged in as many physical activities as possible. The staff took care of the house and the children, though ultimately the children reared themselves. She had little interest in their day-by-day development. Discipline was never consistent, limits never defined. Instead, she could be extremely harsh when she lost her temper, overreacting to the same degree that she underreacted at other times.

David was never given a time to grieve after his father's death. Even worse, his mother was several months pregnant with what would be Bob Kennedy's last child. That birth took attention away from the other children, as though some sort of divine passage had occurred by sperm, death, and new birth. Just as David needed someone to love him, those closest to him were absorbed with the last Kennedy in Bob and Ethel's family.

Ethel became an angry mother after the birth of Rory Elizabeth, the eleventh child. She was frustrated, turning away from her children, who seemed to remind her too much of her late husband. The children's grades changed; they were frustrated and depressed.

David was plagued with recurring nightmares in which he relived watching his father's murder. Instead of seeking meaningful help for him, Ethel teamed him with his cousin Christopher Lawford since they were both thirteen. But Christopher had his own problems with his drug-addicted father, and both boys were highly self-destructive.

Christopher and David were allowed to do things together for which they were ill equipped. They traveled to Austria to a ski and tennis camp called Meyerhoff. There were also girls, and the boys soon found that they could parlay talk of their problems and celebrity into sex.

Mrs. Kennedy regularly warned her staff not to leave money or valuables where her grandchildren could get to them. They would steal anything they could find. In fact, the Lawford children were so hated for that and other reasons that one maid always left during their two weeks' stay. Pat Lawford had to bring along her own.

Christopher Lawford began sneaking his girlfriend into the house so she could stay the night. Meanwhile Ethel was endlessly involved with athletic activities and giving large parties, as though the guests could help protect her from her emotions. She did not want to grieve, did not want to pull her family together. And so Christopher also began using drugs, something he had in common with David.

When the Kennedys did compete with one another, as sometimes happened with the older grandsons, it was feverish. The underlying family loyalty and fierce solidarity that had given the previous generation's competitiveness its meaning was no longer there. In the case of Christopher, David, young Bobby Kennedy, and others, that competitiveness was as likely to be destructive as constructive, to involve heavy drug use as athletics.

What the Kennedy compound needed, I mused, was a strong masculine physical and moral influence.

The Easter weekend when Mrs. Kennedy had her stroke, David Kennedy was staying at the Brazilian Court Hotel in the center of Palm Beach. He was no longer welcome in the Kennedy compound, no longer welcome in his mother's house, no longer welcome anywhere. As was mentioned, he had come to feel that if his grandfather were alive, he would have been given an operation like his aunt Rosemary to change his behavior.

David knew his grandmother might be dying and he wanted to see her. He was staying at the hotel with his brother Douglas, and they decided to visit her.

David was intensely emotional. He was twenty-eight years old, had dropped out of Harvard, and had been working to kick his drug habit for several years. He had been on methadone. He had met with psychiatrists. Before traveling to Palm Beach he had been in St. Paul, Minnesota, at yet another treatment facility. But David was too filled with self-loathing, too filled with fear and sorrow, to let any program reach him. He had needed special attention since he watched his father die, yet no one had bothered to reach out to him.

The nursing staff knew about David, knew he was a drug addict, and did not trust him. They were warm and friendly to him, caring about his pain as he saw his helpless, speechless, seemingly sightless grandmother curled on her bed. But they also never took their eyes off him. They feared that he would steal something from the room, as they had a small cache of all types of drugs needed to handle any emergency with his grandmother.

David was in Mrs. Kennedy's room no more than two minutes before leaving. He took nothing with him.

David had been using both cocaine and alcohol fairly heavily that weekend. He had been aimlessly going to nightclubs. He allegedly obtained some of his cocaine from the hotel's bellman, who had been known to deal drugs on the side.

The story of that long weekend has been told elsewhere. David drank vodka, took drugs, and met at least two women. He stayed with Perrier water when his seventeen-year-old brother was with him, trying to set a good example, but on his own, he was balancing stimulants and depressants in dangerous combinations.

According to the nurses taking care of Rose Kennedy, the pharmacy had supplied a much larger container of the painkiller Demerol than was needed. The bottle was found missing sometime after Sydney Lawford and Caroline Kennedy left their grandmother. The nurses did not recall anyone else coming into the room, but no one knows with certainty if either woman took the medication. (Caroline has passed a polygraph exam concerning many of her actions around the time of David's death. Sydney has refused to take such a test.)

If the cousins took the Demerol, it was undoubtedly taken to ease David's pain. Demerol was not viewed as particularly dangerous, even though it was a controlled substance. What neither they nor David understood was that when you overdose on Demerol, then fall asleep, you can "forget" to breathe. In David's exhausted, drug-ravaged state, he fell into a very deep sleep. At some point on Tuesday morning, April 25, 1984, he forgot to breathe, suffocating quietly on his bed.

It would be the last tragedy involving Rose Kennedy.

Rose Kennedy made some appearances well into her nineties. She was ninety-three when she attended the wedding of her granddaughter Sydney Lawford in 1983. Yet the Rose I had known was gone. She had to be helped up the church steps, looking like a shrunken elf. She sat motionless through the ceremony, and a video taken by friends of the bride's reveal a woman whose mind and body were rapidly deteriorating.

On Good Friday in 1984, Rose collapsed during dinner. She was given oxygen, taken to her bedroom, and an intensive care unit was brought to the mansion. She had probably had yet another of the small strokes that were increasingly incapacitating her.

For all practical purposes, Rose Kennedy died on Easter Sunday.

I talked with the nurse who was present, who would remain with Mrs. Kennedy in the months and years that followed.

Easter Sunday, 1984, was Rose Kennedy's time to die. She had a severe stroke, her heart stopped, the priest who was present administered the last rites.

The death would undoubtedly have been a blessing, and not because of what followed. For a woman reared as Mrs. Kennedy had been, death in the midst of the joyous reminder of the Resurrection would have been a cause for celebration. She was a Child of Mary. She was ready for whatever lay ahead in God's plan.

And so they gathered outside St. Stephen's Church on January 24, 1995, in the dear old North End. Eight hundred mourners filled the pews, one hundred of them members of the Kennedy family.

"She has gone to God," said her surviving son, the senator. "She is home. And at this moment, she is happily presiding at a heavenly table with both of her Joes, with Jack and Kathleen, with Bobby and David.

"And as she did all our lives, whether it was when I walked back through the rain from school as a child, or when a president who was her son came back to Hyannis Port, she will be there ready to welcome the rest of us home someday."

The senator spoke of Mrs. Kennedy's playing "Sweet Rosie O'Grady" on the piano while the family gathered around her, singing. He told of her reciting poetry. And he told of her gently teasing him when he was an unsuccessful candidate for president in 1980.

Ted had said to an interviewer, "If I was president . . ." Mrs. Kennedy heard the incorrect grammar and wrote to him, saying: "You should have said 'If I were president,' which is correct because it is a condition contrary to fact."

Mrs. Kennedy's concerns over the years had frequently been for the retarded, though she did not personally involve herself in the work to which Eunice devoted herself. Ted mentioned this, saying, "Mother had a special place in her heart and prayers for our sister Rosemary, for her bravery and the things she taught us all."

Among the mourners, in addition to the Kennedys, were Boston mayor Thomas Menino; Joan Bennett Kennedy, the senator's former wife; Tipper Gore, wife of Vice President Al Gore; the governor and lieutenant governor of Massachusetts; U.S. Housing and Urban Development official Andrew Cuomo; numerous congressional representatives; and others.

And when it was over, before she was buried, Ted recited the following poem, entitled "The Rose Still Grows Beyond the Wall":

Near a shady wall a rose once grew,
Budded and blossomed in God's free light,
Watered and fed by morning dew.
Shredding its sweetness day and night.

As it grew and blossomed fair and tall,
Slowly rising to loftier height,
It came to a crevice in the wall,
Through which there shone a beam of light.

Onward it crept with added strength,
With never a thought of fear or pride,
It followed the light through the crevice's length,
And unfolded itself on the other side.

The light, the dew, the broadening view,
Were found the same as they were before;
And it lost itself in beauties new,
Breathing its fragrance more and more.

Shall claim of death cause us to grieve,
And make our courage faint or fail?

Nay! Let us faith and hope receive:
The rose still grows beyond the wall,
Scattering fragrance far and wide,
Just as it did in days of yore,
Just as it did on the other side,
Just as it will for evermore.

Rose Fitzgerald Kennedy was laid to rest at the Holyhood Cemetery in Brookline, her body placed beside that of her late husband.

BG: THERE HAD BEEN an earlier time I prefer to recall. Death was not an issue then, but there was a parting. Mrs. Kennedy was leaving Hyannis Port for the winter, and as usual the staff was lined up to say goodbye.

For a few minutes we stood around talking. The mood was relaxed, and for some reason Nellie, the cook, said, "You've had the best of everything, haven't you, Mrs. Kennedy?"

Mrs. Kennedy's eyes looked at Nellie yet seemed to be seeing something more, the past as well as the present. Then she quietly said, "I've had the best of everything, and I've also had the worst of everything."

And so she had.

Notes

11, "Then, after moving to Boston": The details of Rose Kennedy's past should not be in question. However, errors are found in a number of highly respected biographies of the family members. Sometimes this occurred because the family preferred to have an "official" version of an unpleasant incident, such as will be seen in the chapter on Rosemary. In other instances the biographer apparently attempted to add additional credibility to personal belief. At least one highly respected biography contains quotes from an "interview" conducted *after* Mrs. Kennedy's stroke had rendered her speechless.

In this instance, historian Doris Kearns Goodwin lists John Fitzgerald's mother as Rosanna Cox, the daughter of Philip and Mary Cox, in her book *The Kennedys and the Fitzgeralds*. This was repeated in the book *The Kennedy Women* by Larry Leamer. However, Rose Kennedy herself notes in her ghost-written autobiography, *Times to Remember*, as do references in books about her father, that her mother-in-law's name was Rose Mary Murray. This name was also used in the biography of her father *Honey Fitz* by John Henry Cutler. The latter does make reference to what apparently was John Fitzgerald's mother's nickname, Mother Rosanna. No explanation is provided as to the source of the nickname.

A check in the Kennedy Library oddly works against the comments by Rose Kennedy. There is no copy of her mother-in-law's birth certificate, which might clarify everything. What does exist is a December 29, 1976, hand-printed copy (*not* a photocopy, which would have clarified matters) of the 1857 marriage record of Thomas Fitzgerald, son of Michael Fitzgerald, and Rose Cox, daughter of Philip Cox. There is also a December 31, 1976, copy (again, not a photocopy) of the March 10, 1879, death certificate of Rosanna (Cox) Fitzgerald, listed as the wife of Thomas and daughter of Philip and Mary Cox.

15, " 'For some reason or other' ": Among numerous sources are such books as the Cutler biography of Honey Fitz and *Reckless Youth*.

24, "Finally Fitzgerald made a move": John Fitzgerald was strongly disliked by Jack Kennedy, his advisers, and his father, Joe. Yet Fitzgerald was also the most brilliant strategist available to the grandson, and Jack did listen to him.

Notes

The famous Kennedy/Nixon debates probably originated with Fitzgerald's teachings.

One of the great historical ironies was that Congressman O'Neil could probably have successfully debated Fitzgerald. His power as an incumbent exceeded Fitzgerald's. He could point to what he had accomplished, to the fact that he would be able to do even more with the greater seniority of another term, and that Honey Fitz would be a meaningless freshman. But O'Neil felt no need to debate the upstart and lost the election.

By contrast, Jack Kennedy did lose the debates with Nixon. The vice president had a far stronger track record in Congress, was far more liberal than the hawkish senator who challenged him (Jack and the Kennedy family had been close friends with the disgraced senator Joseph McCarthy), and had a far better grasp of the issues. Anyone who listened to the debates on the radio or read transcripts published in some newspapers was convinced that Nixon had soundly trounced his rival. However, the still new medium of television was used, and Nixon's jowly face, his heavy beard, and his deep-set eyes worked against him. Jack Kennedy came across as handsome, aggressive, and dominating. Yet it was all visual. Kennedy even used a trick that Nixon had used when having a casual conversation with Soviet premier Nikita Khrushchev at an exposition of American technology in 1957. Nixon had held out his arm and wagged his finger while talking. The gesture meant nothing in context, but the image, taken out of context, made him appear to be aggressively putting down the enemy. Kennedy used the same gesture against Nixon, and it added to the false television image of winning.

32, "Some of the nuns wore": This idea of suffering by inflicting pain through items that might today be found in a sadomasochistic sex shop was not unique to Blumenthal and the Convent of the Sacred Heart. In New Mexico well into the 1920s, there were a group of religious zealots called Penitentes. During the Easter season they would not only deliberately hurt their bodies, at least one of them would be crucified. A cross would be erected and a man would be nailed to it. He would wear a crown of thorns, and though in theory he would not be allowed to die, in practice the man hoped for and occasionally achieved death. This was not suicide any more than the nuns in Blumenthal considered their actions a fetish. It was an attempt to relate directly to the suffering of Jesus.

32, "It would be too much": From *Times to Remember*, 39.

51, "In the midst of her": Joe Kennedy differentiated between his love affairs and the time or times he felt himself truly in love. He considered his girlfriends to be minor diversions so long as he kept impregnating Rose. However, when he fell in love enough to consider himself "committed" to a girlfriend, as would happen with actress Gloria Swanson, no children would be conceived with Rose. In fact, he would later make a point of reminding Gloria that Rose had gone two full years without giving birth during the time that they were together.

54, "Eunice Shriver Kennedy, Rosemary's younger": In matters of fact not covered by available documents and not obtainable through interviews with the people directly involved, we are relying upon Rose Kennedy's comments to Barbara Gibson during the ten years they worked closely together. Rose was adamant about the birth of Rosemary. She did not say that she thought Rosemary might have been damaged at birth, though that was a possibility she certainly considered later. But she did stress that the nurse held her legs together, forcing her to endure far greater pain than in the past when she was given ether as the contractions began. It is doubtful that she would be mistaken about so dramatic an experience. Most likely Eunice either never discussed the matter so directly with her mother or was uncomfortable with the truth. Either way, it can be assumed that Eunice was mistaken.

60, "Barbara Gibson obtained Rosemary's personal": The Rosemary Kennedy diaries have become controversial because they were never meant to be retained. Rose Kennedy gave them to her assistant Barbara Gibson with instructions to throw them in the trash. However, by that time the Kennedy Library was under development, and Barbara thought they might want to add the diaries to their files. Library head Dave Powers rejected the diaries, and Barbara was told to follow Rose Kennedy's original instructions. Eventually Barbara did, but not before also checking with Pat Kennedy Lawford, who agreed that they should not be kept.

But Barbara Gibson had previously worked for the FBI. She had learned that once someone discards an object, personal writing, or anything else and it is deliberately placed outside with the trash, it essentially enters the public domain for possession. Anyone may legally take the item from the trash and own it with the same rights as if it had been purchased. In fact, a number of major organized-crime cases were won, in part, with documents removed from trash cans set out by the road.

Barbara felt that the diaries should not be destroyed. They provided insights into Rosemary, and since they were written up until a short time before her prefrontal lobotomy, they added to the possible understanding of her "condition." Thus Barbara waited until the trash was put out of the house for collection, then took the diaries for herself.

Today the Kennedy Library staff wishes to own the diaries, though Barbara Gibson has refused to give them up. The handwriting has been analyzed, confirming a longtime suspicion. Rosemary had a learning disability that almost certainly was dyslexia, a condition that has affected many men and women, including Nelson Rockefeller. In fact, years later Rose contacted Rockefeller, dictating a letter to Barbara Gibson thanking him for discussing his dyslexia. As Barbara understood her reasons, Rose Kennedy felt that had there been a discussion of dyslexia when Rosemary was young, there would have been no problems.

60, "Rosemary was born retarded, her": These same tests did not reveal great intellect within the Kennedy family. Jack Kennedy scored slightly above average, in what would be considered the "bright normal" category. While intelligence does not relate to compassion, dedication, courage, and a desire to change society for the better, it does make a difference in more scholarly endeavors. This is why Joe Kennedy senior made certain that Jack's two books— *While England Slept* and *Profiles in Courage* were overtly and covertly supported. In both cases, highly skilled "assistants" did most of the work. And Joe helped make *While England Slept* a bestseller by buying many of the books himself. Joe senior admired intellectuals and writers and decided that his son would join their ranks, even if he had to spend large sums of money to do so.

60, " 'When she was old enough' ": *Times to Remember*, 151.

64, " 'So that's the way it' ": ibid., 153–54.

70, "Although he performed more than": There is some confusion as to when Dr. Freeman began using his ice-pick technique. Our research, and that of some other writers, indicates the ice pick was used on Rosemary. Certainly her brain damage indicates the targeted area was missed by several millimeters, a small distance yet one more common with the ice pick than with standard surgical techniques.

Author Larry Leamer, writing in *The Kennedy Women*, implies on page 320 that the ice-pick procedure was a more precise one than those in effect in the fall of 1941. He notes, "It would not be until half a dozen years later that Freeman would develop the well-known 'ice pick operation' usually associated with lobotomies." If Leamer is correct about the timing, then a more serious mistake was made because the other surgery was well understood.

Leamer described Rosemary's operation in a manner different from what we believe occurred. What he describes was one type of procedure used for this end, though.

According to Leamer's account, Rosemary would have been wheeled into the operating room at 8 A.M. She would be mildly sedated, then given Novocain, the same local anesthetic used by dentists. She would be awake through the procedure, her head placed on a sandbag to keep it steady while the surgeons— Freeman and Dr. James Watts—performed the operation.

Leamer writes: "Watts drilled two burr holes in each side of the cranium and inserted the tubing from a large hypodermic needle about two and a half inches into the brain. Then the doctor took a spatula that looked like a 'blunt butter knife,' pushed it into the cavity left by the tubing, and twisted upward destroying the white matter of the frontal lobe. The surgeon made three other cuts, reinserting the spatula each time."

Rosemary was awake so that she could talk, answer questions, and otherwise respond so they would know how far to go. The depth of cutting was deter-

Notes

mined by how sleepy and disoriented the patient became, a curious reaction to seek. The types of skills Rosemary was asked to show—the ability to add, subtract, sing a song, etc.—were precisely the ones the proper candidates for a prefrontal lobotomy usually could *not* do before the operation.

78, "However, such a history would": The Kennedy family and those trying to protect them overlooked that many others kept records about Joe's dealings. From the men surrounding Franklin D. Roosevelt, who would become a political enemy of Joe's, to such career criminals as Chauncey Holt, formerly one of Meyer Lansky's accountants, numerous records remain. And since the "quiet era" of organized crime began right after World War II, a time when business deals were used instead of violence, some men who became connected with the mob at that time are only in their seventies and still able to talk. They are rich resources on Joe Kennedy, though his world is not the subject of this book.

78, "Since he was breaking no": Kennedy was not unique in this regard. It was long said of industrialist John D. Rockefeller that he never broke a law. However, his business actions were so outrageous, so unfair to competitors, that many a law was passed because of him.

93, "The *Rose Elizabeth* had a": This story is best told in the book *A Question of Character: A Life of John F. Kennedy* by Thomas C. Reeves.

94, "Sending the cardinal may have": It has also been suggested that either Joe or John Fitzgerald sent O'Connell. The idea of Joe Kennedy doing such a thing makes no sense, especially since he was quite comfortable breaking off with Swanson or anyone else.

Having Fitzgerald make the contact is more plausible. However, his relationship with the Catholic Church was more a matter of expediency. He was the type likely to confront Swanson himself. Yet Honey Fitz loved his daughter, and if he thought that asking a cardinal for help would work, he would do so. Since both Fitzgerald and Rose were wealthy and prominent enough to get the cardinal's attention, the idea that one of them made the request seems most plausible.

115, " 'The President's suggestion was a' ": From chapter 1, page 4, of the autobiography being written with James Landis, then never published. Quoted in Nigel Hamilton's *JFK: Reckless Youth.*

129, "She knew of her father's": Jack was the quieter of the two older brothers. He liked the idea of having affairs, but he was gentle. Prostitutes and willing "nice" girls were his style, with the emphasis on *willing.*

Joe, by contrast, had gained the reputation as one of the boys who was NSIT —Not Safe In Taxis. This meant that he would aggressively try to take liberties with any girl with whom he found himself alone, including in the backseat of a cab. Debutantes labeled such young men as NSIT to warn each other at a time when the most wicked act imaginable for most young women was to enjoy a chaste kiss while returning to a party from which they had sneaked out for an hour or so of nightclub hopping. Kathleen was not pleased with Joe's actions, but none of her new friends were overly concerned. They looked out for one another and did not blame "Kick" for her brother's actions.

133, " 'It seems to me that' ": William L. Langer and S. Everett Gleason, *The World Crisis and American Foreign Policy: The Challenge to Isolation, 1937–1940*, 249.

133, " 'The President desires me to' ": ibid., 249–50.

142, " 'It was a system we' ": *Times to Remember*, 277.

147, " 'Teddy is the same and' ": Rose Kennedy's "Dear Children" letter from February 16, 1942. Kennedy Library.

147, " 'To Bobby's amazement when he' ": Rose Kennedy's "Dear Children" letter from March 27, 1942. Kennedy Library.

147, " 'We expected darling Teddy home' ": Rose Kennedy's "Dear Children" letter from October 9, 1942. Kennedy Library.

160, "He arranged for press releases": Doris Kearns Goodwin cites an unidentified war buddy of Jack's quoting Jack as saying, "My story about the collision is getting better all the time. Now I've got a Jew and a nigger in the story and with me being a Catholic, that's great." *The Fitzgeralds and the Kennedys*, 714.

160, " 'Joe was wise in the' ": *Times to Remember*, 308–9.

163, "Shortly before the primary, Joe": Joe was the primary backer of Jack's campaign, though how much money was spent is unknown. Dave Powers was later quoted as saying that when he needed rent for the Charlestown headquarters of the campaign, he would go see Eddie Moore. Moore would take him into a pay toilet, shut the door, and hand him the cash. The action seemed secretive to the point of paranoia, but it also reflected the habits of men who had spent years making deals they never wanted exposed to the light of day.

178, "Meeting academic standards meant more": Anyone familiar with the excellent reputation of the University of Virginia Law School may wonder how Bob could enter if he could not attend Harvard. Then, however, the University of Virginia Law School was still in transition and not particularly respected. The qualifications for attending were far less demanding than they have become, and a degree then meant a less rigid academic course than is required today.

183, "Jacqueline Bouvier had known little": The first name of Jacqueline Bouvier Kennedy Onassis is usually ignored in favor of "Jackie." In notes that she wrote to Rose, she frequently signed them Jackie, the same name that some people used as Jack's nickname. However, when introduced to the sisters and Ethel, she made clear that her name was Jacqueline, pronounced like the French—Jock-Lean. The result was hate at first sight.

219, " 'I didn't sit with him' ": Gail Cameron, *Rose*, 172.

222, "When playing golf in Hyannis": Rita Dallas, RN, with Jeanira Ratcliffe, *The Kennedy Case*, 71.

223, " 'I really don't feel too' ": *New York Herald-Tribune*, December 21, 1961.

223, "He told them not to": *Time*, December 29, 1961.

247, "He became like a protective": A number of sources say that Peter

Lawford was desperately trying to save his marriage in 1964. Allegedly he was pleading with Pat to take him back, seeking to be a part of the family. Yet Lawford's personal papers, interviews with his friends, and interviews with his widow, Patricia Seaton Lawford, all indicate that the marriage was over well before the assassination. He and Pat Kennedy were continuing a public charade solely to keep Jack from facing the embarrassment of a divorce in the family prior to his reelection. But well before the assassination, the couple planned to divorce. Peter never wanted to return to the folds of the Kennedy family or his wife, Pat, on whom he had been cheating for months.

282, " 'I have made Ted promise' ": *New York Times*, January 5, 1976. Article without byline entitled "Kennedy's Mother Recalls Pledge He Wouldn't Run."

283, "Rita Dallas wrote that shortly": Rita Dallas, *The Kennedy Case*, 69.

293, "Like his brothers and sisters": Barbara Gibson's dictation book does not record the date this letter was dictated to the editor of the *New York Times*, but it was the summer of 1976. The quote is from Barbara's notebook.

300, "If the cousins took the": For the complete story of David's death, see *The Kennedys: The Third Generation*, by Gibson and Schwarz.

Bibliography

Ainley, Leslie G. *Boston Mahatma: A Biography of Martin Lomasney*. Boston: Bruce Humphries, Inc., 1949.

Beatty, Jack. *The Rascal King: The Life and Times of James Michael Curley (1874–1958)*. Reading, Mass.; Menlo Park, Calif.; New York: Addison-Wesley Publishing, 1992.

Beschloss, Michael R. *Kennedy and Roosevelt: The Uneasy Alliance*. New York: Norton, 1980.

Birmingham, Stephen. *Real Lace: America's Irish Rich*. New York: Harper & Row, 1973.

Bishop, Jim. *The Day Kennedy Was Shot*. New York: Funk & Wagnalls, 1968.

Blair, John and Clay Jr. *The Search for JFK*. New York: Berkley, 1976.

Bradlee, Ben. *Conversations With Kennedy*. New York: Norton, 1975.

Buck, Pearl. *The Kennedy Women: A Personal Appraisal*. New York: Harcourt, 1969.

Bullitt, Orville H., ed. *For the President: Personal and Secret Correspondence Between Franklin D. Roosevelt and William C. Bullitt*. Boston: Windsor Publications, 1984.

Burke, Richard E. *The Senator: My Ten Years With Ted Kennedy*. New York: St. Martin's Press, 1992.

Burns, James MacGregor. *Edward Kennedy and the Camelot Legacy*. New York: Norton, 1976.

———. *John Kennedy: A Political Profile*. New York: Harcourt, 1960.

Callan, Louise. *The Society of the Sacred Heart in North America*. London: Longmans, Green and Co., 1937.

Cameron, Gail. *Rose: A Biography of Rose Fitzgerald Kennedy*. New York: G. P. Putnam's Sons, 1971.

Chellis, Marcia. *The Joan Kennedy Story: Living With the Kennedys*. New York: Simon and Schuster, 1985.

Clinch, Nancy Gager. *The Kennedy Neurosis*. New York: Grosset & Dunlap, 1973.

Bibliography

Collier, Peter, and David Horowitz. *The Kennedys: An American Drama.* New York: Summit Books, 1984.

Curran, Robert. *The Kennedy Women: Their Triumphs and Tragedies.* New York: Lancer, 1964.

Cutler, John Henry. *"Honey Fitz".* Indianapolis; New York: Bobbs-Merrill, 1962.

Dallas, Rita, RN, with Jeanira Ratcliffe. *The Kennedy Case.* New York: G. P. Putnam's Sons, 1973.

Damore, Leo. *The Cape Cod Years of John Fitzgerald Kennedy.* Englewood Cliffs, N.J.: Prentice-Hall, 1967.

Davis, John. *The Bouviers.* New York: Farrar, Strauss & Giroux, 1969.

————. *The Kennedys: Dynasty and Disaster.* New York: McGraw-Hill, 1984.

Davis, Kenneth. *FDR Into the Storm, 1937–1940: A History.* New York: Random House, 1993.

————. *FDR: The Beckoning of Destiny—1882–1928.* New York: G. P. Putnam's Sons, 1971, 1972.

DeBedts, Ralph F. *Ambassador Joseph Kennedy 1938–1940: An Anatomy of Appeasement.* New York: Peter Lang, 1985.

Diner, Hasia R. *Erin's Daughters in America: Irish Immigrant Women in the Nineteenth Century.* Baltimore and London: Johns Hopkins University Press, 1983.

Dinneen, Joseph. *The Kennedy Family.* Boston and Toronto: Little, Brown, 1959.

Erie, Steven P. *Rainbow's End: Irish-Americans and the Dilemmas of Urban Machine Politics, 1840–1850.* Berkeley: University of California Press, 1988.

Fuchs, Lawrence H. *John F. Kennedy and American Catholicism.* New York: Meredith Press, 1967.

Gallagher, Mary Barelli, and Frances Spatz Leighton. *My Life With Jacqueline Kennedy.* New York: David McKay, Inc., 1969.

Gibson, Barbara, with Caroline Latham. *Life With Rose Kennedy: An Intimate Account.* New York: Warner Books, 1986.

Gibson, Barbara, with Ted Schwarz. *The Kennedys: The Third Generation.* New York: Thunder's Mouth Press, 1993.

Goodwin, Doris Kearns. *The Fitzgeralds and the Kennedys: An American Saga.* New York: St. Martin's Press, 1987.

Hamilton, Nigel. *JFK: Reckless Youth.* New York: Random House, 1992.

Handlin, Oscar. *Boston's Immigrants, 1790–1880.* Cambridge, Mass.: Belknap Press of Harvard University Press, 1991.

Harris, Ruth-Ann M., and Donald M. Jacobs, eds. *The Search for Missing Friends: Irish Immigrant Advertisements Placed in the Boston Pilot.* Boston: New England Historic Genealogical Society, 1989.

Hersh, Burton. *The Education of Edward Kennedy.* New York: William Morrow, 1972.

Heymann, C. David. *A Woman Named Jackie.* New York: Lyle Stuart/Carol Publishing, 1989.

Kelley, Kitty. *Jackie Oh!* Secaucus, N.J.: Lyle Stuart, 1978.

Kennedy, Rose. *Times to Remember.* Garden City, N.Y.: Doubleday, 1974.

Koskoff, David E. *Joseph P. Kennedy: A Life and Times.* Englewood Cliffs, N.J.: Prentice-Hall, 1974.

Langer, William L., and S. Everett Gleason. *The World Crisis and American Foreign Policy: The Challenge to Isolation, 1937–1940.* New York: Harper & Brothers, 1952.

Lasky, Victor. *JFK: The Man and the Myth.* New York: Macmillan, 1963.

Lawford, Patricia Seaton, with Ted Schwarz. *The Peter Lawford Story.* New York: Carroll & Graf, 1988.

Leamer, Laurence. *The Kennedy Women: The Saga of an American Family.* New York: Random House, 1994.

Lieberson, Goddard, ed. *John Fitzgerald Kennedy as We Remember Him.* New York: Atheneum, 1965.

Madsen, Axel. *Gloria and Joe.* New York: Arbor House, 1988.

Manchester, William. *The Glory and the Dream: A Narrative History of America, 1932–1972.* New York: Bantam, 1980.

———. *Portrait of a President: John F. Kennedy in Profile.* Boston and Toronto: Little, Brown, 1962.

McTaggart, Lynne. *Kathleen Kennedy: Her Life and Times.* New York: Dial Press, 1983.

Merrill, Marlene Deahl, ed. *Growing Up in Boston's Gilded Age: The Journal of Alice Stone Blackwell, 1872–1874.* New Haven and London: Yale University Press, 1990.

Oppenheimer, Jerry. *The Other Mrs. Kennedy.* New York: St. Martin's Press, 1994.

Parmet, Herbert S. *Jack: The Struggles of John F. Kennedy.* New York: Dial Press, 1980.

Rainie, Harrison, and John Quinn. *Growing Up Kennedy: The Third Wave Comes of Age.* New York: G. P. Putnam's Sons, 1983.

Reedy, George. *From the Ward to the White House: The Irish in American Politics.* New York: Charles Scribner's Sons, 1991.

Reeves, Thomas C. *A Question of Character: A Life of John F. Kennedy.* New York: Free Press, 1991.

Russell, Francis. *The President Makers: From Mark Hanna to Joseph P. Kennedy.* Boston: Little, Brown, 1976.

Saunders, Frank, with James Southwood. *Torn Lace Curtain.* New York: Holt Rinehart and Winston, 1982.

Schlesinger, Arthur M. Jr. *A Thousand Days.* Boston: Houghton Mifflin, 1965.

Searls, Hank. *The Lost Prince: Young Joe, the Forgotten Kennedy.* New York: World Publishing Company, 1969.

Sherwood, Robert E. *Roosevelt and Hopkins: An Intimate History.* New York: Harper, 1948.

Bibliography

Solomon, Barbara Miller. *Ancestors and Immigrants: A Changing New England Tradition.* Boston: Northeastern University Press, 1956.

Sorensen, Theodore C. *Kennedy.* New York: Bantam Books, 1966.

Spada, James. *Peter Lawford: The Man Who Kept the Secrets.* New York: Bantam, 1991.

Swanson, Gloria. *Swanson on Swanson: An Autobiography.* New York: Random House, 1980.

Travell, Janet, MD. *Office Hours: Day and Night.* New York and Cleveland: World Publishing, 1968.

Wakefield, Edward. *An Account of Ireland, Statistical and Political,* 2 vols. London: 1812.

Whalen, Richard J. *The Founding Father: The Story of Joseph P. Kennedy.* New York: New American Library, 1964.

Williams, Margaret, RSCJ. *The Society of the Sacred Heart: History of a Spirit, 1800–1975.* London: Darton, Longman & Todd, 1978.

Wills, Garry. *The Kennedy Imprisonment: A Meditation on Power.* Boston: Little, Brown, 1981.

Kennedy Library Material

John F. Kennedy Personal Papers, Box 1: early years genealogical papers; souvenirs: clippings, 1940.

John F. Kennedy Personal Papers, Box 4A: correspondence, 1933–50; folder: Rose R. Kennedy, 1941–45; folder letter to Joseph P. Kennedy Sr. from Rose F. Kennedy, 10/12/47; Joseph P. Kennedy Sr. folder: letters to JFK, 1940–45.

Robert F. Kennedy Papers: pre-administration working files—Permanent Subcommittee on Investigations, 1953–56; folder marked "1956 Kennedy Family and New York Office, 4/56–5/56;" folder marked "1956 Kennedy Family and New York Office, 9/56–12/56."

Special Correspondence

The letters and memos of Rose Kennedy as taken in shorthand by Barbara Gibson.

The Peter Lawford Files of the Special Collection division of the Hayden Library, Arizona State University, Tempe, Arizona.

Index

Index

Index

Index

Index

Index

Shrivers, the, 238
Sinatra, Frank, 210
Skakel, Ann, 174, 175
Skakel, Ethel, 167, 171, 174–75, 177–79, 220
  marries Bob Kennedy, 179
  See also Kennedy, Ethel Skakel
Skakel, George, 174, 175, 192
Skakel, Pat, 177, 179
Skakel family, 175–77, 180, 182, 192, 193
Smith, Al, 107
Smith, Amanda Mary, 279
Smith, Jean Kennedy, 72, 103, 104, 109, 116, 192, 202–3, 210, 227, 249, 250, 279, 297
  See also Kennedy, Jean
Smith, Kym Maria, 227, 279
Smith, Stephen, 173–74, 202–3, 214, 235, 264, 266, 267, 279, 292
Smith, Steve Jr., 279
Smith, Dr. William Kennedy, 5, 10, 279
Smith family, 291
Sorensen, Ted, 264
Spalding, Charles, 197–98
Spargo, Bill, 78
Spellman, Francis Cardinal, 151, 212
Stone, Galen, 52, 80
Sulzberger, C. L., 122
Swanson, Gloria, 62, 76, 80, 85–89, 91–97, 146, 149, 183, 205, 217, 247

Terkel, Studs, 211
Thompson, Fred, 81, 84
Thomson, Monsignor, 255

Times to Remember (Rose Kennedy), 32, 60, 62, 64, 98
Timilty, Joe, 148
Tobin, Maurice, 158
Townsend, Kathleen, 292
Trespasser, The (film), 89, 93, 95
Tretter, Charles, 258
Truman, Harry S., 165

United States, in World War II, 117, 119, 130–33, 141, 143
Unruh, Jesse, 282

Vance, Cyrus, 278
vanden Heuvel, William, 264
Victoria, Queen of England, 114, 236, 242
Voboril, Mary, 59
Wagner, Helga, 258
Waldrop, Frank, 144
Walsh, Tom, 201, 229, 279
Walters, Barbara, 190, 292
Watts, Dr. James, 69
Welch, Joseph, 197
White, Byron (Whizzer), 128
White, John, 66, 144
William, Duke of Devonshire, 136
Williams, Andy, 292
Willkie, Wendell, 112
Wilson, Pat, 149
Winchell, Walter, 206
Windsor, Duchess of, 224

Zukor, Adolph, 81